Mosaic and the New Internet

Mosaic and the New Internet

Serving Business and Personal Needs

Steve Karlovsky
Kevin Leininger
Linda Winkler

McGraw-Hill
New York San Francisco Washington, D.C. Auckland Bogotá
Caracas Lisbon London Madrid Mexico City Milan
Montreal New Delhi San Juan Singapore
Sydney Tokyo Toronto

McGraw-Hill

A Division of The McGraw-Hill Companies

pbk 1 2 3 4 5 6 7 8 9 DOC/DOC 9 0 0 9 8 7 6 5

Library of Congress Cataloging-in-Publication Data

Karlovsky, Steve.

Mosaic and the new Internet : serving business and personal needs / by Steve Karlovsky, Kevin Leininger, Linda Winkler.

p. cm.

Includes index.

ISBN 0-07-912097-0 (p)

1. Mosaic (Computer file) 2. Internet (Computer network) 3. Information superhighway. I. Leininger, Kevin E. II. Winkler, Linda. III. Title.

TK5105.882.K37 1995

025.04—dc20 95-22075

CIP

McGraw-Hill books are available at special quantity discounts to use as premiums and sales promotions, or for use in corporate training programs. For more information, please write to the Director of Special Sales, McGraw-Hill, 11 West 19th Street, New York, NY 10011. Or contact your local bookstore.

Acquisitions editor: Jerry Papke

Editorial team: Michael Christopher, Manuscript Editor
David M. McCandless, Managing Editor
Joanne Slike, Executive Editor
Jodi L. Tyler, Indexer

Production team: Katherine G. Brown, Director
Rhonda E. Baker, Coding
Rose McFarland, Desktop Operator
Nancy K. Mickley, Proofreading

Design team: Jaclyn J. Boone, Designer
Katherine Lukaszewicz, Associate Designer

9120970
WK2

Contents

Part 2
How to use the Internet

Acknowledgments

Thanks first to Kevin and Linda for being such skilled and unselfish writing partners, and to McGraw-Hill and TAB for making the ideas that follow available worldwide. Thanks also to John Vomer for dropping such a great opportunity into my lap, and to Argonne National Laboratory for encouraging its employees to expand their professional horizons. Finally, I wish most to thank my wife Gail, and Adrienne and Ian, for giving so much to make my participation in this work possible. And for convincing me to "go for it", sparing me years of pain from kicking myself.

Steve

Thanks to my wife, Karen, and my two sons, Alex and Michael for allowing me to produce this book.

Kevin

I would like to thank my family for their support and encouragement which contributed immeasurably to the successful completion of this project.

Linda

Introduction

The Internet has gone through a revolution in the past three years. One piece of evidence is that you are reading this book, which implies at least three things:

- The book was available in the first place.
- You knew what it was likely to be about.
- You believe that you can actually use the Internet, even at home.

Kevin Savetz maintains, on the Internet, *The Unofficial Internet Book List*. By his count, as of March 6, 1995, there were 239 such books on the market. So what sets this book apart and makes it worth your attention?

First, this book is not a resource directory, though you might decide to own one of those, too. Neither do we provide list after list of Internet resources grouped by topic or by resource type. Instead, we describe useful tools and techniques to help you find what you are looking for once you are connected.

Second, this book is not a survey of Internet tools. We could recommend several such books, but our intention is to explain the various types of Internet resources in the context of what we will call the *New Internet* throughout this book. You do not need to know the details of the old tools like FTP, Archie, or Telnet anymore.

Third, even though this book is centered around an application called Mosaic it is not really about Mosaic itself (some other books are). Rather, this book is about how the availability of Mosaic, coupled with other factors, has fundamentally changed the Internet. It's about what that could mean to you, not merely in technological terms but in terms of your business and your home life.

Finally, on the enclosed CD we provide the latest commercial Mosaic software for your Microsoft Windows PC or UNIX workstation. You'll find Spyglass Enhanced Mosaic, distributed by Luckman Interactive (v2.01), for both platforms. You'll also find the software you need to establish a free trial connection to Portal, an Internet service provider, for dial-up World Wide Web access over a modem and telephone line.

What's so exciting about the New Internet? As you'll see in Chapter 1, there are several elements. Some appeal to the mind and others appeal to the spirit. For one thing, the New Internet probably gives us the clearest picture we presently have of what our future holds in store. It's the whole world of information, of words and pictures and movies and sound, available to you as if it were all stored up in your own computer.

If you are a business person you might gain from this book a concise understanding of the Internet's potential benefits and risks. You will understand why the Internet culture is what it is, and how you can function effectively within that culture while better addressing your business needs. The New Internet is headed in your direction, and your needs are aggressively being met.

If you are a home user, we hope to give you a feeling of insight and inclusion in a growing global community, using straightforward, uncomplicated dialog with only sprinkles of techno-gibberish inserted where necessary. You will see why many believe the New Internet is destined to take its place in your home, next to your telephone and your television. It has already begun to rival traditional print media.

It is important that a book like this be directed to both home and business users, for two reasons. First, much of what we offer applies equally to both environments—the history, Web terminology, the Mosaic interface, and so on. Second, and perhaps more important, the line between work and home is becoming harder and harder to draw. The major growth in employment today is in home-based businesses, so home-connectivity issues can also be business issues. And Tom's experience in Chapter 1 is by no means the exception; people who are exposed to Mosaic on the job want to know how to use it at home.

Your roadmap to this book

Part 1 (Chapters 1 through 3) focuses on the possibilities of the New Internet. What is it like to discover the New Internet first-hand for the first time? Where did it come from, and why has it caught on like wildfire? What impact is it already having on society and in our daily lives? How could the New Internet help you attain your business goals? Your personal goals? A few Mosaic and Internet terms are introduced for later discussion, but in principle these chapters are for the intuitive part of your mind to absorb.

Part 2 (Chapters 4 through 8) gets the other half of your brain involved. We explain how to get Mosaic up and running in your own environment. And that might not require you to load the CD-ROM at all, for Microsoft Windows 95 is expected to ship Internet-ready with Mosaic included, and World Wide Web access is becoming available even on the online services like America Online. We'll then discuss the terminology of the World Wide Web and Mosaic, and help you understand how to reach long-established resources like Anonymous FTP sites and Gopher servers, all from within the context of the New Internet.

Part 3 (Chapters 9 through 13) pulls it all together, focusing on making the "how-to" of the New Internet fulfill the possibilities. We'll offer strategies for browsing the World Wide Web, and for keeping up with new resources. We'll also discuss practical approaches for effective searching, using old paradigm tools like Archie and

Veronica, as well as the growing collection of Web-based robotic search tools such as Lycos and the World Wide Web Worm.

Then, what about establishing your own presence? We'll cover, at a basic level, what it takes for you to start creating and serving your own World Wide Web Home Pages. Finally, we'll offer additional insights to help you position yourself and those around you for what lies just over the Internet horizon.

Now . . . if you're ready, let's join Tom as his colleagues welcome him, and you, to the New Internet.

1

Welcome to the New Internet

Tom [Hanging up the telephone] . . . and we'll schedule a meeting with them both on Monday. Thanks. [click] Come in!

Tracy Busy, Tom?

Tom No, Tracy. Show me what you installed on my PC last night.

Tracy Sure. It's here in this program group. The icon labeled Mosaic.

Tom So what do I need to do?

Tracy Just click on it, Tom.

Tom OK, looks like it's doing something . . . it's taking a while, though.

Tracy Five or ten seconds. It'll be worth the wait. (Fig. 1-1.)

Tom Not bad. Logo looks nice! So, this page is on my hard disk?

Tracy No, Tom. It's in Dallas.

Tom Dallas? And I can see it like this on my desk?

Tracy You bet. You're accessing a piece of the Internet called the World Wide Web. This is our Very Own Corporation Home Page.

Tom Why is some of the text blue and underlined?

Tracy Those are called hyperlinks. Click on one. Use the left button on the mouse.

Tom How about 'Dallas, Texas' . . . ah, that was easy! (Fig. 1-2.)

Figure 1-1

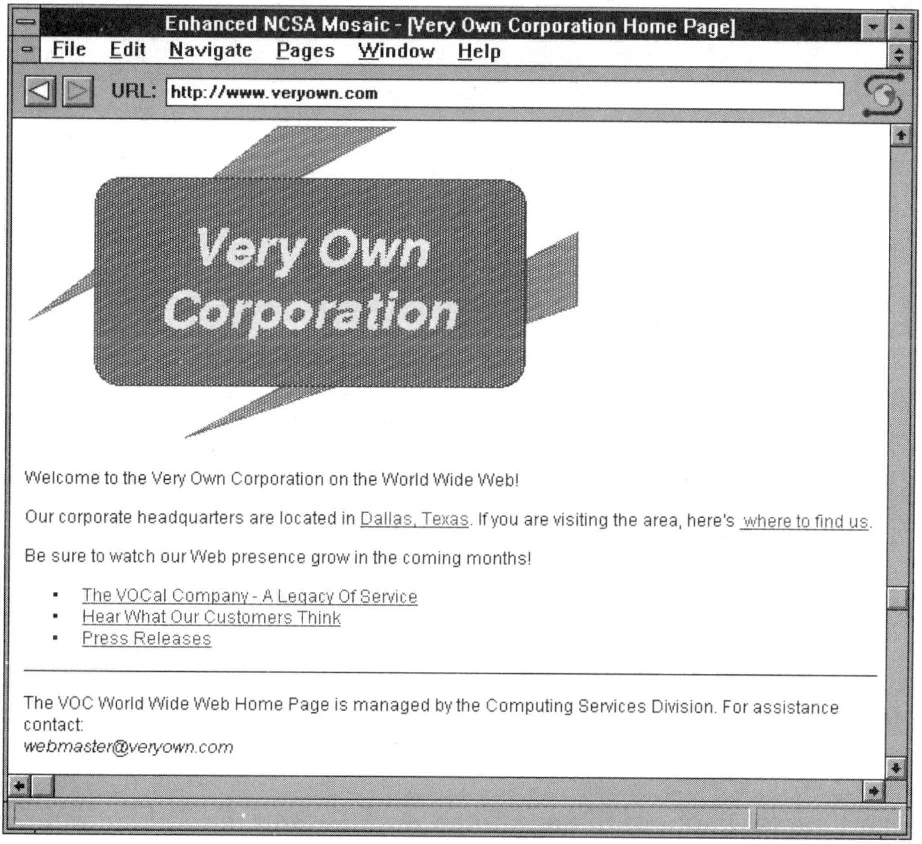

Windows Mosaic window, home page example

Tracy There are buttons on the screen that let you step back a page or go back home. Either one will suffice here. Or, you can try out your hotlist.

Tom What's a hotlist?

Tracy A hotlist stores pointers to your favorite Internet locations—you can save the ones you want. I added a few in there already for you to see. The list is up here in this menu. (See Fig. 1-3.)

Figure 1-2

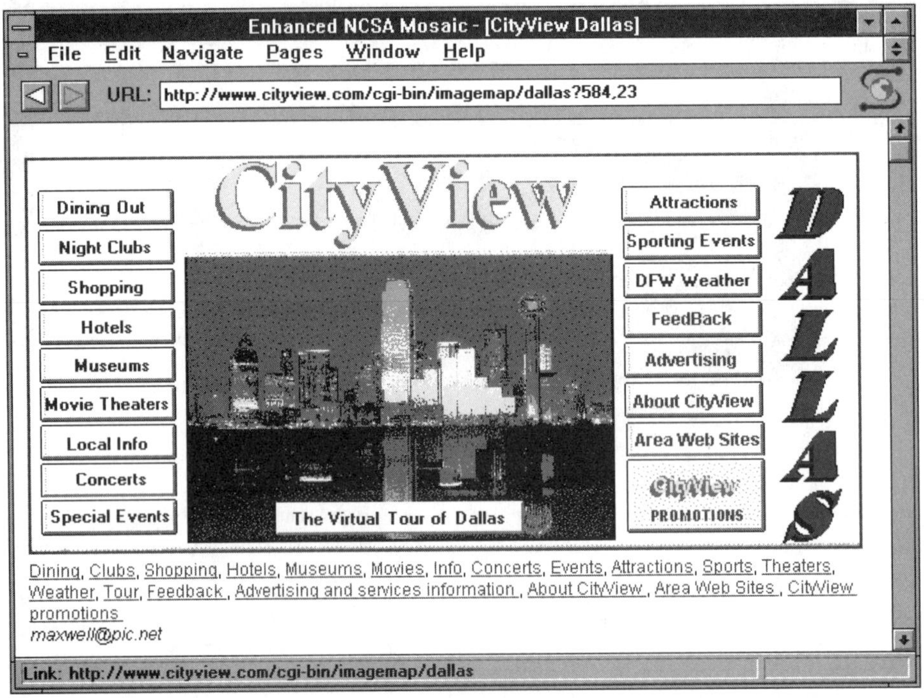

Windows Mosaic window, CityView Dallas Home Page— ***http://www.pic.net/cityview/dallas.html***

Figure 1-3

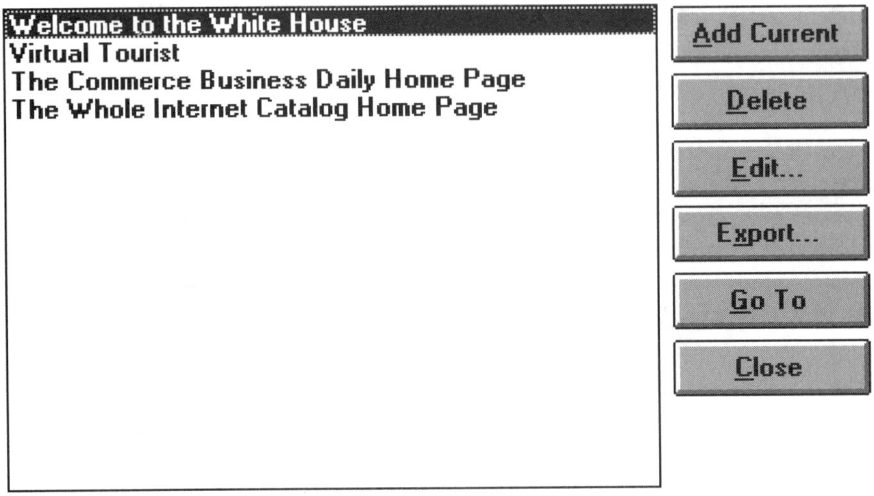

Tom's hotlist

Tom I'd love to understand what the Internet is really about. I see it mentioned all over but I barely know where to start.

Tracy Well, there's this great book . . .

Tom Should I click on 'White House'?

Tracy Sure.

Figure 1-4

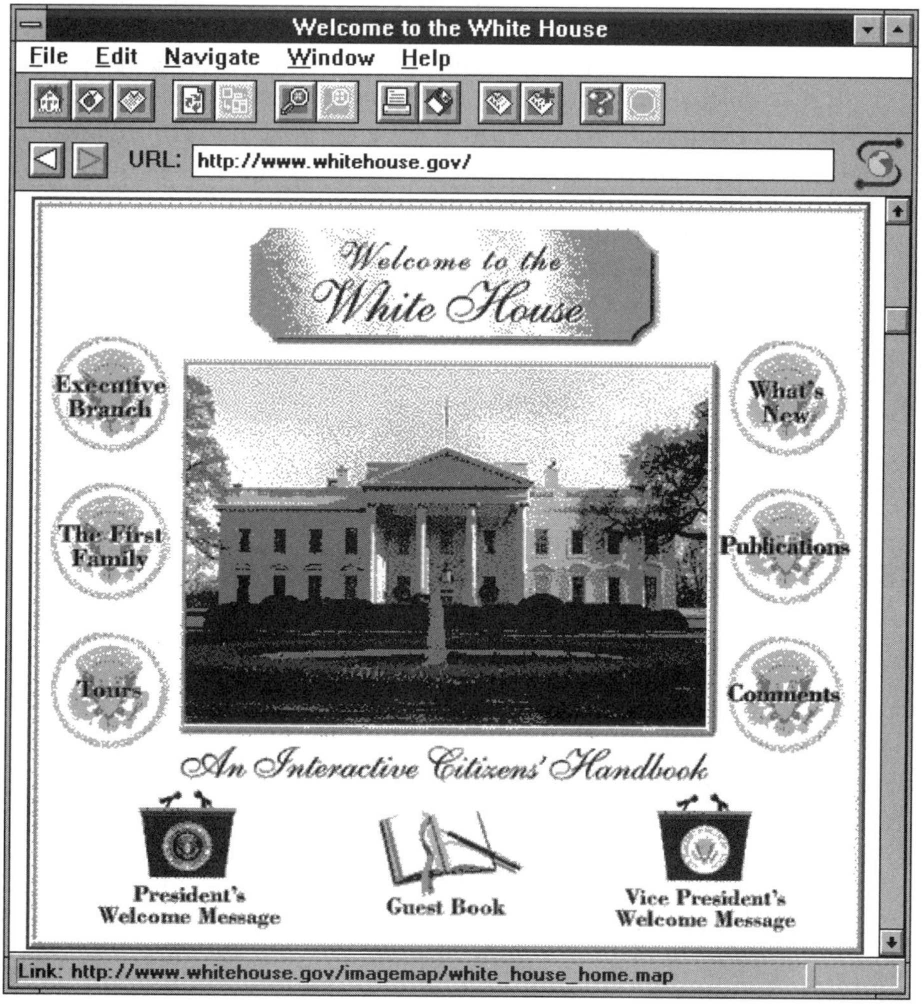

Windows Mosaic window, The White House Home Page—
http://www.whitehouse.gov/

Tom Son of a gun. There it is! Now what?

Tracy This is called a clickable image. Click the mouse somewhere on the page and see what happens.

Tom Let's see what Mr. Clinton has to say.

Tracy Not 'see,' 'hear.'

Tom's PC *Welcome to the White House—our first on-line citizen's handbook. I hope you find this a useful way to find answers to your questions, a better way to let me know what you think, and a powerful way to find information you can use—whether you are in Nome, Alaska or right down Pennsylvania Avenue. Please don't forget to sign the guest book and let us know what you think of this new service.*

Tom Could we do this with our own—you called it a home page?

Tracy It's already in the works. All of our divisions will be represented, including full descriptions of their product lines. And they'll each be running their own servers at their own sites.

Tom And our main home page can point to them all?

Tracy Sure, that's what the White House did. All the government agencies are tied in. The SEC, the Library of Congress, the CIA . . .

Tom The CIA? They would NEVER let you see anything!

Tracy Sure they would! There's a revolution going on, Tom. The base of information on the Internet is huge and it's growing every day. And not just in the U.S. Pull down on the hotlist again and click on Virtual Tourist.

[A few moments later . . .]

Figure 1-5

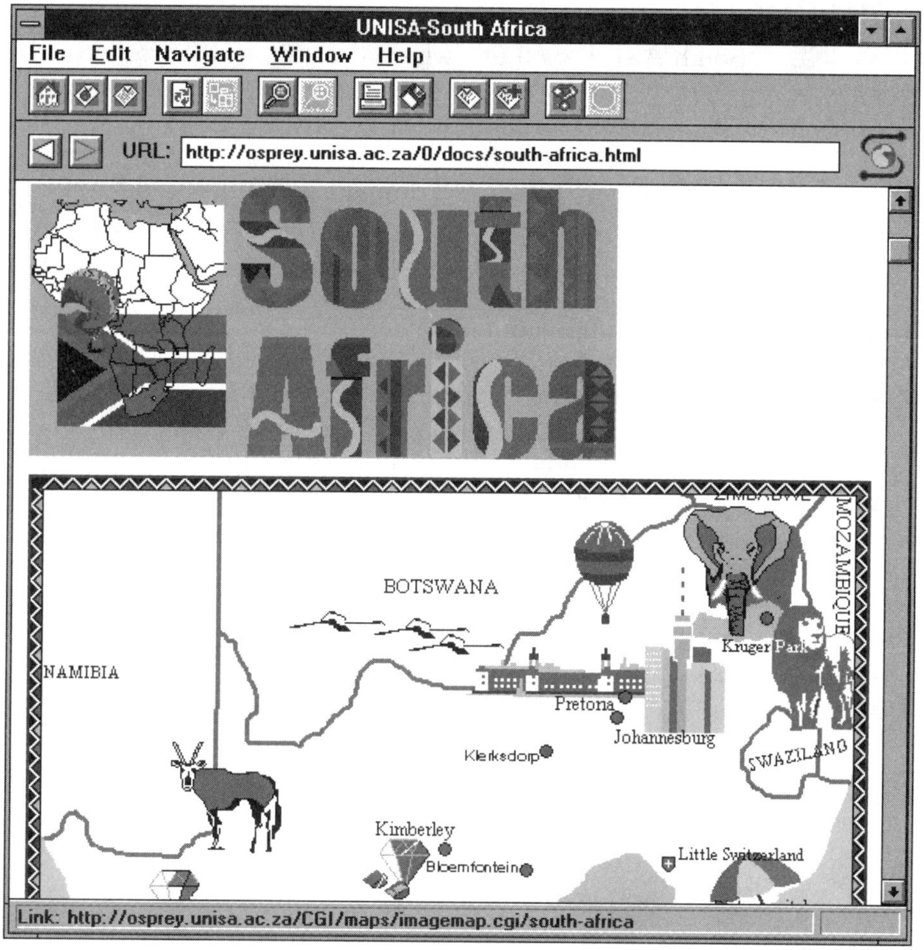

Windows Mosaic window, Welcome to South Africa—
http://osprey.unisa.ac.za/0/docs/south-africa.html

Tom This is amazing! I'm in South Africa! At least I think I am. How can I tell?

Tracy By looking at the URL[1] near the top of the window. That first part, *http://*, just means this page is coming from a World Wide Web server somewhere. But the next part up to the next slash identifies the computer by its Internet

1 URL stands for the Universal Resource Locator (often called an *Internet address*) that helps locate documents and provides the ability to address any object anywhere on the Internet. More in Chapter 7.

domain name. *za* is the international country code for South Africa, so that's where the page came from.

Tom So *.us* means United States?

Tracy Well, yes, but most U.S. domain names use a different convention. They end with *.com* for companies, *.gov* for the government, *.edu* for schools and universities . . .

Tom Who came up with all this?

Tracy Which part? The core of the Internet has been around for more than twenty years. The World Wide Web technology and all of the information servers have been developed all over the world. Mosaic knows how to present all of it to you when you ask for it. Mosaic was developed at the University of Illinois.

Phil Excuse me, Tom.

Tom Come in, Phil. What's up?

Phil Fictional Enterprises just announced a new product. It could be trouble.

Tracy Let's see if they have a Web server.

Tom Where did that dialog box come from?

Figure 1-6

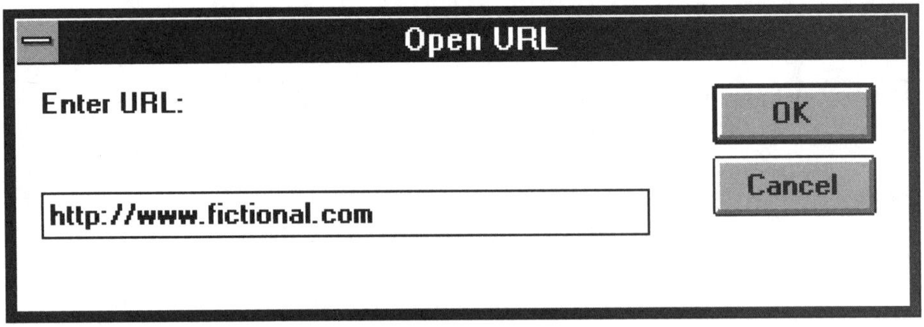

URL dialog box, URL example

Tracy Oh . . . sorry, Tom. Under the File menu.

Tom And how did you know what URL to type?

Tracy It's a pretty standard naming convention. You can try names and acronyms and locate lots of companies this way. Looks like this is going to work.

[They watch the screen intently. A few minutes later . . .]

Figure 1-7

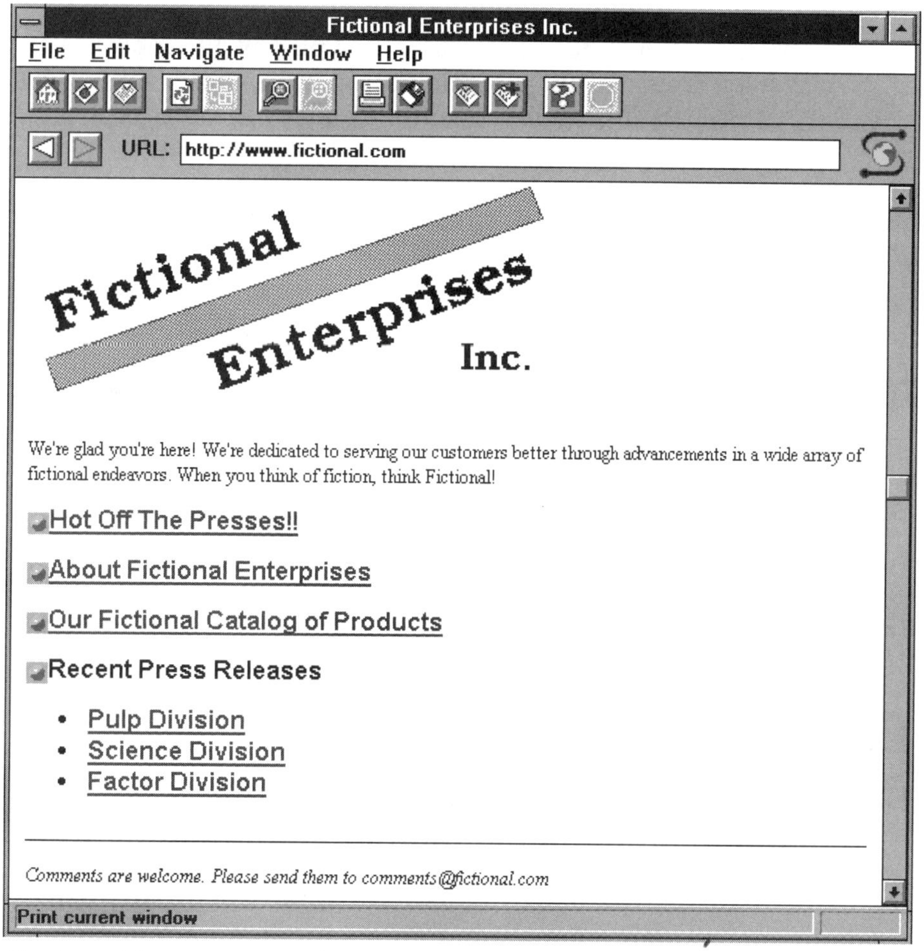

Windows Mosaic window, home page example

Tom	We wouldn't see this in the trades until next week!
Phil	I'll download a copy and circulate it right away.
Tom	Thanks, Phil! And I'll save this URL in my hotlist. Tracy, can Phil do this from his Macintosh, too?
Tracy	Sure, and I run Mosaic from my UNIX workstation. They all look and feel basically the same.
Tom	Does Mosaic always work this well?
Tracy	No, sometimes you click on a hyperlink and Mosaic just spins its wheels. But think about it. All those servers all over the world tied together by all those networks. Systems occasionally fail. So you try again later.
Tom	One more thing before you go. All the resources that I'd like to access for personal use . . . I can't honestly justify using the company's facilities. Can I run Mosaic at home?
Tracy	Sure. You'll need to dial-up to an Internet service provider to make your connection. The graphics take longer to load over a modem, but there are strategies you can use to soften the blow.
Tom	How can I get started?
Tracy	Let me go get that book . . .

Epilogue: The New Internet defined

Scenes such as this are being played out every day at thousands of companies and in thousands of homes all over the world. They depict the discovery and embracing of what we call the New Internet.

You might have heard about the Internet and developed your own preconceptions—it's too hard to understand, only "techies" are welcome, or what have you. So what's truly significant about this so-called *New* Internet?

First, and most visibly, text, video, graphics and sound are all available, and all can be fully integrated. Information can be conveyed more clearly with a higher degree of creativity.

Second, people can work within it in human terms and not merely in computer terms. It means pointing into an illustrated book versus conversing in addresses and protocols—a world of difference.

Third, it's available to the masses, not just to the technologically privileged few. We'll see that, before long, virtually everyone with a computer will have available to them at least one economical access path to the New Internet, and probably several.

Finally, the New Internet is rapidly breaking down the traditional boundaries of our lives. It means visiting your office without leaving your home or your hotel. And it means speeding off to faraway lands without going through customs.

We also hoped to illustrate a few subtler points with our story. For example, not everything about the Internet works properly all the time. Failures do occur and servers get busy, but such situations are temporary.

Also, not everything is speedy, especially over phone lines. Patience is a virtue here, but it's worth the wait.

And, people catch on to the New Internet *very* quickly—even novices. And they love to tell their friends about it.

If you are excited (or even merely intrigued) by all this, read on. The next two chapters will explain, with as few technical details as possible, how the New Internet came into being, and will describe its potential roles in your business and in your home.

2

Understanding the Internet revolution

CHAPTER 2

WE keep tossing around the word *revolution* in these early chapters. The word conjures up images of Paul Revere and the American Revolution, or of cotton gins or Model Ts. One way to define a revolution is to call it the collision of a long-established system with a new invention or a new approach that changes the system by meeting a built-in need. The need can be long-repressed or entirely new, but either way, the result is a fundamentally different system that carries forward from that point.

A revolution is precisely what has been occurring across the Internet over the last five years. We therefore offer this chapter to help you:

- Feel more comfortable with the emerging culture before you dive in, as you would when visiting a newly aligned foreign country for the first time
- Understand some of the tensions that exist right now on the Internet, caused by rapid change and a clash of cultures
- Appreciate what is driving the course of the New Internet, and why

Laying the groundwork—The Internet that *was*

Despite all the attention the Internet has received in the last year or two, its core is not the least bit new. The U.S. Defense Advanced Research Projects Agency built an experimental network called the *ARPAnet* in 1973. ARPAnet and its successors and siblings, which collectively comprise the Internet, existed in relative obscurity for nearly 20 years, known only to the computer and telecommunications researchers and researchers in other sciences who were "on the net."

Within this context, over the course of the next 20 years there evolved an expansive interconnection of networks and computers; a recognized set of software tools and protocols to serve and retrieve information; a global collection of information and discussions of great depth but limited breadth; and, a philosophy or culture not necessarily aligned with that of the world around it.

Physical connectivity

Computers on the ARPAnet ultimately communicated with each other using a protocol called IP, the Internet Protocol. IP was invented as a protocol that would run on both local area and wide area networks (LANs and WANs).

When the University of California at Berkeley began distributing IP with their BSD UNIX kernels in the early 1980s, a new de facto standard network protocol was born. UNIX users on the ARPAnet could easily use IP-based tools to send electronic mail to other users, log into accounts on other computers to do work, and transfer files to and from other computers.

Along with Berkeley, a number of new agencies were beginning to build computer centers. Because most of the universities and research laboratories selected as homes to these centers were already on the ARPAnet, it was the most economical way to connect the centers together.

As UNIX computers became more popular, scores of localized IP networks called LANs were built on campuses and in research centers. In 1986, the National Science Foundation (NSF) put a 56-kbps-wide area network architecture in place, interconnecting the regional supercomputer centers that used IP. Today, 45 Mbps facilities carry on the order of 12 billion packets per month.

The NSF began promoting educational access to NSFnet and helping to defer costs, intending to help place all educational institutions on NSFnet. The local networks were linked in, and NSFnet became the most influential "backbone" network in the Internet. In addition, as students graduated from their educational environments and moved into the commercial world they began convincing corporations to connect to the Internet as well.

While this activity expanded the Internet somewhat, UNIX systems made up only a small fraction of the total number of computers in use worldwide. Three technical advances made Internet connectivity possible for the rest of us:

- **Gateways to other types of networks**. BITNET gateways, for example, allowed electronic mail to pass between Internet hosts and BITNET-connected, IBM mainframe computers. Packets of information passing through a gateway were converted from one protocol to the other.
- **IP software for non-UNIX computers**. Those IBM mainframes, as well as DEC computers, IBM PCs, and Apple Macintoshes could now talk IP as well.
- **SLIP and PPP protocols**. These protocols made it possible to communicate using IP using a modem over a telephone line. Home computers could now establish temporary Internet connections.

So, over 20 years of evolution, the word *Internet* began to refer to the global interconnection of IP-supporting networks spanning more than three dozen countries.

Software tools & protocols

Early on, the gurus of the Internet began working out ways to offer public repositories and information services to Internet users at large. This meant creating servers that users could contact without needing to register for user names and passwords in advance, while at the same time maintaining a measure of security from hackers. Over time, the Internet-user community found several types of public resources to be the most useful.

Discussion groups/bulletin boards. These were forums for discussion of technical and social issues, and places to tap the collective expertise of the Internet community. Examples included Listserv groups and other electronic mail discussion groups, and USENET Newsgroups.

Public file repositories. These were places you could go to find software, either public domain or shareware, or other types of files such as graphics images or documents. Examples included Anonymous FTP sites, electronic mail file servers, and WAIS servers.

Local information servers. These were kiosks of sorts, announcing events for an organization or serving information such as weather forecasts. An example would be Telnet servers.

Distributed information servers. These were similar to local information servers, but they connected many servers with related information and let you, as a user, jump from one to another. A good example would be Gopher.

Search tools into these resources. These were tools that would help you find the information you needed. Examples would include WAIS, Archie, Veronica, and Jughead.

The electronic-mail-based schemes were initially the most popular, because users on non-IP networks could reach them across the early gateways. Using electronic mail to retrieve files over the Internet is cumbersome and has long been superseded by better tools such as Anonymous FTP. But electronic mail discussion groups, or mailing lists, are more popular than ever.

Even though it essentially *contained* or could *deliver* a great deal of information, the Internet was never one monolithic database or resource. Instead, it evolved into a loosely interrelated collection of resources, with corresponding vehicles or tools for accessing those resources. The most popular tools were written by many different people with different objectives, and therefore had little in common in how they worked or how one used them.

In a sense, traveling the Internet was much like traveling in the *real* world. A car might get you to where you wanted to go, but if you had to haul anything back you might need a truck or moving van. If you were crossing the mountains you might need to ride the train and leave the car at home. Overseas? You sailed your boat or flew a plane. No one vehicle could take you everywhere.

We'll talk more about the various tools of the Internet in Chapter 8.

The information base

The information that collected throughout the Internet reflected and catered to the user community. The users were primarily researchers and scientists in various disciplines, including computing itself.

What, then, would a scientist want to discuss? Several possibilities, including advances in their respective research areas; current events; their hobbies; the Internet itself (because they needed to know a lot about it to use it); and their computers themselves, especially software. Interestingly, we'll see in Chapter 8 how well these areas of discussion are reflected in the original USENET newsgroup categories.

Note that no one was out there publishing information for the Internet-user community per se. Discussions about current events were just that, with plenty of opinions and personal bias, and everyone on the Internet was invited to participate.

There was plenty of uncharted territory (personal finance, for instance). But if there *was* material about a particular topic it was often quite extensive. If you decided to become a curator for online material about a given subject you did so out of a love for that subject, and a desire to share your interest with others.

The Internet culture

The makeup of the user community did not merely influence what types of information were available. It also shaped the overall culture and philosophy of the Internet. Also, without being overly simplistic we know that researchers tend to share certain qualities:

- They frown on regulation but still desire order and classification. They try to balance the creation of an orderly world with the freedom to "do their own thing."
- They dislike advertising in the traditional sense, but nonetheless want to know what products and services will be available when they need them.

- They are comfortable with an active approach to information gathering. The ability to investigate and follow references to even more references is a fundamental skill to a good researcher.
- They abhor censorship and rely on the ability to freely exchange ideas and opinions. Agreeing to disagree is fundamental.

As the Internet evolved, these characteristics became the tenets of the Internet culture. The Internet community became generally self-policing, and rather proud of that.

Users also came to appreciate both the benefits and the pitfalls of such an instantaneous communications medium. On one hand, questions and responses and followups could be exchanged very quickly, so problems could be resolved quickly. You could post a question to a USENET newsgroup and collect responses from all over the world within an hour or two.

When the dialogue became impassioned, however, there was danger in being able to compose a message and fire it off in seconds, where cooler heads might have otherwise prevailed. In addition, the lack of verbal and visual cues in electronic communication increases the chance of serious misunderstanding. So *smileys* were invented as tools for communicating those missing cues. Some of the more popular smileys are shown in Fig. 2-1.

Figure 2-1

```
We all know the alderman is a man of his word. :-)

We all know the alderman is a man of his word. :-(

We all know the alderman is a man of his word. ;-)
```

Examples of smileys; same phrase with different meanings

Disclaimers attached to Internet communications also became important and popular, to clearly separate one's personal views from those of his or her employer. They are usually tied into the signature portion of the message, positioned at the bottom, and are often composed in a humorous vein.

The paradigm shift begins

By the late 1980s the Internet was all at once an extensive *network of networks*, a worldwide body of public information with a corresponding collection of software tools to access it, and a culture all its own. Then three developments took place that changed the course of the Internet dramatically. By name these were: The World Wide Web, NCSA Mosaic, and the National Information Infrastructure. The Internet would never be the same.

The conception of the World Wide Web

In 1989, Tim Berners-Lee of the CERN European Particle Physics laboratory in Geneva, Switzerland, saw a way to connect together the scattered and diverse resources of the Internet and present them to even a novice user in a natural way. A new Internet resource type called the World Wide Web was born, with modest intentions, to provide an intuitive way for high-energy physicists to organize and share their work.

The Web is hypertext-based. You, as the user, see text on your screen—a research abstract or instructions for a process, for example—as if you were reading a page of a book. But key areas of the text are highlighted, and if you select one of these areas a new page appears that elaborates on or relates to the highlighted text. Such a system represented a real breakthrough, first because it provided a natural way to organize and sift through related information and second because the next page you might select could reside anywhere on the Internet.

The World Wide Web was first introduced as a prototype in 1990, and was made widely available, free, on the Internet in 1991. Beyond the goal of advancing science and education, the WWW project has had a tremendous impact on other areas as well. It might revolutionize commerce, politics, and literature to name just a few.

The arrival of NCSA Mosaic

If you wanted to access World Wide Web resources you needed a Web browser—a program to run on your computer that communicated with the Web server and retrieved whichever documents or files you selected. The early Web browsers were developed at CERN.

The National Center for Supercomputing Applications (NCSA) was established at the University of Illinois at Urbana-Champaign, in 1985, for the study of computational science. NCSA began to develop the premier browser for the World Wide Web, called Mosaic. NCSA released Mosaic for the three common platforms (UNIX, Microsoft Windows PC, and Apple Macintosh) by the fall of 1993.

Almost overnight, Mosaic took the Internet by storm. Mosaic refined the early browsers and took the World Wide Web to an entirely new level. There were several keys to its success.

- It had a terrific GUI, or graphical user interface. Web pages looked pretty, complete with graphics. Viewers for other data formats, such as audio files or animation clips, could be launched on the fly. There was room for creativity for Web page authors and plenty of *Wow!* for the users (more on this in Chapter 7).
- It understood several protocols. It was all at once a Web browser, a Gopher client, an Anonymous FTP tool, a WAIS client, a USENET newsreader, and more, all the while taking full advantage of the benefits of hypertext. You no longer needed to obtain all the different tools and learn how to use them (which is explained in detail in Chapter 8).
- It ran on all of the most popular computers. You could be a businessperson with a PC, an educator with a Macintosh, or a scientist with a UNIX workstation and reap the same benefits.
- It was *easy* and *fun* to use! Mosaic unleashed an exciting commercial medium and, in the process, did for the Internet what the Apple Macintosh and Microsoft Windows did for personal computing. It transformed the technology beyond the realm of "computer jocks" and put it within the grasp of everyone.

Mosaic became particularly popular among electronic publishers and computer vendors who wanted to incorporate it into their own products. In less than a year the demand for Mosaic skyrocketed, and in August 1994 NCSA granted all future commercial licensing rights to Spyglass, Incorporated, which, in turn, developed the Enhanced Mosaic software included with this book. NCSA continues to develop Mosaic for noncommercial use.

The birth of the NII

These advances in Internet technology did not go unnoticed in the political arena. During the 1992 presidential race, vice-president-to-be Al Gore and the Democratic Party made the National Information Infrastructure a key component of their campaign. Thus many people heard about the *Information Superhighway*, and how it would eventually lead to every home and business, for the first time.

The fundamental goals of the NII were to

- enhance the competitiveness of American manufacturers
- increase the speed and efficiency of electronic commerce
- improve healthcare delivery and control costs
- promote the development and accessibility of quality education and lifelong learning
- enable more effective environmental monitoring
- provide government information to citizens more quickly and more efficiently

These goals were ambitious and wide-reaching, and clearly were intended to touch the lives of virtually everyone.

By the time the Clinton-Gore administration began acting on the NII, there was already an increased public awareness of the Internet, a new perception of governmental commitment, and a greater focus on issues of global competitiveness. The Internet had been discovered and was being directed toward serving the best interests of the nation.

The great commercial awakening

In 1992, the Internet took one step toward commercialization when the NSF clarified its acceptable use policy (AUP). The NSF stressed that the AUP, which placed restrictions on commercial use, applied only to backbone traffic of the federal agencies. Many big corporations had been on the Internet for years. For the most part, their participation had been limited to their research and engineering departments. The same corporations used a private network for their business communications.

However, while Amoco and IBM might be able to afford to run nationwide networks connecting their sites, Joe's Software Service might not have the same capability. But if Joe had an office in Ann Arbor, Michigan, and another in Berkeley, California, all those offices needed was an Internet connection at each one. For all practical purposes, with Internet they could have an international network connection for the cost of two local access lines.

By the end of 1993 the picture had changed even more dramatically, in two important respects. First, average people were aware that something like the Internet could become important in their own lives. And second, a fun and engaging tool that anyone could use was now available for navigating the Internet. The free enterprise system being what it is, commercial interests suddenly became very interested in the Internet and found it to be full of opportunity.

On the surface this might sound like the beginning of the end, with the evil forces of capitalism leveling sacred ground and putting up shopping malls. But that assumption has proved to be too hasty. The original Internet culture is deeply entrenched, and those who have tried to run roughshod into the Internet with traditional commercial philosophies have been soundly rebuked.

Meanwhile, commercial companies have identified many ways to incorporate the Internet into their business plans along one or more of three lines: by helping to expand the Internet, letting the Internet add value to what they already do, and actually conducting business on the Internet.

Internet expansion

Expanding the Internet has meant a lot of things, most of them to the direct benefit of the user community, including the following:

- Providing Internet connectivity to homes and businesses
- Providing education and training in the form of books (such as this one), courses or online information
- Developing more robust, industrial-strength tools with better technical support
- Making important technology enhancements, such as data-encryption options for secure communication and commerce
- Improving usability by collecting pointers to resources on particular topics, or developing more sophisticated search tools
- Creating new and interesting Internet locations to visit

Most of these efforts can be subsidized directly, through monthly charges for a connection, tuition for courses, and so on. However, other efforts benefit those involved less directly. Visibility on the Internet has value, as does the perception that a company is closely associated with the Internet and is therefore an insider.

Internet as added value

Without a doubt, the Internet is "in." Thoughout 1994 and 1995, the Internet was featured in more magazines, newspapers, and television and radio broadcasts than one could have ever imagined, many having little to do with computing per se, such as *Vogue* and *People*. Publishing a company's electronic mail address also became fashionable.

Beyond legitimately reporting on the Internet as news, or merely becoming associated with something hip and trendy, some companies, like the home online services, were positioned to incorporate Internet access into their existing service packages. Others, like Encyclopedia Britannica, would actually produce Internet-accessible editions of their products.

Internet as a new marketplace

Perhaps the most visionary of commercial Internet players have been those who have seen the Internet as not just a new communications media, but as a new marketplace. As you might expect, this category of business opportunity has been the slowest to be recognized and exploited, because it relies first on Internet expansion and visibility for its success.

To be sure, legions of companies have begun marketing their products on the Internet, first by establishing a presence (a storefront, if you will) and then by posting complete, detailed product catalogs (some with full color illustrations) and contact information. Their ultimate goal, however, is the ability to conduct business and complete orders over the Internet.

This vision of the Internet opened an interesting niche. Companies began leasing electronic storefronts to other companies that wanted to establish a presence on the Internet without investing in their own servers and staff to run them. We'll discuss all this in more detail in Chapter 12.

The revolution continues

In this chapter, we have traced the course of the Internet from its obscure beginnings and initial growth through its transformation into what we now call the *New* Internet, and have traced the role of commercial interests in the process. But the revolution goes on, and public and commercial interest continues to grow.

The Internet & society

As this book goes to press, the Internet remains in the news. When the now famous Pentium processor bug was discovered, consumers on the Internet were in the know in a matter of hours, long before Intel itself could respond. When another deadly package bomb was delivered, the FBI turned to the Internet community for help in tracking down the responsible party. When two attorneys in California broadcast an advertisement for their services wildly across the Internet, the outcry from the user community made headlines (and, to the dismay of many, created a new pair of celebrities). Candidates for office, political action committees, and even an inmate on death row in Illinois used the New Internet to try to influence public opinion directly, outside the editorial boundaries of traditional media.

Competition & standards

The World Wide Web browser market is changing. NCSA Mosaic is no longer the only premier graphical interface to the New Internet, though it still fits into an important niche as *the* quality browser that's available free on the Internet. Spyglass Enhanced Mosaic is commercially available in large quantities to third-party vendors. Luckman Interactive is such a vendor which, in turn, makes Enhanced Mosaic available to you on CD with this book.

The other major player across all three major platforms, as of this writing, is Netscape, developed by Netscape Communications Corporation. One of NCC's first acts was to hire several of the original Mosaic developers away from NCSA. Netscape is available for download from the Internet, but for a small charge. NCSA Mosaic, Spyglass Enhanced Mosaic, and Netscape are all developing their own loyal followings, and several other commercial browsers are also available.

With increased competition, however, comes concern that standards for the Internet, and particularly Mosaic and the World Wide Web, will be ignored in favor of proprietary enhancements. CERN and the Laboratory for Computer Science at MIT have founded the WWW Consortium (W3C) to ensure the evolution of WWW into a true information infrastructure. Under the direction of Tim Berners-Lee, the organization was established as a vendor-neutral forum for formalizing and evolving Web standards.

Internet privatization

For years, the networking community has called upon the telephone companies and other for-profit ventures to provide off-the-shelf IP connections. That is, just as you can now place an order for an extra telephone jack in your house, purchasing an Internet connection should be just as easy. You order, the telephone installer leaves, and you plug your computer into the Internet.

The telephone companies have historically said, "We'll sell you phone lines and you can do whatever you like with them." But now that large corporations have become interested in the Internet, the attitude of the phone companies has begun to change. As commercially available services become viable, government subsidies are being withdrawn.

Although many people in the networking community think that privatization is a good idea, there are some obstacles to overcome. Most revolve around the funding for the connections. Many schools are connected because the government pays part, and in some cases all, of the bill. If they had to pay their own way some schools would probably decide to spend their money elsewhere. Major research institutions would find financial support to remain connected but some smaller colleges might not, and the costs would probably be prohibitive for most secondary schools. The Internet has not yet become a necessity in the minds of many.

Moving on

So this is where the Internet has been and where it is headed, at least in the near term. But what impact could the New Internet have on you in today's business and social climate? We'll explore these questions in Chapter 3.

3

You & the New Internet

CHAPTER 3

AS we pointed out in the introduction to this book, the boundaries between home and the workplace are blurring. Dial-up access for employees to company computers is becoming more common, especially as businesses become motivated to encourage telecommuting. Many small businesses are now being run out of home offices, where a computer, a modem, and a fax machine can allow you to operate on even a global scale. And personal home access to the Internet has become complementary to access on the job, where company policies might prohibit Internet use for personal aims.

This chapter addresses the question, "What can the New Internet do for you?" To answer that question we need to take both professional and personal needs into account. We'll explore the work-related aspects first. What fundamental information needs of business does the Internet serve? Does it make sense, in turn, to serve the Internet? What concerns business about the Internet today, and are these concerns justified? Then we'll turn to the home user. What do you need to feel comfortable in welcoming the Internet into your home? What purposes can it serve once you are connected? How do you get started?

The New Internet at work

The research arms of the corporate world have known about the Internet since it began. They've used it for electronic mail communication outside the organization, collaborative information sharing, remote computing, and locating and collecting software.

Today, the Internet influences a company's bottom line in a whole new array of ways. We'll be discussing them in the upcoming sections. Businesses have also raised additional concerns over being connected to the Internet as well. We'll look at those concerns, too, with an eye toward how they are being met right now. To be sure, regardless of your industry or profession, failing to be *Internet aware* will eventually put you and your business at a competitive disadvantage.

Filling the information needs of business

A wealth of electronic information is out there, much of it useful and important to business and industry. Certainly, some of this information is available through sources outside the boundaries of the Internet. But Mosaic has the power to help manage the flow and pull widely varying types of data together in one place. You can keep the LEXIS-NEXIS information services, state and local regulatory agencies, and your competitors' Internet servers right there in your hotlist for quick access, alongside the rest of your most valued Internet resources.

Among other things, Mosaic and the Internet can help you:

- Expand your customer base
- Keep up with developments in your industry or profession
- Access standards and regulations
- Research economic and statistical information
- Learn to manage your work more effectively
- See what your competition is doing

In these sections we'll highlight through examples some of the ways that the New Internet can meet the fundamental information needs of business. The Internet addresses shown (the lines beginning with **http://** and set in **boldface** type) are called *URLs*. We'll be describing how they are used in Chapter 7. Also, the resource examples we offer are notable but not unique. In Chapter 9 you'll learn how to find many more related Internet resources that you can use in various areas of your professional life.

Company data

Among the most valuable types of information for businesspeople are those relating to other companies. Through online sources on the Internet it's possible to know about another company's market position, financial resources, key decision makers, and more.

Perhaps the most visible provider of company information in the business world is Dun and Bradstreet. Their Internet home page is shown in Fig. 3-1. The D&B information base includes data on 36 million companies worldwide, gathered from interviews, news sources, public records, legal filings, trade associations, and other sources.

Figure 3-1

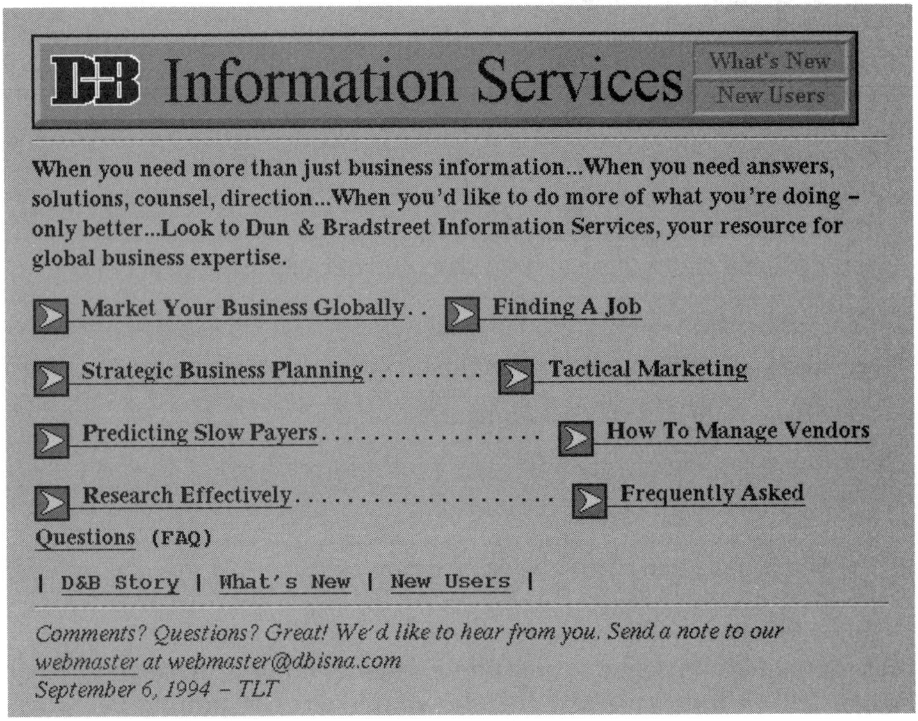

Dun & Bradstreet Information Services Home Page—
http://www.dbisna.com/

Another useful source of company data on the Internet is the EDGAR database, where anyone can search the archives of electronic, public filings to the Securities and Exchange Commission since 1994. The Internet EDGAR Dissemination project (its home page is shown in Fig. 3-2) is actually a research project not affiliated with the SEC. It's also free, and therefore within the reach of even the smallest of business concerns and concerned individuals as well.

Figure 3-2

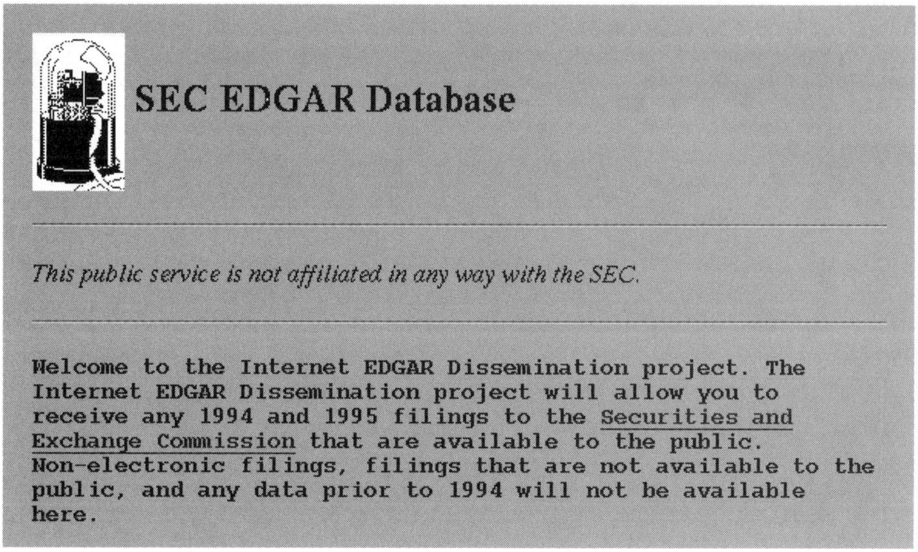

*SEC EDGAR Home Page—**http://town.hall.org/edgar/edgar.html***

✳ Entrepreneurial & small business resources

If you are about to launch a new business or have just started out, the Internet might be your best source for information and assistance. Some of the traditional sources are there, such as the U.S. Small Business Administration (see Fig. 3-3). SBA Online offers valuable information for starting, financing, and expanding your business.

In addition, there are sites that evolved directly out of the Internet information infrastructure, such as Entrepreneur Net (shown in Fig. 3-4). Also called ENET, this resource contains sites of interest to entrepreneurs and the like, including links to several other entrepreneur-related home pages, finance information, tax information, other commercial sites, newsgroups, and links to most of the major search engines on the Web.

✳ Financial market data

Internet sites have started appearing, which address the needs of business for financial market data. QuoteCom is one such service, shown in Fig. 3-5. Registered users might retrieve stock and commodity quotes, and might reference various stock guides and news wire

Figure 3-3

Small Business Administration Home Page—
http://www.sbaonline.sba.gov/

reports. Quite coincidentally, you can sample any of the QuoteCom services at no cost for the ticker symbol MHP—McGraw-Hill.

Information research services

Online research services have been around for more than twenty years. They allow business professionals to search electronically across thousands of magazines, newspapers, journals and reports for news and information related to their markets. Such services are by no means free, of course, even on the Internet. But once you are a

Figure 3-4

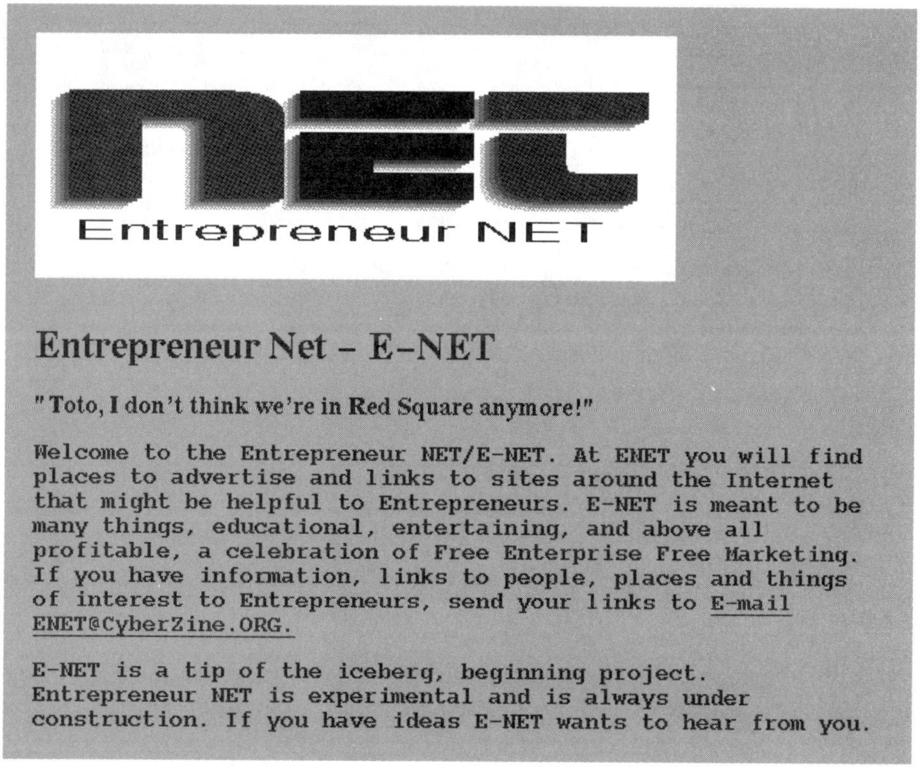

Entrepreneur Net Home Page—
http://www.cyberzine.org/html/Entrepreneur/enetpage2.html

subscriber, Internet access makes it very easy to use these services within the Mosaic environment.

DIALOG has a home page, as shown in Fig. 3-6. With a DIALOG subscription you have searchable access to over 100 newspapers, thousands of magazines and journals, intellectual property files, and millions of other documents across a diverse spectrum of disciplines.

The LEXIS-NEXIS services are also on the Internet (see Fig. 3-7). Launched in 1973, LEXIS bills itself as the first commercial full-text legal information service. NEXIS is a companion news and information service. LEXIS-NEXIS indexes nearly half a *billion* documents in more than 5000 databases.

Figure 3-5

QuoteCom Home Page—***http://www.quote.com/***

Figure 3-6

DIALOG Home Page—***http://www.dialog.com/***

Figure 3-7

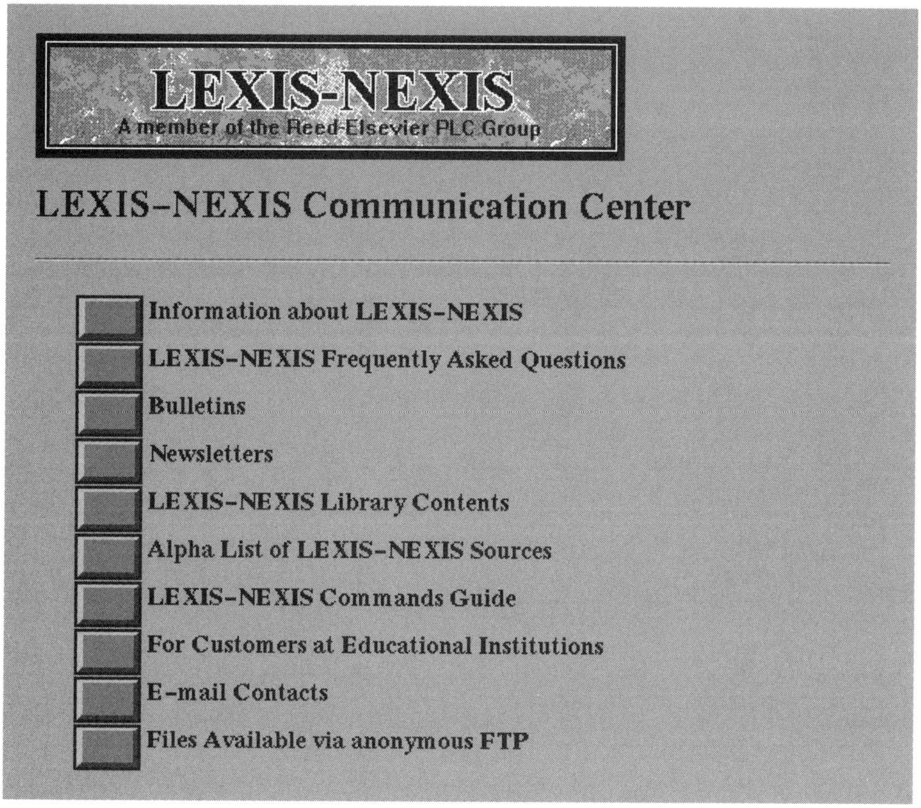

LEXIS-NEXIS Home Page—***http://www.lexis-nexis.com/***

✳ Market opportunities

How can the Internet help you expand your business? One way is by helping you understand foreign markets. The National Trade Data Bank is on the Internet (shown in Fig. 3-8). The NTDB is the U.S. Government's most comprehensive source of world trade data.

Also notable here is the ability to access The Commerce Business Daily on the Internet (see Fig. 3-9). The CBD lists notices of U.S. Government procurement activities, including all proposed procurements of over $25,000. This is where most companies identify government contract opportunities.

Figure 3-8

National Trade Data Bank Home Page— ***http://www.stat-usa.gov/BEN/Services/ntdbhome.html*** STAT-USA is a trademark of the U.S. Department of Commerce, Economics, and Statistics Administration.

Figure 3-9

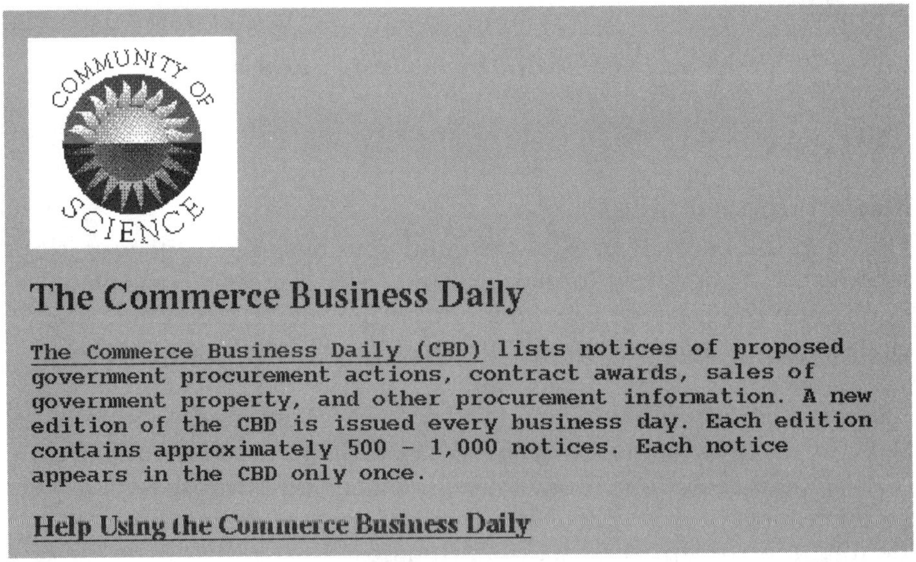

The Commerce Business Daily Home Page— ***http://cos.gdb.org/repos/cbd/cbd-intro.html***

⁜ Standards & regulations

Virtually all businesses are subject to various regulations and standards pertaining to the workplace, the environment, and their own products and services. Much of this information is Internet-accessible in convenient ways. The IEEE (Institute of Electrical and Electronics Engineers), OSHA (Occupational Safety and Health Administration), and NIST (National Institute of Standards and Technology) all operate World Wide Web servers. The IEEE home page is shown in Fig. 3-10.

Figure 3-10

IEEE Home Page—***http://www.ieee.org/***

⁜ Statistics & economic data

The Internet contains some wonderful sources of economic and statistical data. Inforum EconData, at the University of Maryland, makes hundreds of thousands of economic time series available for downloading (see Fig. 3-11). These include national income and product accounts (NIPA), labor statistics, price indices, current business indicators, industrial production, and more. The U.S. Bureau of the Census and the U.S. Department of Commerce Economic Bulletin Board are also on the Internet.

Figure 3-11

*Inforum EconData Home Page—***http://info.umd.edu:86/ Educational_Resources/AcademicResourcesByTopic/Economics Resources/EconData/.www/econdata.html**

Establishing an Internet presence

The potential business benefits of a connection to the Internet extend beyond the collection of information served up by others. Consider the various types of home pages depicted in this book. What makes the companies, agencies, and individuals they represent useful to you as a potential user? More important, what makes them worthwhile to those that serve them? You're likely to discover that the answers to these two questions go hand in hand. Both UPS and Federal Express, for example, let you track your shipments over the Internet quickly and easily.

There are several reasons why your company might choose to establish a presence on the Internet. For example:

- Making product catalogs, press releases and other information available electronically. For some kinds of goods and services the availability of such information on the Internet can significantly reduce the costs and environmental effects associated with using paper for the same purposes.
- Making the product itself available over the Internet, if that product is a form of information. This is what DIALOG, Dun and Bradstreet, and Encyclopedia Britannica are already doing.

- Sustaining relationships with customers in an inexpensive way. Customers can have a responsive place to go for technical assistance or to initiate new business.
- Eventually taking orders and conducting business over the Internet. In Chapter 12, we'll review a few of the tools currently being developed to make Internet electronic commerce possible very soon.

Chapter 12 will also explain how to establish a multimedia presence on the Internet, either by maintaining your own server or by leasing space from a third party.

Home field advantage—Enterprise-wide webs

In this discussion about the New Internet at work we first saw how Mosaic gives you a powerful window into the vast Internet storehouse of facts, figures, charts, graphs, and more. We then discussed something of how serving multimedia information to other Mosaic users can meet certain customer-oriented business needs.

But there's also a way to combine many of the benefits of both of these notions to address a different class of business problems, while sidestepping some of the concerns to be discussed in the next sections. The idea is that of an enterprise-wide Web.

Many companies are using World Wide Web servers and Mosaic browsers to build information delivery systems for internal use. At least initially, the servers are not accessible from the Internet at large. But employees throughout a group, division, or entire company have fast access to project information, training resources, strategic plans, human resource information, and more. Mosaic is also becoming the tool of choice for viewing legacy data—Web servers can now act as gateways to Oracle databases and Excel spreadsheets, for example.

The underlying concerns of business

We've written a lot of wonderfully positive things about the New Internet so far in this chapter. But if you have already explored Internet connectivity even casually for your business, you know that there is much to be concerned about as well. Business criticisms of the Internet tend to fall into five categories, which we will discuss in the following sections—education, effort, misuse, reliability, and security.

Educational concerns

Companies have traditionally believed that learning how to use the Internet is too difficult for it to be useful on a large scale, and that it's particularly difficult if you are not experienced with UNIX. When you needed to rely on the traditional tools like FTP, for instance, in a line-terminal environment, this was true. In a way, effective Internet users needed to be multilingual in terms of protocols. Moreover, Internet books for nontechnical users were scarce or nonexistent—you found your way around because a techie was willing to hold your hand, or by limiting your approach to a single tool that gained you access to only a small fraction of the Internet.

By the time you have completed this book we hope you will be convinced that this is no longer the case. The New Internet is well within the realm of comfort and competence for virtually anyone.

Effort concerns

Hand in hand with the educational concerns, it has also been widely believed that setting up and maintaining Internet connectivity throughout a company required too much effort for the benefits that could actually be realized. There has also been concern that the Internet is just too large and disorganized for the average user to locate anything in it easily.

Connectivity can indeed be difficult, especially when dealing with PC LANs. You might want to bring in some expertise to get your Novell server connected to your firewall, for instance. And installing Mosaic and all the required support software on a PC has always been tricky and time-consuming. However, you should read through the middle chapters of this book carefully. Given the software provided on the CD, you might discover that the situation is not nearly as ominous as it might have seemed in the past.

As for locating resources, Chapter 9 aims to put that concern to rest once and for all. It *is* possible to find extensive collections of information on most any topic, by using the tools we recommend and the methods we propose.

❊ Misuse concerns

Concerns about misuse of the Internet are of still a different nature. In the best case, misuse might simply mean that employees are wasting time exploring resources not related to their work. This is an accountability issue and your company might institute whatever controls it deems worthwhile to limit nonproductive use as best it can. You probably already have an acceptable-use policy for long distance calls and fax transmissions. Plan to have one for Internet use as well.

In the worst case, however, misuse can mean public embarrassment or worse. For example, if an employee is discovered to have used company networks and computers to download pornographic images from the Internet the reputations of the company and the employee might suffer. Legal issues come into play here too—pornography might not be illegal in the country it was obtained from, but what about its importation into *your* country? Your company should assess its tolerance for risk in this area.

❊ Reliability concerns

Much of business' concerns about reliability come from the heavily distributed nature of the Internet, and to some extent from the cultural differences between the Internet community and the business community. Much of the software involved in Internet connectivity and use is public domain or shareware. Is it reliable? Is it supported? Business is accustomed to formal support organizations and products backed by reputable companies. Discovering that you are sending electronic mail to a university student for product support might come as a shock. By now, however, there are commercial versions of any software you might need, though until more tightly integrated software solutions become available, issues of coordinating support remain.

Also at the core of this issue is the concern that "Nobody owns the Internet," and the corollary assumption that any system of this magnitude with no central administrative body must be a breeding ground for unreliable service. But the fact is, each component of the

Internet is owned by somebody and each owner has a heavily vested interest in keeping his or her corner of the Internet running smoothly.

There are also a handful of organizations that oversee Internet activities at a more holistic level. The Internet Engineering Task Force (IETF) is responsible for short-term technical deliverables across the Internet. The IETF produces documents describing protocol and application standards, and information of general technical interest to the Internet community. The Internet Society is an international oversight organization founded to maintain and extend the development and availability of the Internet and its associated technologies and applications. There is also the WWW Consortium, whose goal is to ensure the smooth evolution of the World Wide Web and its protocols into a true information infrastructure. Many of the major players in internetworking are participants in the W3C, including AT&T, Digital Equipment Corporation, IBM, NCSA, Novell, and many others.

Security concerns

When it comes to Internet connectivity or most anything else, nothing raises the red flags faster for company executives than concerns about security. Internet intruders, like intruders from within an organization, can compromise the confidentiality of stored information, or perhaps even compromise the data itself.

Even if they do not modify the data they can disrupt the normal availability of your computers. Or, they can simply watch your employees' usage patterns to glean information to be used for competitive advantage.

The key to addressing security concerns is to raise security awareness among your users and system administrators. Here are some of the basic considerations:

- Nothing sent out into the Internet can be expected to remain private without special handling.
- Logging in remotely across the Internet in an unencrypted fashion leaves your username and password—the keys to the kingdom—available to "sniffing" and interception.

- Computers on your network that are not hidden behind network firewalls are potential targets for skilled hackers.
- Divulging your password to anyone—especially over the phone—can defeat even the best security precautions.

Encryption schemes and firewall systems do exist, and recent books, such as *Firewalls and Internet Security—Repelling the Wily Hacker* by Cheswick and Bellovin, have struck a responsive chord. So how can you reduce your risks in this area?

Start by attending a reputable class or two on Internet security. Get acquainted with CERT, the Computer Emergency Response Team, at Carnegie Mellon University (try the URL **ftp://cert.org/pub/** when you reach Chapter 8). Keep your network computer up to date with the latest operating system security patches. And above all, provide written guidelines to your users to help prevent their unwittingly giving away the store.

The New Internet at home

So much for the Internet at work. What about the home front? To the average person, connecting to the Internet can seem like entering the vast unknown, evoking feelings of excitement, fear, and wonder all at once. While home Internet usage had grown dramatically in the last year or so, huge numbers of households have yet to take the plunge, either because people just don't know about the Internet or how to get it, they lack the confidence or the know-how to handle the technology, or they have not yet seen the potential value. In other words, the prerequisites have not yet been met for the acceptance of the Internet into their homes. If you are among this group we hope that this chapter and book will speak to you.

Of the many people who *have* welcomed the Internet into their homes, some approach it with some technical background. Perhaps they already dial-up to the computer at the office, for instance. Others are users of the commercial online services. They might even use their America Online, Prodigy, CompuServe, or GEnie account to reach the Internet. And then there are those who, as with many other technologies, are learning about *surfing the Net* from their kids.

For these folks, the prerequisites have been met. They visit interesting and informative resources for personal use. They tap sources of professional information—perhaps they lack an Internet connection at the office, or their home *is* their office. They seek educational benefits for their children—collecting facts and figures for school projects, witnessing cultural diversity, or just learning networking concepts and skills that are increasingly valuable in tomorrow's world. They have fun being electronic explorers. Or possibly, it's just the trendy thing to do . . . and there's nothing wrong with that!

In the next sections we'll discuss what the New Internet is all about from the home user's perspective. We'll look at those original in-home prerequisites and how we as authors, and countless others, are helping you to meet them. We'll see how the roots of the home users' concerns about the Internet actually represent more global concerns. Many of these are addressed by Internet resources that you can readily use. Finally, we'll see how a home user can gain access to the New Internet, and how it stacks up against other home information sources.

Accepting the New Internet into your home

Whether you will connect your business to the Internet is ultimately a financial decision. On the other hand, whether you will invite the Internet into your home is a personal decision, and personal decisions require that you factor in your values and your fears—your heart as well as your head. There are prerequisites to be met in both respects, and we explain the major ones here. Whether you are currently a home *Internaut* or not, think about the following needs and consider which among them are the most important to you.

Connecting to and using the Internet must not evoke high levels of frustration and embarrassment. Nobody wants to emerge from a new experience feeling inadequate or incompetent, and the fear of failure grips people's lives more than anyone cares to admit. When you are at work and you can't make your PC or software work, you probably have someone to call and help you out. When you are at home, however, you can feel very much alone with the technology.

Unfortunately, all the initial media hype about the Internet preceded its practical use in the home by at least a year, and until very recently, home access to the World Wide Web has been very difficult to accomplish. In writing this book we aim to be reassuring above all else, and to make the New Internet easy to comprehend, install, configure, use, and use effectively. We hope we will be at least somewhat successful.

The cost of connecting and navigating the Internet must be both reasonable and predictable. There are at least four components:

- Cost of the software for your PC
- One-time subscription fee and monthly base charges from your service provider
- Usage fees from your service provider, based on the number of hours you are connected
- Your phone bill

No matter how you obtain your Internet access, most if not all of these factors will come into play. Your software cost might be limited to what you have paid for this book and CD, or your particular provider might sell or give you the software you need. As for the other charges, shop around. Some providers charge a flat monthly fee for Internet access with unlimited use. If they also have a point of presence close to your home (local phone call), and if your local phone company charges nonmetered rates for local calls, this is probably your least expensive service provider in the long run. And if you don't understand how your phone company charges, ask them to explain their metering rates.

Access to the Internet must add value to your life, not detract from it. It must deliver what has been promised. Try to sort out the hype in advance to make the most accurate possible judgment. Will the Internet enhance your life? To a large degree, it depends on how you choose to use it. There is no question that the Internet offers timely information and enriching experiences to those who look for them. Yet there's some pretty troubling stuff out there, too.

If you insist that the Internet be a playground where you can turn your kids loose for hours of unsupervised, totally wholesome fun and education, reality will not meet your demands. For all that was said in Chapter 2 about the Internet culture, the Internet *does* reflect humanity, good and bad—more accurately than television does, which we believe is an asset. We urge you to be willing to view the Internet as a teacher in the same way the world around us is a teacher. There are benefits to the Internet in education, expertise, consumerism, convenience, and entertainment. And it's possible to avoid the negatives with a little care.

Meeting the home user's needs

We have just identified at least three important needs to be met if you are to welcome the Internet into your home. There's nothing at all unusual about these needs. In fact, they could be considered in conjunction with virtually any decision you make that affects you personally. When it comes right down to it, the Internet is just a vast interconnecting of people with the same needs. This is what can make the Internet so valuable to you, for it gives you a place to turn to as you face the problems and choices of everyday life.

The Internet can go a long way toward alleviating frustration and isolation. You can find helpful advice and information on virtually any topic. Perhaps more important, you can see first-hand that others have been in your shoes and might even be willing to connect with you directly. And don't assume that members of the Internet community hide behind their computers, either. For example, there is an Internet discussion forum on the subject of parenting (the USENET newsgroup **misc.kids**—USENET is described in Chapter 8). Not only do the many hundreds of participants share their child rearing experiences, but some also contribute their family photos to an annual yearbook, and travel many miles to meet up with each other for picnics in the summer. As you face decisions about how to manage your finances, or how to judge the value of a good, a service, or a relationship, the Internet can help you there as well.

A home user's Internet sampler

Once you have at least entertained the possibility of Internet access from your home, think for a moment about the specific ways a resource like the Internet might fit into your daily life. We've thought of some possibilities, and have even found a few Internet locations you could visit to get yourself started. As we said in the business sections, you will learn all about how to use these addresses (called URLs) and how to find many, many more related to Internet resources later in this book.

Career & employment

There are several Internet sites containing job openings and other useful resources for both job seekers and human resource managers. One example is the NCS Career Magazine (see Fig. 3-12), maintained by National Career Search. They combine job postings, employer profiles, recent news articles about careers, guidelines for resumé writing, and more.

Figure 3-12

*NCS Career Magazine Home Page—**http://plaza.xor.com/careermag/index.html***

Consider as well that thousands of prospective employers are on the Internet. By visiting their home pages you can explore career opportunities and gather valuable background information about them.

Consumer assistance

On the whole, you're likely to find that the best information on the Internet for consumers comes from other users sharing their opinions and experiences. We mentioned in Chapter 2 how Internet users knew more about the Intel Pentium division bug, and knew it sooner, than anyone else in business or the media.

Internet sites dedicated to consumer assistance and consumer advocacy are also springing up. You probably know of the U.S. Government Consumer Information Center (Pueblo, Colorado 81009). Their catalog and services are on the World Wide Web, as shown in Fig. 3-13.

Figure 3-13

Consumer Information Center Home Page—***http://www.gsa.gov/staff/pa/cic/cic.htm*** This service is provided by the Consumer Information Center of the U.S. General Services Administration.

⁎ Current events

One of the aspects of the Internet that makes us most gratified to be writing about it is the way individuals and organizations step forward to serve the public interest when significant events occur. Some of these events can be anticipated—elections, for example. Digital Equipment Corporation and the State of California joined together in the fall of 1994 to provide voter information and returns for the 1994 California general election. The home page is shown in Fig. 3-14. Note that it was offered in several languages.

Figure 3-14

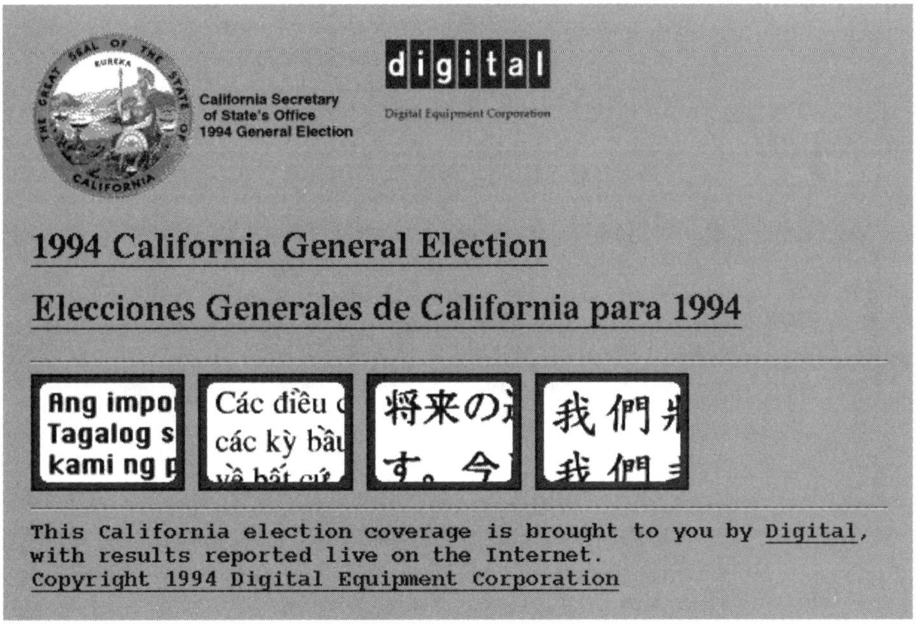

*1994 California General Election Home Page—**http://www.election.ca.gov/*** ©1994 Digital Equipment Corp.

Another pilot project called VOICE (Voter Online Information and Communication Exchange) has provided candidate profile and voter information from the Leagues of Women Voters and other sources, with public libraries serving as the access points. Such services are likely to proliferate in the future.

Other important events, however, cannot be anticipated. Immediately after a magnitude 7.2 earthquake shook Kobe, Japan, in January 1995 the Kobe Earthquake Reference Page appeared (as shown in Fig. 3-15), with up-to-date damage and injury reports and links to many valuable related information sources. For many with relatives in Japan, the Internet was among the most reliable sources of comprehensive information in those first few days after the quake. Similar home pages appeared during the January 1995 flooding in California, and in the aftermath of the April 1995 bombing in Oklahoma City. In the former case, more than ten organizations contributed weather and highway data, emergency assistance, food/shelter information, damage assessments, and other valuable information.

Figure 3-15

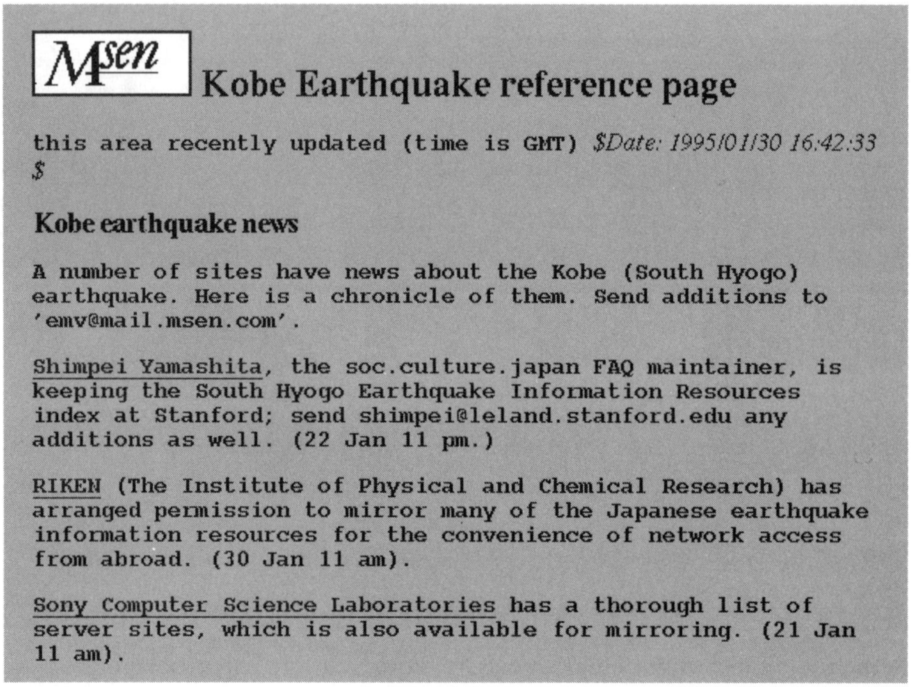

Msen Kobe Earthquake reference page

this area recently updated (time is GMT) *$Date: 1995/01/30 16:42:33 $*

Kobe earthquake news

A number of sites have news about the Kobe (South Hyogo) earthquake. Here is a chronicle of them. Send additions to 'emv@mail.msen.com'.

Shimpei Yamashita, the soc.culture.japan FAQ maintainer, is keeping the South Hyogo Earthquake Information Resources index at Stanford; send shimpei@leland.stanford.edu any additions as well. (22 Jan 11 pm.)

RIKEN (The Institute of Physical and Chemical Research) has arranged permission to mirror many of the Japanese earthquake information resources for the convenience of network access from abroad. (30 Jan 11 am).

Sony Computer Science Laboratories has a thorough list of server sites, which is also available for mirroring. (21 Jan 11 am).

Kobe Earthquake Information Home Page—***http://www.msen.com/~emv/kobe.html*** Maintained by Edward Vielmetti.

✳ Education

The possible applications of Internet exploration toward learning are inherently limitless. You will be able to use the tools and strategies explained in Chapter 9 of this book to find information about topics, cultures, organizations, and more.

But there are also places on the Internet where more structured learning environments are being established for people of various age groups. One is the Cyberspace Middle School, shown in Fig. 3-16. It's geared toward 7th, 8th, and 9th grade students and their teachers, with funding from the U.S. National Science Foundation.

Figure 3-16

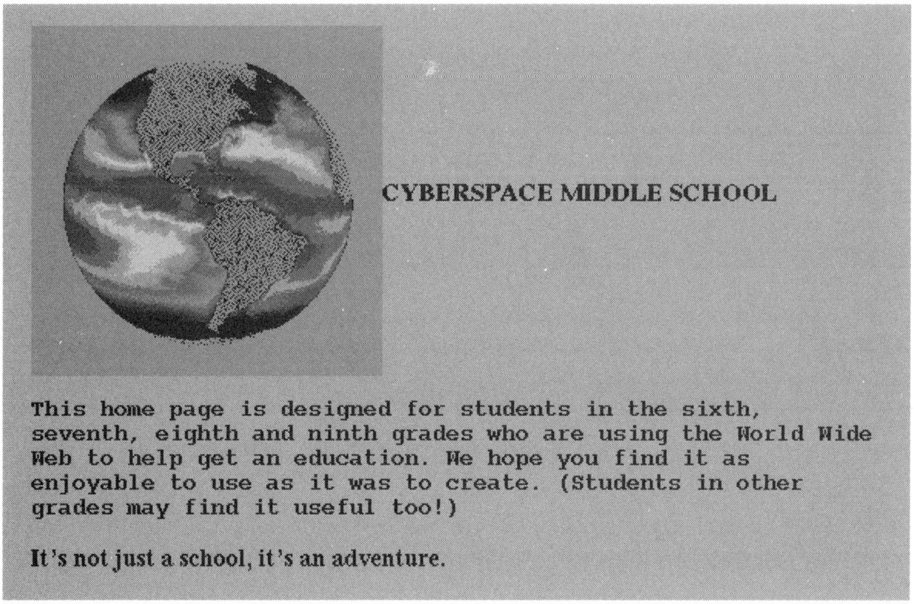

*Cyberspace Middle School Home Page—**http://www.scri.fsu.edu/~dennisl/CMS.html***

Entertainment

Given the nature of multimedia, the New Internet is a natural place both for providing entertainment and for promoting or complementing entertainment in other media—television, recordings, live performances, and so on.

The CBS Television Home Page (see Fig. 3-17) is just one example. It focuses on promoting CBS shows and personalities.

Figure 3-17

CBS Television Home Page—***http://www.cbs.com/*** CBS "eye device" is a registered trademark of CBS, Inc. ©MCMXCV CBS, Inc. All rights reserved.

In addition, fans of actors, musicians, and artists proudly create home pages about them, full of biographical information and text and multimedia references to their works. The search techniques discussed in Chapter 9 will lead you directly to sites about many of your favorites.

✳ Health & medicine

Regardless of your level of sophistication on the subject, there are many sources of health and medical information available to you on the Internet, from basic information on nutrition on up to the latest research findings on cancer or AIDS. Healthwise is but one example, shown in Fig. 3-18. It's provided by the Columbia University Health Service, and is oriented to a question and answer system called *Ask Alice*. Compared to calling your family doctor, Healthwise offers at least two potential benefits—you can ask questions anonymously, and you can search the archives of past questions and responses.

Figure 3-18

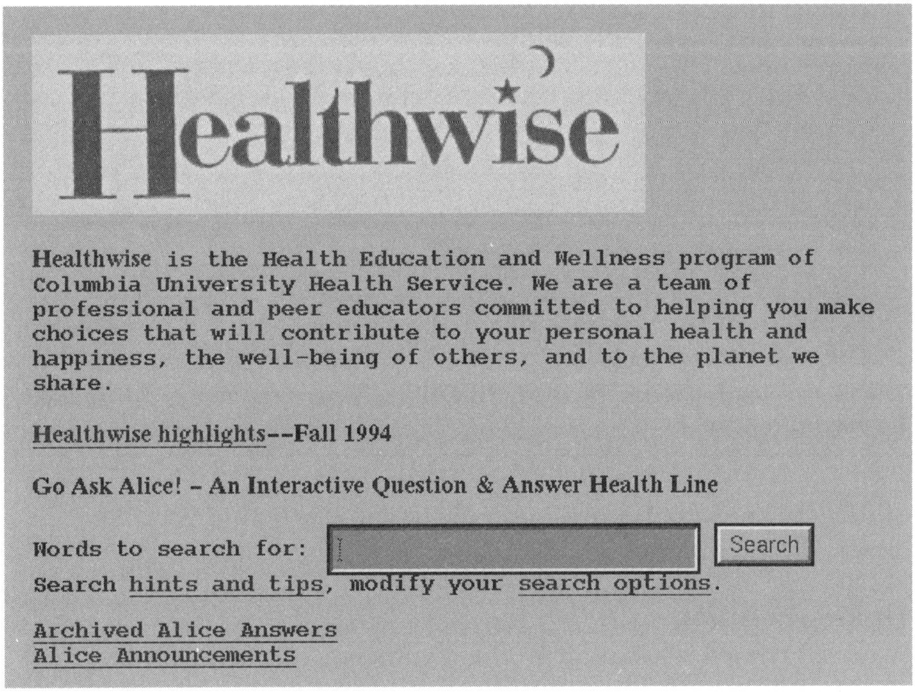

Healthwise Home Page—***http://www.columbia.edu/cu/healthwise/index.html***

⁂ Hobbies

The Internet is fertile ground for discussions of hobbies—hiking, horses, photography, ham radio, scuba diving—you name it, including gardening. There's The Garden Gate, for instance (shown in Fig. 3-19). Not only have links to a vast variety of online gardening resources been pulled together in one place, but because the curator is located in Eastern Illinois (on the Prairienet Free-Net), there is also horticultural information tailored specifically to that region. This sort

Figure 3-19

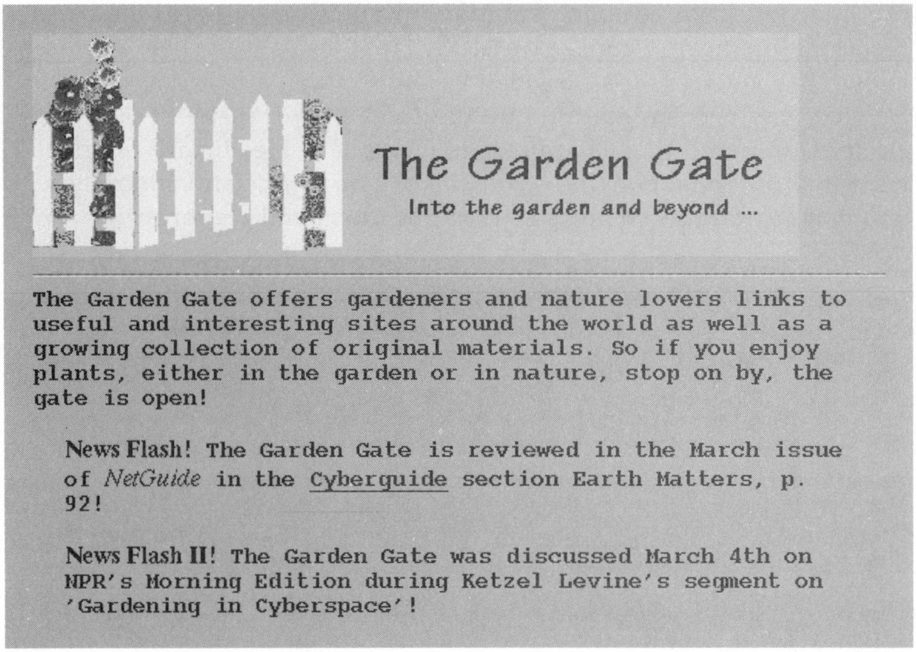

The Garden Gate Home Page—***http://www.prairienet.org/ag/garden/homepage.htm*** © 1994-95 Karen Fletcher.

of focus is hard to find in a book about gardening, but is rather typical on the Internet.

Home shopping

As we discussed in Chapter 2, the commercial world is working very hard to find successful ways to sell their wares on the Internet. There are indeed such things as "shopping malls" on the Internet. The television-based Home Shopping Network runs one of the largest, called the Internet Shopping Network. Relatively few online shopping storefronts have profited so far, but they are out there for you to visit to gather product and service information, and will become even more convenient to use once secure credit card transactions become possible over the Internet within the next year or so.

How else can the Internet make home shopping easier? One way is to be able to browse or search 1-800 long-distance telephone directories, such as AT&T's (shown in Fig. 3-20). If you are Internet-connected

Figure 3-20

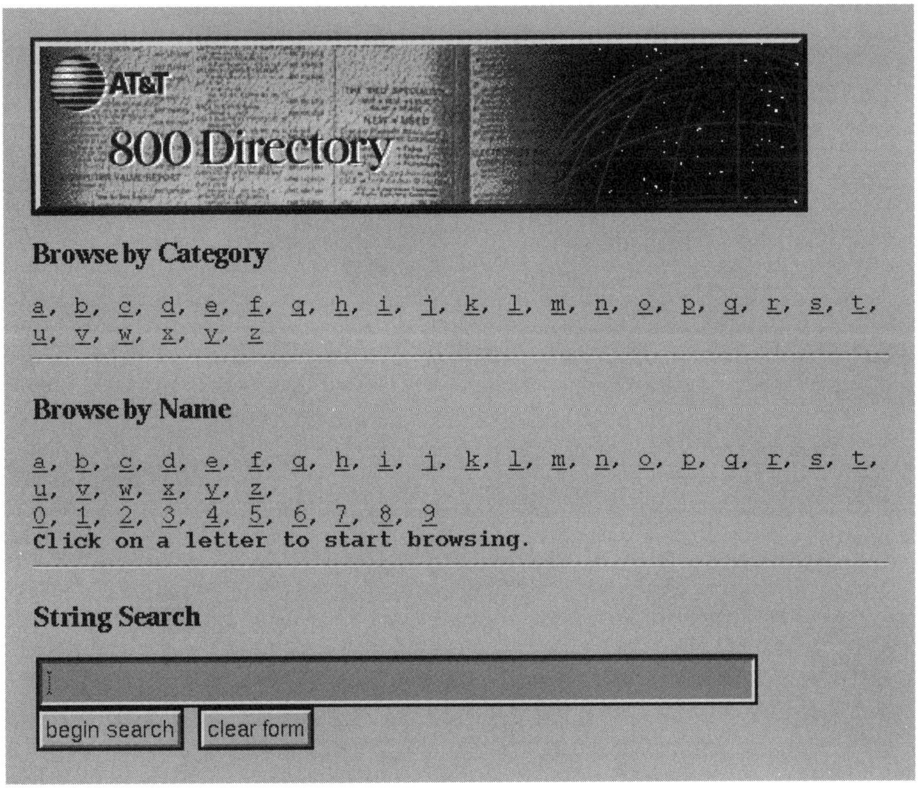

*AT&T 800 Directory Home Page—**http://att.net/dir800/***

you'll find the online directory offers more flexibility than calling 1-800 directory assistance or thumbing through the paper directory.

Personal finance

Most people would place their finances near the top of their list of personal issues. The Internet reflects this, now that the user community had grown so large.

If you are an investor, you might be interested in a free service called NETworth by Galt Technologies, shown in Fig. 3-21. They provide stock quotes, mutual fund prospecti, tips for individual investing, detailed weekly market updates, and other services.

Figure 3-21

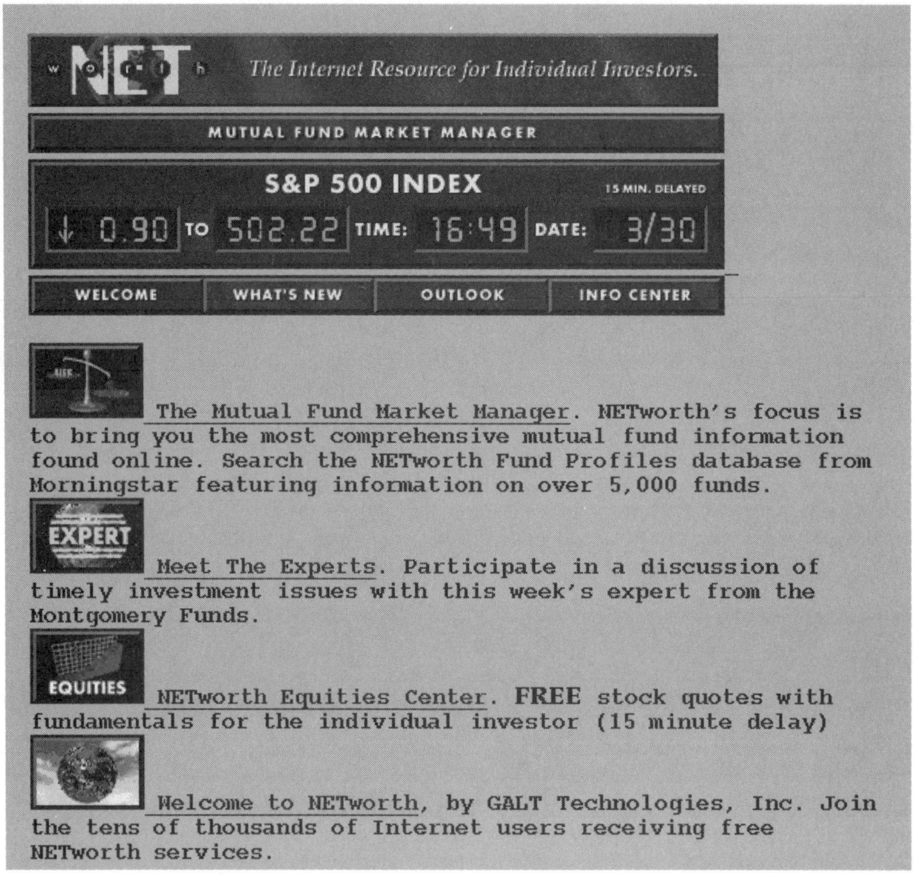

NETworth Home Page—
http://networth.galt.com/www/home/networth.html

Other types of finance-related resources are available on the Internet, too. If you are a U.S. taxpayer, you can obtain federal tax forms online directly from the Internal Revenue Service (see Fig. 3-22). The IRS Web site also maintains a frequently asked questions list, which you might find even more useful. Similar services might be available on the Internet for your home state as well.

Figure 3-22

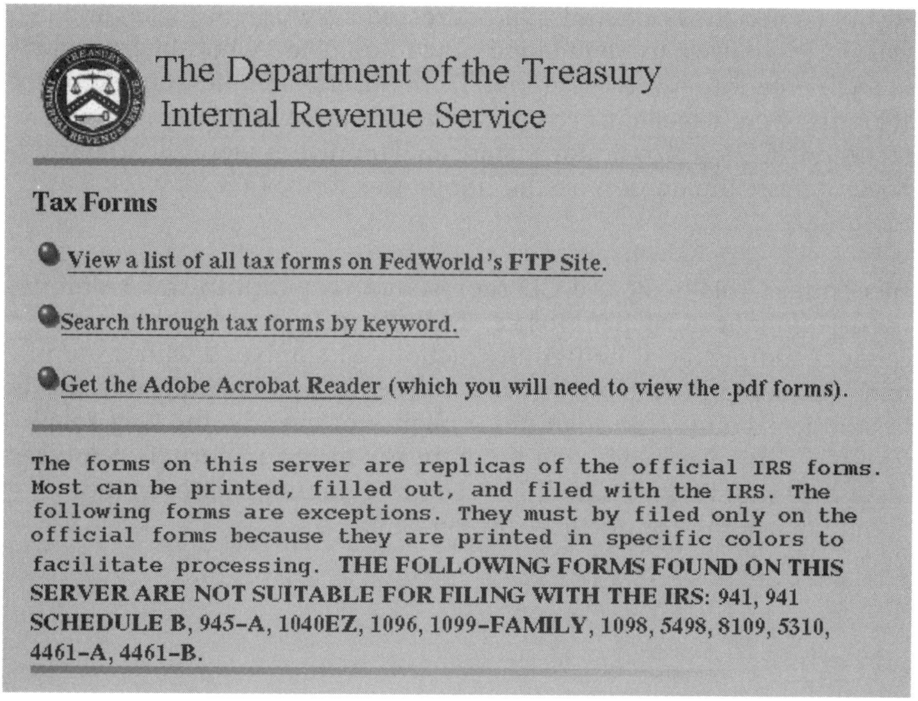

The Department of the Treasury
Internal Revenue Service

Tax Forms

- View a list of all tax forms on FedWorld's FTP Site.
- Search through tax forms by keyword.
- Get the Adobe Acrobat Reader (which you will need to view the .pdf forms).

The forms on this server are replicas of the official IRS forms. Most can be printed, filled out, and filed with the IRS. The following forms are exceptions. They must by filed only on the official forms because they are printed in specific colors to facilitate processing. **THE FOLLOWING FORMS FOUND ON THIS SERVER ARE NOT SUITABLE FOR FILING WITH THE IRS:** 941, 941 SCHEDULE B, 945-A, 1040EZ, 1096, 1099-FAMILY, 1098, 5498, 8109, 5310, 4461-A, 4461-B.

Internal Revenue Service Tax Forms Home Page— ***http://www.ustreas.gov/cgi-bin/searchforms***

Internet alternatives at home

As we mentioned earlier, the tremendous hype surrounding the New Internet (browsing hypertext with a tool like Mosaic) was well underway long before it was practical to use any of the newer options at home. The early Internet connectivity solutions for the home were far from straightforward and not for the faint-of-heart. In *The Great Commercial Awakening* in Chapter 2 we discussed how some companies and individuals sought to profit from helping to expand the Internet, including into the home. Advances were made and continue to be made in four areas: software tools for users, low-level communication software, service offerings over standard phone lines, and education.

At first, solutions appeared that addressed only one of these, and it was up to the user to understand how to combine what they needed in each area into a total solution. To the users' benefit, some of these solutions were excellent because, in large part, the providers were focused (NCSA's Mosaic for instance). The niches were filled, but nevertheless, the burden on the home user to make it all work was too great.

By contrast, this book and CD represent an attempt to serve all four needs—Enhanced NCSA Mosaic, TCP/IP software, Portal Internet service, and plenty of written instruction, all combined with a *plug-and-play* setup program. We are the first to say, however, that this is by no means a utopian solution. It might not even be the best solution for your particular needs, but if you're not already Internet-connected, it's a nice way to get started. Proceed to Chapter 4 to learn more about your home connectivity options.

4

Connecting to the New Internet

WHILE the information in this book is interesting and exciting, it will not do you much good unless you get your own Internet access functioning properly. This chapter outlines how to establish a connection to the Internet that makes it possible to enjoy the multimedia assets of Mosaic and the New Internet.

This chapter presents information for Mosaic requirements if you are using your own Internet connection. It focuses on helping you establish your access to the Internet. However, even if you have already crossed this hurdle, you'll want to read on to find out where your Internet service fits into the array of alternatives.

A roadmap for users of America OnLine, CompuServe, GEnie, & Prodigy

Capitalizing on the business user's and consumer's voracious appetites for information, the growth of online bureaus such as Prodigy is due in part to the affordability of personal computers, the low cost of switched telephone services, and the wealth of printed material that is being transformed into electronic formats. Commercial services such as Prodigy, America Online, and CompuServe have been optimized to give information providers, whose medium is typically print, a digital electronic distribution facility.

Much of the information available from these online services is similar. However, the format and content detail is keyed to each provider's targeted audience. For example, CompuServe satisfies its targeted audience of sophisticated business users and techies by providing comprehensive search and retrieval databases related to MS-DOS and Windows technical reference material. In contrast, America Online's information sources on the same subject matter are intended for its home-user/consumer audience and are therefore relatively high level, with few details. Many of these services provide interactive communication applications enabling users to conduct real-time conversations with other users, and to send/receive mail with electronic mail users on any number of different online service bureaus and networks.

If you are a user of one of the four major commercial online services you either have a Mosaic-like browser for the World Wide Web available to you already or you probably will soon. If you are satisfied with your online service's World Wide Web solution you should use it. You can then bypass much of Chapters 4 and 5 and consult only their instructions for installing your browser and any necessary external viewers. However, if your service recommends that you obtain your own viewers you might wish to read Chapter 6 of this book for guidance. Otherwise, the material in Chapter 6 will not apply to you, either.

If your service provides Mosaic as your browser, pick up our trail again at Chapter 7. If not, rejoin us in Chapter 8 where we discuss a Web browser's relationship with the rest of the Internet.

Available levels of Internet service

If you are interested in bringing up Mosaic to access the New Internet but are still in need of a pathway to the Internet, turn to an Internet Service Provider, or ISP. Some ISPs have been around for a long time, and over the years several levels of Internet service have evolved. In order of increasing functionality they are:

- UUCP-type access (UNIX to UNIX Copy Program) for intermittent batch dial-up operations, such as sending and receiving electronic mail
- Terminal dial-up access to an Internet-ready computer in a text mode
- Full interactive access with your computer acting as a full node on the Internet

Each of the above offers benefits and drawbacks based on your need to accomplish certain tasks. Your need as a Mosaic user, however, is for the third option, with the ability for your computer to participate fully as an Internet node even if only for the duration of a dial-up session. Put in slightly more technical terms, your computer must communicate using the IP protocol, which we introduced in Chapter 2. There are two basic methods for establishing a full IP connection to the Internet: dial-up line (analog or ISDN) or leased line.

The dial-up connection

The most basic (and generally the slowest) type of IP connection, shown in Fig. 4-1, is the dial-up line. There are a variety of types of dial-up lines, including standard analog telephone lines that support speeds of 14.4 Kbps or 28.8 Kbps. This will be the lowest cost solution that can still provide you with a full function IP connection.

Figure 4-1

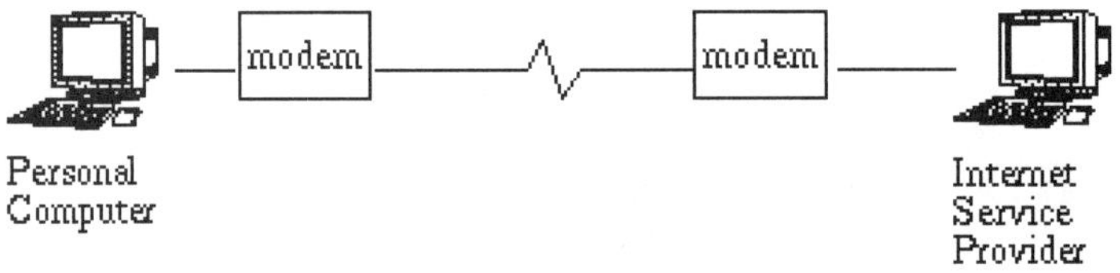

Dial-up connection with modem

This option provides a full-function IP connection without the cost of the leased line or associated hardware. This is the most common configuration used from the home today; however, with the emergence of ISDN, that might change.

ISDN is rapidly emerging as a choice for the home market (see Fig. 4-2). ISDN stands for Integrated Services Digital Network and represents the next major push by the telephone companies to provide higher-speed, lower-cost lines into the home and work environment. ISDN is a technology that has been touted as perfect for home use because it is dial-up (so you only pay for the line when you are connected), low cost (doesn't cost much more than a standard phone line), and relatively high-speed (either 64 Kbps or 128 Kbps depending on your ISDN interface). Many of the Internet providers in large

Figure 4-2

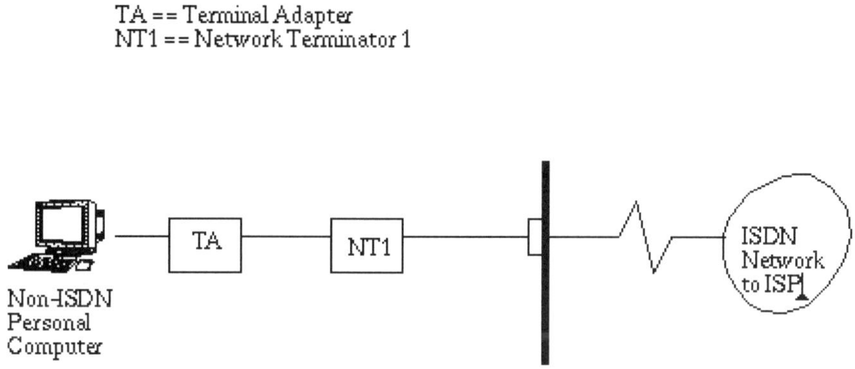

Dial-up connection with ISDN

metropolitan areas are getting ready or actually offering ISDN-capable service and support. What they can offer is mostly a function of the availability of ISDN to your location. Ask your local telephone company or local Internet access provider for more information.

IP over a dial-up line

Whether you are using standard modems or higher-speed ISDN technologies you are using a dial-up line for your Internet access. This means that you need some technology to make IP available on this dial-up line. Two technologies available today can provide IP capabilities over a dial-up line: SLIP and PPP.

SLIP (Serial Line Internet Protocol) is the original software that allows you to run IP over a dial-up phone line. It is free software that has been ported and implemented on almost every piece of computer hardware available. Because of its easy availability there are many versions, some better than others, available for your platform including Microsoft Windows and most flavors of UNIX.

PPP (Point-to-Point Protocol) is the other option available for providing IP over standard dial-up lines. PPP is the successor to SLIP and implements a more robust and capable dial-up protocol. Through the use of more sophisticated transmission techniques, PPP provides higher and more reliable throughput than SLIP. PPP is also free software and is commonly implemented on most available platforms.

Both SLIP and PPP provide merely the underlying support for IP over a dial-up line; they don't provide the actual IP itself. You must also install and configure an IP protocol along with the SLIP or PPP. IP can run over a variety of physical mediums including Ethernet, token ring, high-speed leased lines, and dial-up lines. For dial-up lines you need either SLIP or PPP, which essentially makes the dial-up line look like a leased line and allows the IP software to work correctly. Example installations and configurations are described later in this chapter.

The choice between SLIP and PPP will be determined mostly by which of the two your Internet access provider supports. From a usability point of view there is very little difference between them. There are differences in reliability and scalability that favor PPP, however, and you should choose PPP if given the option. Talk with your access provider for more details.

As stated earlier, both SLIP and PPP are free software packages and are available from a variety of sources on the Internet. These packages are also available from a variety of commercial IP providers, including FTP Software, Novell, Sun Microsystems, and others. The issue of using the freeware version versus the commercial version is mostly one of support. Most freeware versions work quite well. These will be documented later in this chapter and are available on the accompanying CD. However, the level of installation and usage support is minimal. The commercial versions offer more support but at a cost. This is a choice that you must make based on your level of expertise and willingness to work on installing and configuring the software.

The leased-line connection

The leased line consists of relatively low-speed digital circuits such as DS0 (56 Kbps) up to high-speed circuits such as DS1 (1.544 Mbps) and DS3 (45 Mbps). Due to the maturation of this market and the increasing competition among long distance carriers (such as AT&T and MCI), and the Regional telecommunications providers (such as Ameritech or Pacific Bell), the cost of these lines has dropped dramatically in the last few years. You can now lease high-speed lines for hundreds of dollars a month instead of the thousands of dollars per month they once cost. Because of this people are beginning to invest in these types of lines for business, even at home.

The leased line is the simplest but least cost-effective way to connect yourself to the Internet. However, it does provide the advantage of giving you a full-time link to the Internet. This is obviously essential if you are planning on providing any type of server environment. If you are not planning on providing this type of environment you might want to consider a dial-up connection as a lower cost alternative.

The typical leased line configuration is shown in Fig. 4-3.

Figure 4-3

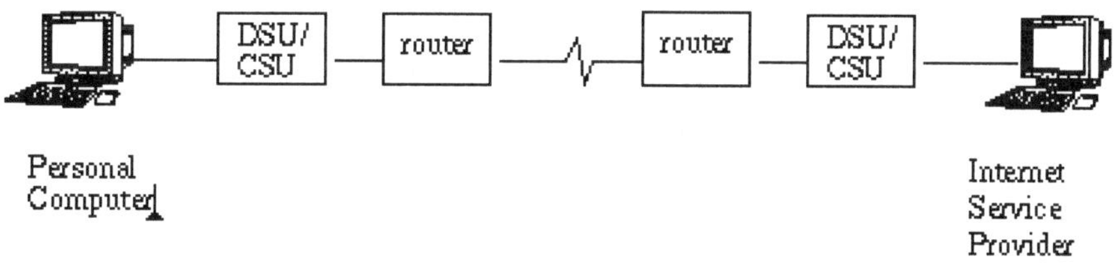

Router as a gateway to the Internet . . . include DSU/CSU devices

IP over a leased line

The DSU/CSU is a digital device that translates the signals from your serial port to the leased line. For all intents and purposes it is a digital modem (even though this is an oxymoron of sorts), and this is the best way to think of a DSU/CSU. This can either be purchased or you can lease it along with your line from your telephone carrier. However, unless you have other uses for it you might want to consider leasing this device to avoid some of the initial costs of making the Internet connection.

While a router is the preferred method of connection to a leased line, you can also avoid the router and simply connect the CSU/DSU to your serial port and use SLIP or PPP as described in the discussion of dial-up lines above. This has the advantage of lower cost but doesn't provide the robustness or off-loading capability that the router provides. The DSU/CSU will handle the connection and line for you just as it did before. This solution will provide higher bandwidth than a standard dial-up line; however, you will pay slightly more because you are using a leased line.

Unless you are a large organization or a not-for-profit, such as a University or research laboratory, you will probably have to purchase access to the Internet from a commercial access provider instead of having direct Internet access yourself. This means that you will pay a monthly fee to a provider who has direct access to the Internet, who will provide you either a leased line or dial-up line capability into his facility. From your perspective the type of connection doesn't matter, because it appears that you are directly connected to the Internet backbone and all programs and services are available to you as you would expect. The Internet provider might help you coordinate the installation and configuration of your leased line. Ask your provider and/or your local telephone company for more details.

Considerations for home & office

Connecting at work

The basic connection to the Internet you have at work is based on the current Internet connection within your company. Many companies have high-speed (T1) Internet connections, which allow you to simply tap into the link through your LAN. If this is the case, your connection to the Internet will be relatively straightforward: IP, a windowing environment such as the X Window System or Microsoft Windows, and Mosaic will be all you need to begin using the Internet to its fullest (see more details in Chapters 5 and 6). Because there are often performance and security issues related to the use of your company's Internet connection you should check with your network administrator before attempting to access Internet via your company's connection. However, once you have established IP and have installed and have configured Mosaic you are ready to begin navigating the Internet with the click of a mouse.

If your company does not have Internet access you will need to contact any one of several Internet service providers who provide such access, as described later in this chapter. Contact the providers that serve your area and begin getting information and quotes on an IP connection to the Internet. You will probably want to invest in a higher-speed network capability such as a leased line of 56 Kbps or ISDN. Either one will significantly enhance your capabilities and the reliability of your Internet link, and it will support more users.

Basic Mosaic usage and capabilities will be based on the speed of your link to the Internet. While this might seem strange, it will become evident as you begin to use Mosaic that bandwidth to the Internet is the single most critical component of your Mosaic usage. If you have a high-speed link, such as a T1 or greater, you can use all the capabilities and power of Mosaic, including in-line video, sounds, and pictures without experiencing any real difficulties. This will not be true, however, if you have a lower-speed link.

If you are running a link such as a 56 Kbps circuit it will become painfully evident that running movies, downloading pictures and other bandwidth-hogging activities will be too slow to execute efficiently on the lower-speed lines. There are things you can do to increase the usefulness of Mosaic over the lower-speed lines, and some of these are documented in the section entitled *Connection speed impact on Mosaic*. However, nothing will substitute for obtaining the highest-speed connection you can.

Connecting at home

In contrast to your work environment, you probably do not have high-speed or even medium-speed capabilities to your home. You probably have one or more analog phone lines that are capable of operating at speeds of 14.4 kbs or 28.8 kbs maximum. The option of purchasing a leased line is unreasonable based on the relatively high cost of leased lines.

If you choose a dial-up analog line configuration you will be limited in terms of your bandwidth to the Internet. This does not mean, however, that you cannot use tools like Mosaic to browse the Internet and have all or most of the capabilities of the World Wide Web at home. In fact, the beauty of a tool like Mosaic is that you can use it on a low-speed line and achieve many of the benefits of the tool without paying a high cost. While you might not want to pull down large graphics files with a low-speed line, you can still access the same basic information on a low-speed line. More on this in the next section.

If you choose a higher-speed dial-up technology, such as ISDN, you obviously have more options in terms of Mosaic usage. It is much quicker to download files and move data around the network with a higher-speed link, such as an ISDN line. Because of this higher speed you can more easily use the full power of Mosaic, including in-line graphics, sound, video, and other multimedia capabilities included within Mosaic.

Connection speed impact on Mosaic

Several comments on Mosaic usage and line speed were made in the earlier sections, but we did not include in-depth discussion. This section will outline the general requirements and usage characteristics of Mosaic over lower-speed lines.

First, it is important to outline what lower-speed line means. Anything below a 56 kbps line is a low-speed line. This encompasses all conventional modem speeds, including 9.6 kbps, 14.4 kbps, and 28.8 kbps. Speeds below 9.6 kbps won't support even the basic functions of Mosaic. You simply don't have enough bandwidth to run IP, and therefore you cannot run the newer tools, such as Mosaic, or even Gopher or Telnet. Fortunately, 28.8 kbps modems have now dropped below $200 so you won't have to pay a lot to get enough performance to make Mosaic usable.

If you have modem speeds at 9.6 kbps or above you can begin to use Mosaic in a reasonable fashion. Even though your response will not be as fast as with a higher-speed link, the basic functionality is the same. The most important thing to remember is that, every time you click on a hypertext link (more on this later), you generate a series of commands to download information to your Mosaic client. This might include very large files, such as graphics, audio, and video files. Or it might consist of smaller files, such as ASCII text or HTML files. Depending on how much information you are downloading, and what type of file it is, it will take a varying amount of time to download and display this information.

To give you a feeling for just how long these downloads can take, let's consider a 500-KB audio file (this is not an unusual size for an audio file), which is probably less than 30 seconds of actual audio. If you are using a 14.4 Kbps modem this means that you can transmit 14,400 bits per second. Due to the error correction and parity bits, this means that you can transfer roughly 1440 bytes per second. This assumes that you are using the entire bandwidth of the line. With SLIP or PPP you will probably achieve closer to 75% of the available bandwidth.

To transfer 500,000 bytes could take almost eight minutes. Unless you sit there for eight minutes while the download occurs you might miss this entire process. This is why the speed of your link to the Internet is the most critical piece and the one on which you should spend the most money you can afford, to obtain the highest possible bandwidth.

While it will be somewhat painful to download large images and multimedia files, the vast majority of the Web servers don't contain documents that will automatically download large amounts of data that will overload your low-speed line. Most administrators of Web servers recognize that Web clients often come in over low-speed lines. They therefore structure their home pages to minimize the amount of data to be downloaded. Often, a Web page will include a small image that you can then click on to download the larger version. This allows those with lower-speed lines to determine whether they want to wait for this to occur. Most of the time you will be able to reference just about anything on the Web servers without too much difficulty.

How to find a service provider

Locating a service provider can sometimes be a catch-22 situation. The latest lists of service providers by region are available on the Internet, which you can't access unless you already have a service provider. Some people can circumvent the problem by using an existing connection elsewhere to facilitate the research. For others, though, the problem remains.

If you are in need of Internet service and do not currently have an access path to the Internet, here's the approach we recommend. Go ahead and sign up for the free trial service with Portal. It's a simple procedure that's part of the Spyglass Enhanced Mosaic installation from the attached CD. Use some of the free access time to investigate Portal's pricing, and to explore the Internet for alternatives. One extensive source for ISP information is PDIAL, the Public Dial-Up Internet Access List. Once you have Mosaic up and running, visit the following URL:

http://www.cis.ohio-state.edu /hypertext/faq/usenet/pdial/faq.html

Items on the menu will explain how PDIAL is organized and will explain how to locate service providers that serve your area. If you need Internet service outside the United States, there's another site that keeps track of Internet access providers around the world. Visit URL:

http://www.earth.org/~lips/

There are other ISP directories out on the Internet, too. You can find many more by perusing the subject catalogs described in Chapter 9.

Questions to ask a service provider

We strongly recommend comparison shopping. The following list of questions will give you a good starting point for comparisons.

1. Who provides your link to the Internet? How fast is it?
2. What modem speeds (14.4 and 28.8 Kbps) and standards (v.32, v.fast) do you support?

3 How many modems are available at the access point I am most likely to use?

4 Do you offer local as well as 800-number dial-up access?

5 What is your subscriber-to-modem ratio?

6 What is the size of your support staff? At what hours can I reach them? How do I get assistance?

7 What services/account types do you offer?

8 What do I get in terms of bandwidth, services, and software?

9 What else will I need?

10 What is the true cost of the service?

11 How will I be billed?

12 Is there a time limit or a price penalty for prime-time usage?

13 Are there time of day or usage restrictions?

Question 1 attempts to ascertain the quality of the provider's Internet connection. Is it provided by a well-established, reliable provider? Questions 2 through 5 are intended to ensure that the provider is capable of meeting customer demands for service.

Question 6 will tell you how available support personnel will be. Who will you call when you need help? Question 7 will help you determine what services, such as Netnews or electronic mail, are included in the basic package and which involve extra charges?

Questions 8 through 10 will help you avoid hidden costs and charges. Does the provider offer a shrink-wrapped software kit for connectivity or is that left up to the buyer to acquire? Along those lines, if the provider asks for a credit card number (question 11), be cautious. What is the billing cycle? monthly? quarterly? How will you cancel service if you are dissatisfied?

Questions 12 and 13 will help you evaluate the provider's scheme to ensure that it will meet your needs. For example, some providers include four to six hours of dial-in access with the basic charge. Others charge a premium for use during normal business hours.

Summary

There are minimum connectivity requirements that must be met in order to use Mosaic in either Microsoft Windows or UNIX. But once these requirements are met Mosaic becomes a very powerful multimedia tool for accessing the Internet.

This chapter outlined the basic information you need to know to begin to install Mosaic. Other chapters outline installation procedures for particular platforms in greater detail; however, it is important to understand the basic material in this chapter before proceeding to the installation and configuration of Mosaic itself.

5

Getting Mosaic up & running in UNIX

CHAPTER 4 outlined the basic connectivity requirements for Mosaic in a platform independent way. If you are a UNIX user, we assume your UNIX workstation affords you full interactive access to the Internet and that it has an IP address assigned to it. Assuming requirements have been met, this chapter outlines specific tasks to install and begin to use Mosaic in a UNIX and the X Window System environment.

Your Mosaic software alternatives

On the accompanying CD we have provided you a solid, high-quality, World Wide Web browser—Spyglass Enhanced Mosaic, version 2.0, from Luckman Interactive. If you have a CD-ROM drive attached to your workstation, this CD will make it easy for you to get up and running, especially if you are just starting out.

However, we intend this book to be of value to you regardless of which Web browser you choose, and other quality browsers are available for downloading from the Internet. At this time, version 2.5 of the original Mosaic for the X Window System is available from NCSA. Also, Netscape Navigator, version 1.1, is available from Netscape Communications Corporation. Each of these alternatives has its relative strengths, and as you become more experienced in the New Internet you might find it worthwhile to compare them yourself.

Loading software from the CD

Here's how to load the software you've chosen from the CD. The CD includes Spyglass Enhanced Mosaic from Luckman Interactive, precompiled for several UNIX platforms. The installation of Mosaic from this medium is very straightforward. See Appendix A.

The structure of the CD

Because the accompanying CD must support both UNIX and Microsoft Windows platforms it has a particular format known as ISO 9660. This format specifies more rigid specifications for filenames and formats than UNIX alone requires.

ISO 9660 specifies all filenames as uppercase, and limits them to eight characters with a three-character suffix. You are also limited to eight directory levels, which can sometimes create problems with certain UNIX utilities.

However, you should not encounter such a situation here because device drivers on different UNIX machines will interpret these filenames differently. You might see the filenames in uppercase or lowercase, depending on the driver. You might also see versions preceded by a semicolon, while other drivers will ignore this specification. Once you mount the CD you will be able to quickly tell how your device driver is interpreting the information on it. This will allow you to quickly and easily get the appropriate information from the CD onto your local disk. Simply specify the filename that you are presented with upon issuing the ls command and you will be able to directly access and control the files on the CD.

Mounting the CD

First you need to mount the CD. Depending on the type of machine you are on, the syntax will vary. The basic syntax of the mount command is:

```
$ mount CDROM_device mount_point
```

The CD-ROM device will vary from operating system to operating system and is something that you must determine. See your system administrator if you need assistance with this. Once you have determined the CD-ROM device name you can choose any empty directory to use as a mount point. /cdrom is the typical choice for CD-ROM device mount points.

The basic syntax for several machine types is shown below:

SunOS 4.1.X `$ mount -r -t hsfs /dev/sr0 /cdrom`

Solaris 2.3 `$ mount -r -F hsfs /dev/dsk/c0t6d0s0 /cdrom`
(Note: If you are running the volume management subsystem, the CD will mount automatically.)

AIX 3.2 `$ mount -r -v cdrfs /dev/cd0 /cdrom`

HP-UX `$ mount -r -s cdfs -o noversion /dev/rz3c /cdrom`

Irix `$ mount -r -t iso9660 /dev/scsi/sc0d410 /cdrom`

If you want more information, see the man page (UNIX manual page) on mount.

Installing Mosaic from the CD

Take the following steps (subject to possible last-minute software changes) to install Mosaic from the accompanying CD:

1. First, copy the appropriate tar file to a local directory. If you are a system administrator, this could be **/usr/local**, for instance.
2. Type the command tar xvf followed by the name of the tar file.
3. Type chdir Enhanced_Mosaic.
4. Type install-mosaic and follow the directions.

Customizing Mosaic

The easiest method for controlling Mosaic's behavior is the *Options...* menu within Mosaic. Several options are available, including Fonts selections. Mosaic uses various fonts within a font family to display the different types of information within the Mosaic window. You can control the fonts through either the resource definitions as described above or, more easily, through the *Options...* menu. There is a Fonts option within the *Options...* pulldown menu. Select this and choose one of the many font families available to Mosaic. The changed fonts will become available immediately; however, only during the current session. You need to use resource definitions if you want the changes to become permanent.

The *Options...* menu also allows you to specify whether to download images, load files to the local disk, flush image caches, clear global history files, and control underline styles. Each is relatively self explanatory and is simple to execute within the Mosaic environment.

This is a simplistic introduction to the customization capabilities of Mosaic. You can customize many more variables in Mosaic, and you will learn which ones are important to you as you begin to use Mosaic more frequently.

Changing or adding viewers

Mosaic comes with a series of predefined viewers for multimedia type files, as described in Chapter 7. These are customizable based on both the file extension as well as the viewer, which acts on a particular file type. Mosaic will allow you to configure a new viewer each time an unrecognized filetype is encountered. We discuss how to find viewers on the Internet in Appendix B.

Summary

Mosaic is an extremely powerful tool which, at a basic level, is simple to install and use. Yet Mosaic does have a significant amount of power and customizability. This chapter has outlined the basic installation procedures for Mosaic, plus many of the customization options available on a UNIX platform. By utilizing these capabilities you will find Mosaic to be one of the most powerful and flexible Internet navigation tools available today.

6

Getting Mosaic up & running in Microsoft Windows

CHAPTER 4 outlined the basic requirements for Mosaic in a platform-independent environment. This chapter outlines specific tasks for installing and beginning to use Mosaic in a Microsoft Windows environment.

Your Mosaic software alternatives

There are two basic installation methodologies for Mosaic, one for the version that comes with the CD and another for the version that is available on the Internet. The first is described in detail in this chapter. The second method is described in Appendix B.

The installation of Mosaic is relatively straightforward in a Windows environment. There are binaries for Windows available on the Internet, which are also included on the accompanying CD. Once the binaries have been copied to your local disk you must define some file locations, and then you are ready to go.

Software from both the Internet and from our CD will be similar. There are differences, however, relating to both the Mosaic software and the TCP/IP interface software. The CD that accompanies this book contains a commercial version of Mosaic known as Luckman Super Mosaic (based on Spyglass Enhanced Mosaic version 2.0), as well as a commercial version of a TCP/IP stack that provides connectivity to the Internet. These are commercial products not available from the Internet. Issues related to support and functionality are the primary differences between these two solutions. Based on your needs and capabilities, you will have to determine whether you need a package from the Internet. The software on the CD should be more than sufficient for most readers of this book, but you can still get different versions of this software from the Internet if you so desire.

Your external viewer alternatives

Super Mosaic comes with built-in GIF and JPEG viewers and a built-in audio player for AU and AIFF files. Otherwise, due to licensing restrictions on the viewers available for Mosaic, none are contained on the CD and you will therefore need to get the appropriate viewers from the Internet. The best way to get these viewers is to invoke Enhanced Mosaic and go through a relatively well-defined screen on the Internet.

Loading software from the CD-ROM

Now that you have taken stock of your software alternatives, we will explain how to load the software you've chosen from the CD-ROM.

This CD includes Super Mosaic 2 from Luckman Interactive. Several files are contained on the CD, including the Mosaic binary, installation files, dynamic link libraries, and the relevant text files for documentations. The CD also contains a commercial version of TCP/IP software, which provides you with access to the Internet. Both of these are necessary to get Mosaic up and running in a Windows environment.

Before we proceed with the installation and configuration of Mosaic, it is necessary to explain the structure of the CD that accompanies this book. Once you understand this the installation will be relatively straightforward.

The structure of the CD

Because the accompanying CD must support many platforms, including UNIX and Microsoft Windows, it has a particular format known as ISO 9660. This format stipulates fairly rigid specifications for filenames and formats. While this would not have been the structure of choice if this were a UNIX-only CD, it was necessary to support other platforms, including Microsoft Windows.

ISO 9660 specifies all filenames as uppercase and limits each one to eight characters with a three character suffix. You are also limited to eight directory levels. ISO 9660 also supports file versioning to allow you to have more than one version of a particular file.

Accessing the CD

With Microsoft Windows you will see what appear to be standard DOS filenames, so you might proceed as you normally would. Once you insert the CD you will be able to access the information on a particular drive (normally D or E). This will allow you to quickly and easily get the appropriate information from the CD onto your local disk. There are no commands you have to type or any extra effort involved in accessing a CD. Simply insert it into your CD player and proceed as if this were a standard hard drive in your computer.

Installing Mosaic from the CD

The installation of Super Mosaic 2.0 from Luckman Interactive on a Windows platform is very straightforward. From within Windows execute File...Run... and select SETUP.EXE from the DISK1 directory of the CD-ROM which accompanies this book. This will invoke the Super Mosaic 2.0 setup application. This application prompts you for installation locations, TCP/IP configuration information and tool selections. By answering a few simple questions, you can completely configure Mosaic and begin to access the Internet. The initial screen is shown in Fig. 6-1.

The first thing the installation procedure does is check to see if you have WIN32S installed on your system. WIN32S allows 32-bit applications, such as Super Mosaic 2.0, to run within Windows 3.1. Normally, Windows 3.1 and earlier versions support only 16-bit applications. Super Mosaic 2.0 is a 32-bit application and requires WIN32S to run properly.

If you need to install WIN32S, the installation procedure will inform you of that and then ask you if you want to proceed. If it tells you that you have WIN32S installed, continue without installing WIN32S; otherwise select the INSTALL option to ensure that WIN32S is installed.

Figure 6-1

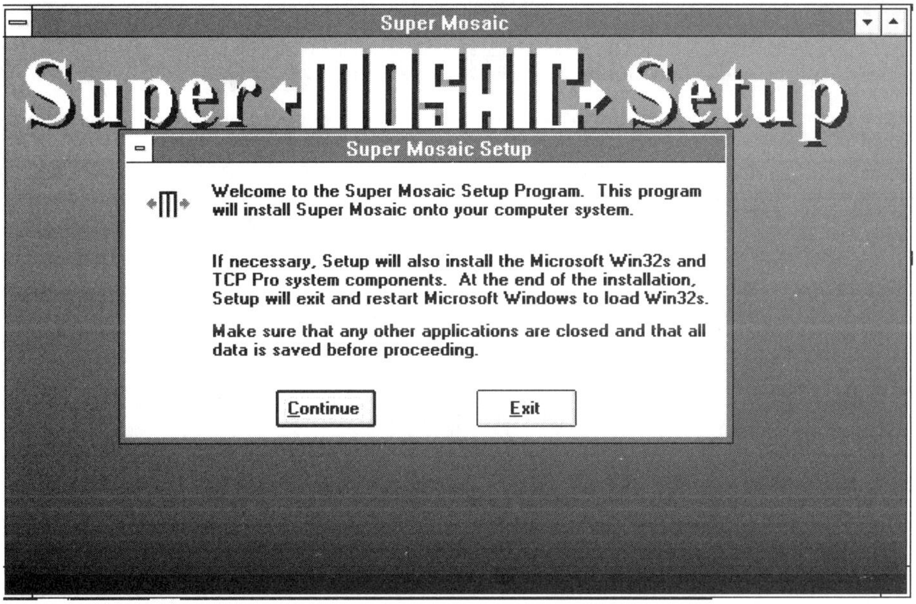

Luckman Super Mosaic Setup screen

Once you have installed WIN32S, the setup program will begin to prompt you for file locations to install the Super Mosaic 2.0 software. It is strongly recommended that you accept the default location; otherwise you might create additional steps later in the installation process. After you have specified the locations of the software, the SETUP.EXE application will place the files in the specified locations.

Once the setup is complete, a new program group will be created containing the Super Mosaic icon.

Next you will be requested to restart Windows.

After Windows restarts, the Internet registration screen will appear, as shown in Fig. 6-2.

The information entered will be forwarded to an Internet service provider (ISP) for processing. Portal is one such ISP. As the notice informs you, a 30-day Portal trial is provided free with this book. The following paragraphs address how to proceed depending on whether you choose to use Portal or another ISP.

Figure 6-2

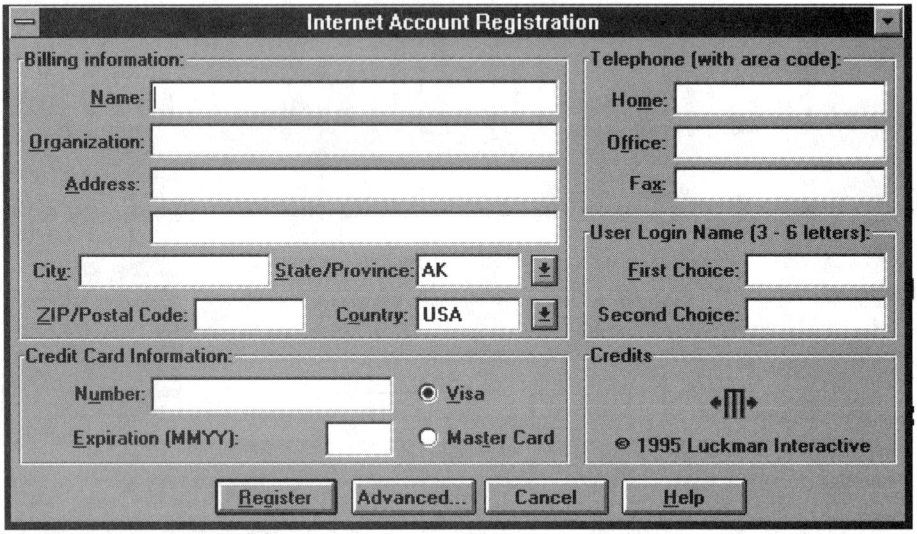

Internet account registration

If you choose Portal as your ISP, fill in the registration information and select Register. This will dial your modem, connecting to the nearest Portal office, and establish your account. Super Mosaic displays a status message as it processes the series of commands. If you receive a message that a connection to the provider cannot be made, click OK to close the message and try selecting Register again. At times, you might experience busy lines.

If you choose another ISP, you will need to make a few adjustments in the way you configure Super Mosaic. Select Cancel on the Internet Account Registration screen. You will need to edit the file SITE.INI and SITES.INI located in the directory where you installed Super Mosaic (the default is C:\TCPPRO\APP). These files contain configuration information used to establish your Internet connection.

First examine the SITES.INI file to determine if your ISP is listed. If your ISP is listed, you need to append that ISP's relevant section into the SITE.INI file. Doing so will include a new Site Option to the Super Mosaic configuration information.

If you do not find your ISP listed, pick one which has features in common with those of your ISP and make the necessary modification to the information before including it in your SITE.INI file. You may need to contact your ISP for assistance with this information.

Configuring TCP & your session

Next you will see the Connect screen shown in Fig. 6-3.

Figure 6-3

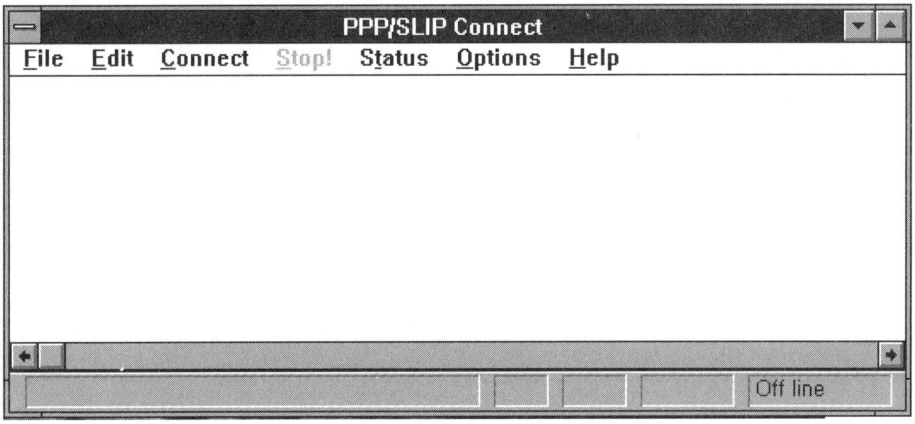

PPP/SLIP Connect screen

First select the Options menu and select Site Setup. The screen shown in Fig. 6-4 will appear.

You should see your ISP listed in the Site field and the appropriate phone numbers listed below. This information is read from your SITE.INI file. If the correct information is displayed, click OK. Otherwise edit the fields and then click OK.

Next, you need to configure your account information. Pull down the Options menu and select Session Setup. Choose PINACC if Portal is your ISP, or Unregistered for other ISPs. From the next screen, click on Handshake Login. Next you will be prompted for your user name and password. These should have been supplied by your ISP. Enter the information exactly as given. Remember that most computers pay

Figure 6-4

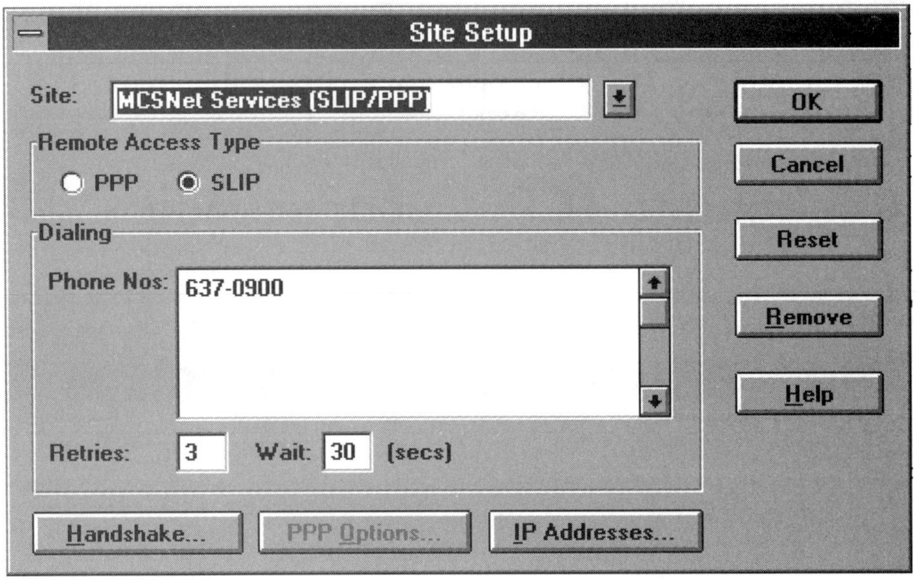

Site Setup screen

attention to the case used to enter text. Once entered, select OK to accept.

Under the Options pulldown menu, select Modem Port Setup to configure your modem parameters, such as communications port and speed, appropriately.

Invoking Super Mosaic 2.0

You are now ready to connect to your ISP. Pull down the Connect menu, select your session name (PINACC or Unregistered) and click on OK to dial the modem and begin your session. Figure 6-5 shows a basic screen during the connection phase. Watch this screen for indicators that your connection attempt was successful.

You are now ready to start Super Mosaic 2.0 by double clicking on the Super Mosaic icon. Chapter 7 will guide you through the Mosaic screen and tell you how to get the most out of your Mosaic configuration.

Figure 6-5

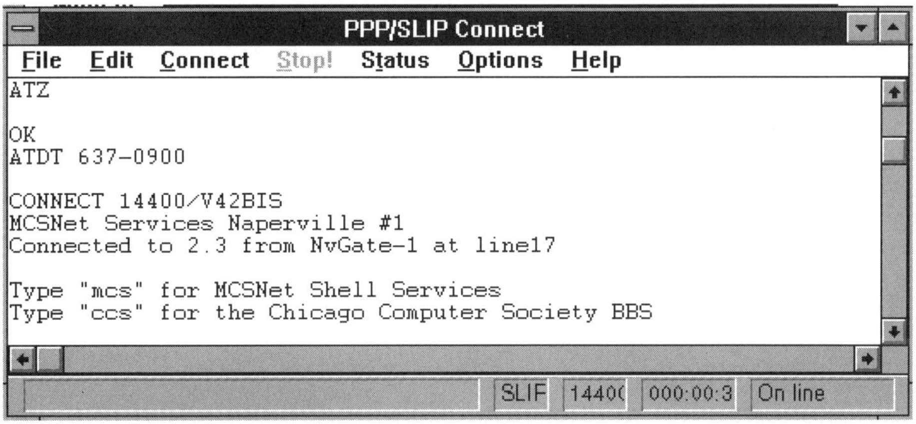

Connecting to the Internet

Under the Connect Options pulldown menu, you may want to select Auto Connect Setup and Auto Connect Enable to automatically bring up your modem connection to the Internet whenever you invoke Super Mosaic 2.0. This handy feature lets you skip the manual connect step.

Disconnecting from the Internet

From the PPP/SLIP Window, pull down the Connect menu and select Disconnect. This will immediately disconnect your modem and terminate any Internet applications communication over that connection. You may want to configure your connection preferences (under the Options pulldown menu) so that your modem is disconnected when you exit the Connect Window.

Summary

Mosaic is an extremely powerful tool that, at a basic level, is simple to install and use. At the same time, Mosaic does have a significant amount of power and customizability. This chapter has outlined the basic installation procedures for Mosaic. You will find Mosaic to be one of the most powerful and flexible systems available today.

7

Getting started with the Web & Mosaic

CHAPTER 7

NOW that we have described this new Internet climate, why you should be excited to learn more, and how to install the software included with this book, it is time to describe the basics of the underlying technology in just enough detail to let you know what is going on and what to expect. In this chapter we will give you the details on the Web and Mosaic, to help you get started in navigating this interesting new milieu.

What is the Web & how is it different than Mosaic?

The World Wide Web model defines the following things:

- An architecture for a distributed-information system of servers.
- A navigation tool enabling access to other Internet services in addition to Web servers.
- A common interface to and presentation of multimedia information.
- A dynamic format (hyperlinks) for mass and personal communications that allows the user to interact with the information and choose the information that he wishes to view next.

The World Wide Web initiative can be described as a wide-area hypermedia information-retrieval system designed to give seamless universal access to a large universe of multimedia information objects. The WWW is based on the hypertext paradigm; i.e., documents contain links to related materials/objects. Hypertext presents information in a nonlinear fashion conducive to searching, retrieval, and comprehension. It is an interactive medium to which hyperlinks contribute additional dimensions. Web documents can contain graphics, audio, video, or plain text, and a link might point to a file residing on a local server or a server halfway around the world.

The Web has transformed the Internet from a distributed network of computers to a distributed information space without boundaries.

Instead of transferring files between computers, a user navigates the global information space using a graphical user interface to control the display of information objects. The user is free to interact with the information without regard to the location of the objects. The user concentrates on the logical structure of the interconnection of information and objects rather than on the underlying physical structure of computers and communications systems.

The powerful multimedia Web browser known as Mosaic has transformed the use of the Internet, from inputting a series of cryptic command strings into taking an exciting voyage as the user jumps from topic to topic, computer to computer, and place to place, an activity sometimes referred to as *surfing the Net*. While the Web is mostly used on the Internet, they are not synonymous. The World Wide Web architecture is designed to handle a widely distributed collection of heterogeneous set of computers running different applications that use different data formats. Several large corporations have implemented internal corporate information distribution systems based on WWW technology. Web traffic is composed of thousands of virtual network transactions (requests for objects) taking place per hour throughout the world, creating a virtual web of information flow.

From the beginning, the WWW project sought to encompass all existing methods of network information navigation and retrieval, so that WWW browsers would be able to communicate with all forms of network information sources and present a unified information space to the users. The WWW has become a superset of all common Internet networked information services: FTP, Gopher, HTTP, news, Telnet, and WAIS. More on this in Chapter 8.

⇨ How big is the Web?

The Internet Society portrays the exponential growth of the Internet by its reachable host computers, shown in Fig. 7-1, which has been attributed in large part to the development of the Web and the release of Mosaic.

Figure 7-1

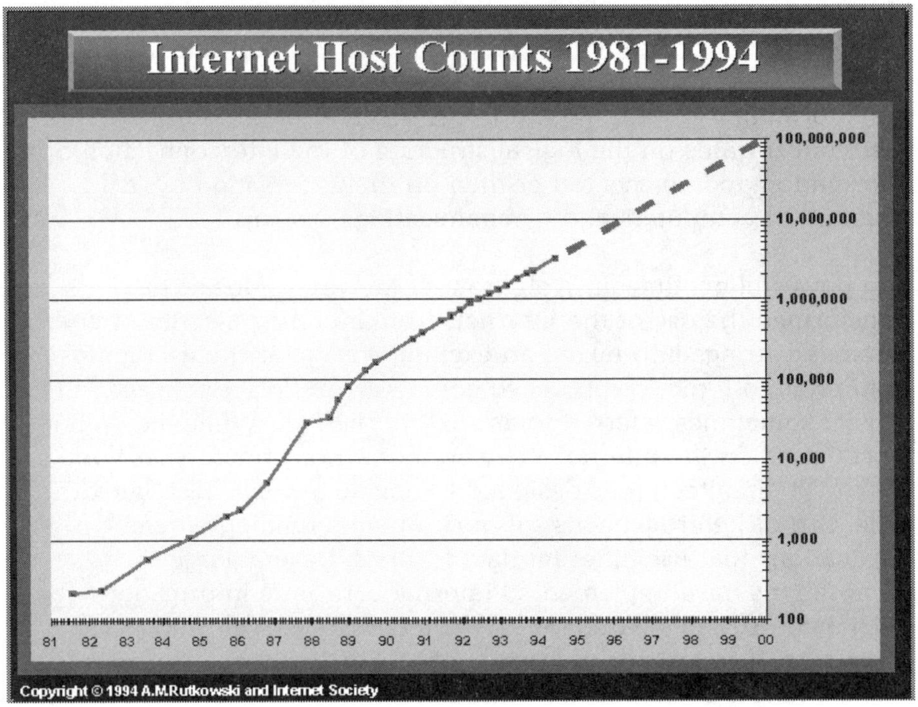

Growth of Internet hosts, 1981–1994

How does the Web work?

The Web architecture operates on the client-server model, as shown in Fig. 7-2. A Web server is a program that runs on a computer for the purpose of storing hypermedia documents and transferring documents to other computers when requested to do so. The server sends the data and waits for the next request.

A Web client or browser, such as Mosaic, is a program that runs on a computer for the purpose of sending requests to servers and receiving documents from servers, interpreting document content and running the appropriate viewers at the front end, and formatting documents for display. You might be starting to realize that the Web browser does a lot of work. It receives raw HTML or other data and has to perform formatting or launch a helper application, such as a movie player, after determining what type of data it has received. Web

Figure 7-2

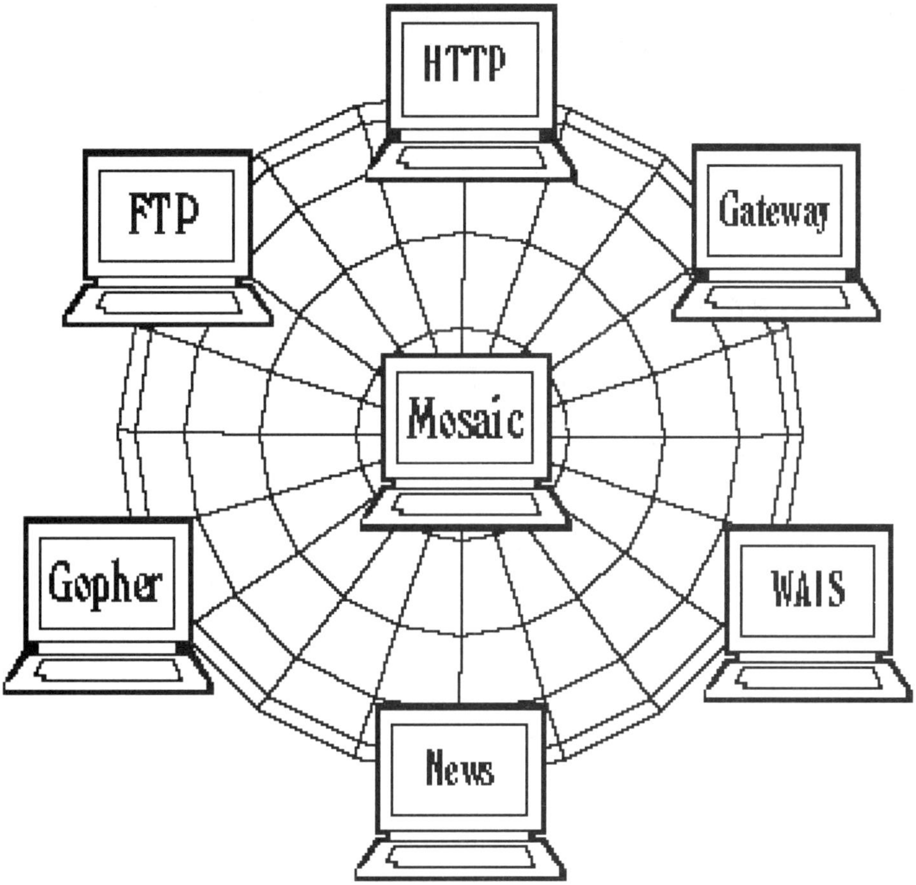

WWW architecture

browsers are also responsible for interacting with non-HTTP servers, such as FTP or Gopher, directly, and for creating a virtual HTML document while doing so.

The pieces of the Web in greater detail

The WWW specifications are public, meaning anyone can follow them to build a client or server. There are three key specifications with which to be concerned:

1 A transfer protocol to specify a way to request and send a document over the network
2 A markup language to describe document formatting and a way of including links within documents
3 A naming system to define a way to uniquely specify the location of any document on the Internet

The transfer protocol

HyperText Transfer Protocol (HTTP) is the language the Web servers and clients use to communicate. HTTP is a stateless protocol, which means there is no continuous connection between the server and client. The term *Web* is often used to describe the collective network of servers speaking HTTP, as well as the vast global body of information available using this protocol. HTTP is used to retrieve documents in an unbounded and extensible set of formats. For more details on extensible formats, refer to the section on viewing multimedia information later in this chapter.

The markup language

World Wide Web documents are written in a simple Hypertext Markup Language (HTML). Every Web browser must be able to interpret HTML. HTML documents are standard, 7-bit ASCII files containing formatting codes that provide information about layout, text styles, document titles, paragraphs, lists, and hyperlinks. Within documents, HTML uses the naming scheme described below to represent hypermedia links to network services and objects.

The naming system

The Web uses a naming scheme known as the Universal Resource Locator (URL) that helps locate documents and provides the ability to uniquely address an object anywhere on the Internet, all of which is essential for the system to scale and for the information space to be independent of the network and server topology. The URL identifies the requested object, the protocol or method of access, the physical locations of the server, and the filename of the document or object. You need to understand the importance of URLs in order to directly access objects via the Web. Understanding URLs will also help you avoid aimlessly wandering the Web in search of information.

One of the most powerful features of the Web is its capability for serendipitous browsing, similar in concept to browsing the library stacks or channel hopping with your remote control. The direct approach to information retrieval, however, requires the user to input the URL of the desired resource. A typical URL request, such as **http://www.w3.org/DataSources/top.html** can be entered in Mosaic by selecting the Open URL function under the File menu. A generic format of the URL is shown below:

protocol://server/directory/filename

The first part of the URL (before the colon) specifies the method of access or the protocol to use in accessing the server. The characters **://** placed right after the protocol type act as separators. The second part is the location or address of the computer in which the information resides. The server field is the fully qualified domain-style Internet address of the server, and optionally the port number to connect to. Following the server name is a directory path. The final part specifies the name of the file, or the text to search for in a database. Note that filenames usually end with a file extension indicative of the file's contents (i.e., .gif for graphics or .html for Web documents).

Table 7-1 summarizes the common Internet protocol URLs.

Once you are viewing a file, a partial (relative) URL may be used to point to another file in the same directory, or on the same server. The missing server and path information is taken by the browser from the URL of the document that contains the link. A partial URL can be distinguished from an absolute URL in that the partial form lacks a colon. For example, with the file **http://www.myown.com/pub/home/html**, another file may be addressed with the partial URL **anotherfile.html**.

Table 7-1 **Summary of Common Internet Protocol URLs**

Protocol	Meaning	Typical URL syntax
file	download a file	**file://server/directory/filename**
ftp	contact a file transfer protocol (FTP) server	**ftp://server/directory/filename**
gopher	contact a Gopher server	**gopher://server**
http	contact a Web server	**http://server/directory/filename**
mailto	send mail	**mailto:who@where**
news	contact an NNTP server	**news:newsgroup**
telnet	contact a Telnet server	**telnet://server**
wais	contact a Wide Area Information Server	**wais://host/database?search**

The following URLs list references for each of the Web specifications, for those interested in learning more:

HTTP reference	**http://www.w3.org/hypertext/WWW/Protocols/Overview.html**
HTML reference	**http://www.w3.org.hypertext/WWW/MarkUp/MarkUp.html**
Beginner's Guide to URLs	**http://www.ncsa.uiuc.edu/demoweb/url-primer.html**
	http://info.cern.ch/hypertext/WWW/Addressing/Addressing.html

The basic transaction

You begin your search for information by launching Mosaic. The first document presented to you is known as your browser's *home page*, described here. By placing your mouse on a hypertext link and clicking, you instruct the browser to retrieve specific information or objects. The status line indicates, *Connecting to server.* Once connected, the client sends a request to the server requesting a specific protocol (FTP, Gopher, HTTP, Netnews, Telnet, or WAIS) and the object it wishes to download. If the client is unable to complete the connection, the connection attempt "times out," yielding an explanatory error message. Otherwise, the server responds and the status line indicates *Reading Response,*followed by a message indicating the protocol being used for the transfer and the "Transferring" message. When the transfer is complete the connection is closed.

Mosaic loads the requested document and displays it or takes appropriate steps to handle the document content type. The most common document types the browser displays are HTML documents that contains imbedded graphics, hyperlinks, and icons. It will display text files as ASCII documents. Other document types (graphic images, sound or video files) require the browser to launch the appropriate viewers (players) that are specified in the configuration files, as discussed later in this chapter.

Mosaic basics

The Mosaic interface

The first information presented by Mosaic is known as a home page. The home page is the initial document displayed and contains hyperlinks to other documents and resources. The home page, along with the hyperlinked resources, might be stored on your local computer or on a computer out on the Internet. Should you become lost during your navigation of the net, use the Home function under the Navigate Menu to return to the beginning.

Navigation basics

In any document, highlighted text (colored or underlined) and graphics with colored borders are hyperlinked to other information. As you place the mouse (or other pointing device) over the hyperlink, the URL of the hyperlink will appear in the Status Bar at the bottom of the window. Clicking on the hyperlink downloads the designated information to your computer. If you click once on a hyperlink for a multimedia file Mosaic will download the file and then open the appropriate external viewer (or player) for that type of file.

A tour of the Mosaic screen

Although using Mosaic is somewhat intuitive, before beginning to explore this brave new world it is useful to learn some keys to using Mosaic, how Mosaic displays information, and how you can control it. Many of the concepts described here apply to most versions of Mosaic, including other browsers such as Netscape, a product of Netscape Communications Corp. However, the details described and the screens shown are unique to the Luckman Interactive Enhanced Mosaic version 2.0 (a.k.a., Super Mosaic) included with this manuscript. Let's begin with the Luckman Home Page shown in Fig. 7-3.

Menu Bar	Contains the names of available commands.
Tool Bar	Allows quick access to frequently used menu commands.
Document Title	Contains the title of the current document in the document view window.
Document URL	Gives the URL of the document currently in the document view window.
Document View Window	Displays the current document.
Progress Indicator	When the Mosaic logo (the globe) at the upper right edge of the page spins, the page is loading.
Status Bar	Displays the URL of the hyperlink to which you are currently pointing. If it is blank you are not pointing at a hyperlink.

Figure 7-3

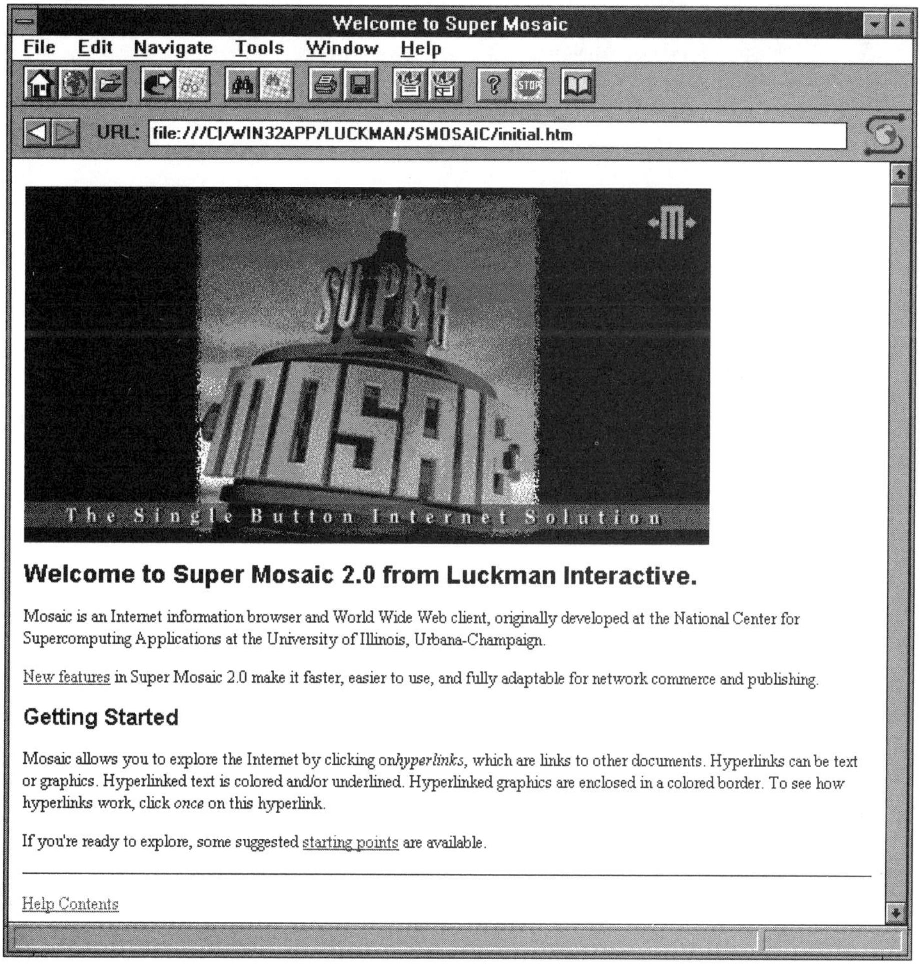

The Mosaic interface

Vertical Scroll Bar The slide control on the right side of the screen allows the user to move through the current document.

✳ Menu bar commands

File Figure 7-4 shows the File pulldown menu.

New Window Opens Enhanced Mosaic in a new window.

Figure 7-4

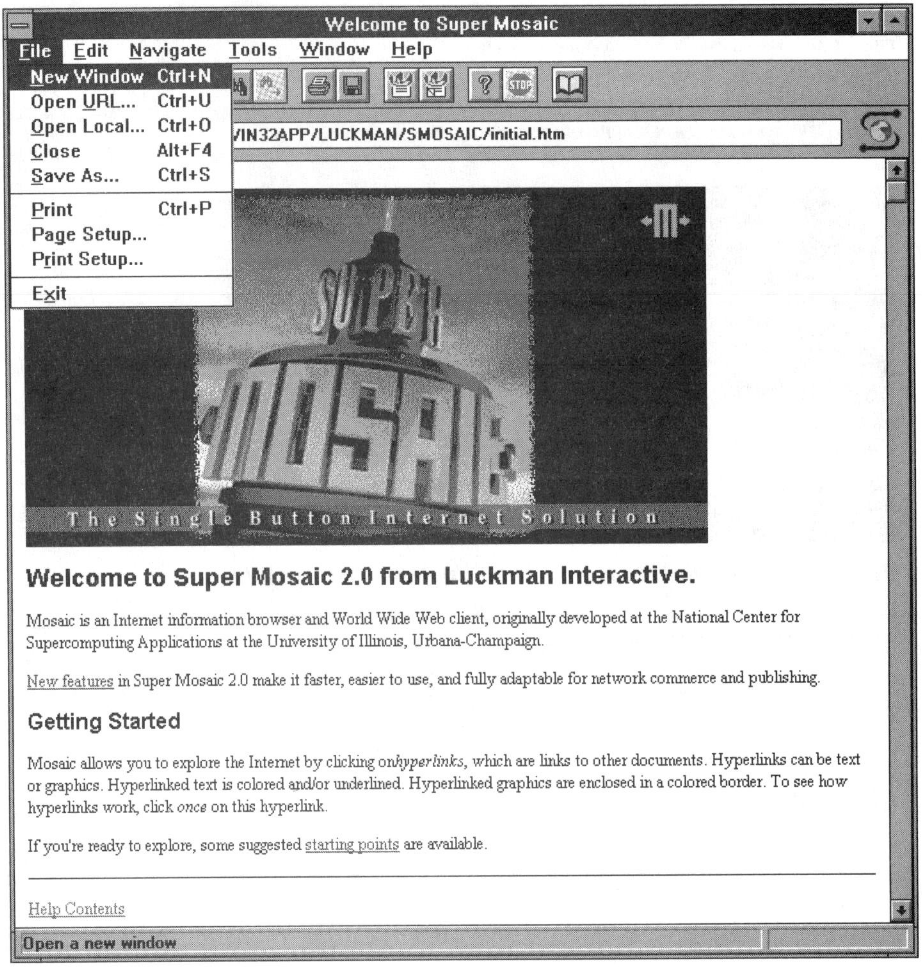

The File menu

Open URL	Jumps to a document by specifying its URL address.
Open Local	Opens a document on your local computer.
Close	Closes the current window.
Save As	Stores a document to a file as HTML or plain ASCII text.

Print	Prints the contents of the current window.
Page Setup	Allows you to control page margins and header and footer spacing.
Print Setup	Sets printer options.
Exit	Ends Enhanced Mosaic.

Edit Figure 7-5 shows the Edit pulldown menu.

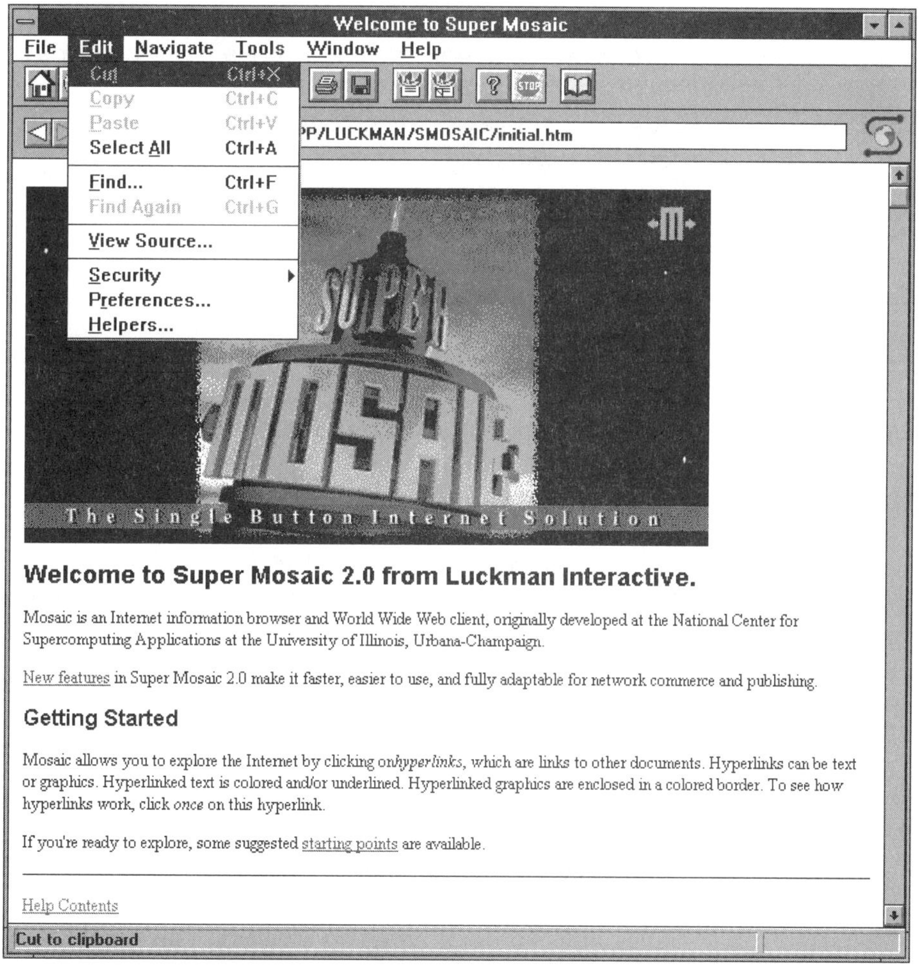

Figure 7-5

The Edit menu

Cut	Removes selected text and saves it to the Windows clipboard.
Copy	Copies text to the Windows clipboard for inclusion in other applications.
Paste	Pastes the contents of the Windows clipboard at the current cursor location.
Select All	Selects all text on the current page for subsequent action.
Find	Searches the current document for a word or phrase.
Find Again	Finds the next occurrence of the word or phrase previously searched.
View Source	Displays the HTML source of the current document.
Security	Sets up security modules.
Preferences	Configures user options.
Helpers	Configures additional external viewers.

Navigate Figure 7-6 shows the Navigate pulldown menu.

Back	Re-displays the last document viewed. Same as the Back button in the upper left corner of the window.
Forward	Displays the next document.
Home	Displays the home page.
History	Displays a list of documents viewed during the session. Use the History Dialog to return to a previously viewed document quickly.
Hotlist	Saves links to documents so that you can quickly find them again.

Figure 7-6

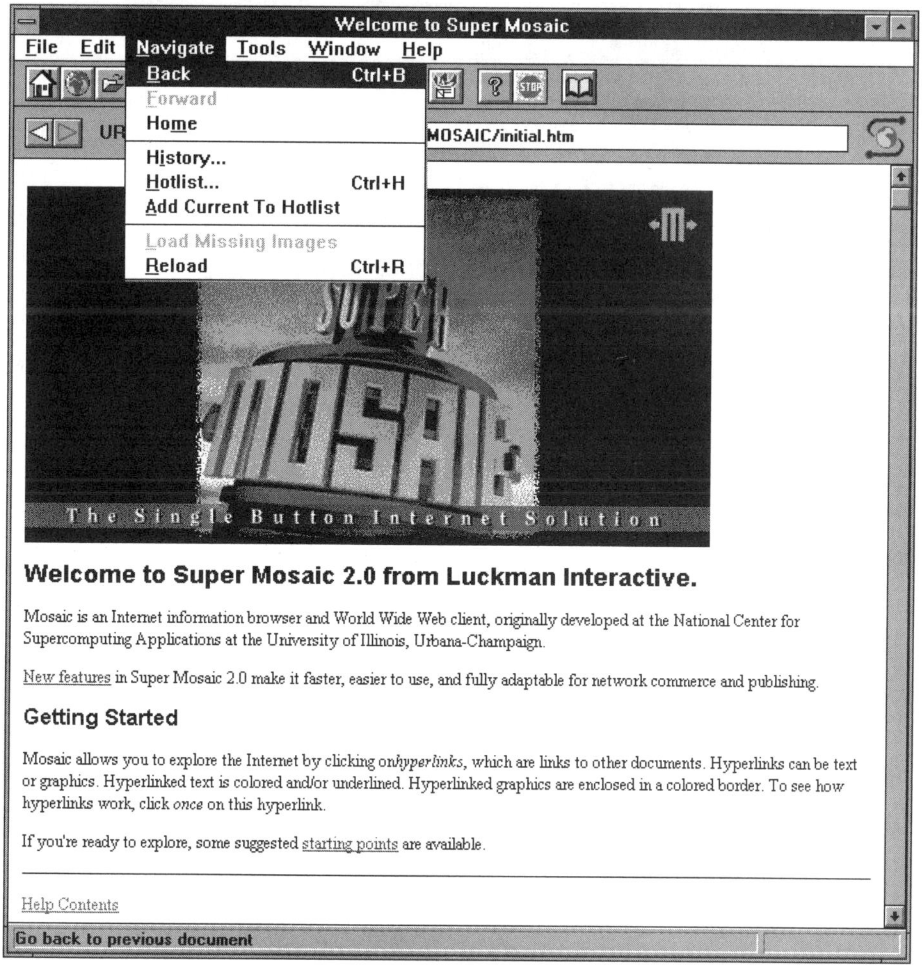

The Navigate menu

Add Current to Hotlist Adds the current document to your hotlist.

Load Missing Images Loads any images that were not loaded in the current document.

Reload Reloads the current document.

Window The Window pulldown menu appears in Fig. 7-7.

Figure 7-7

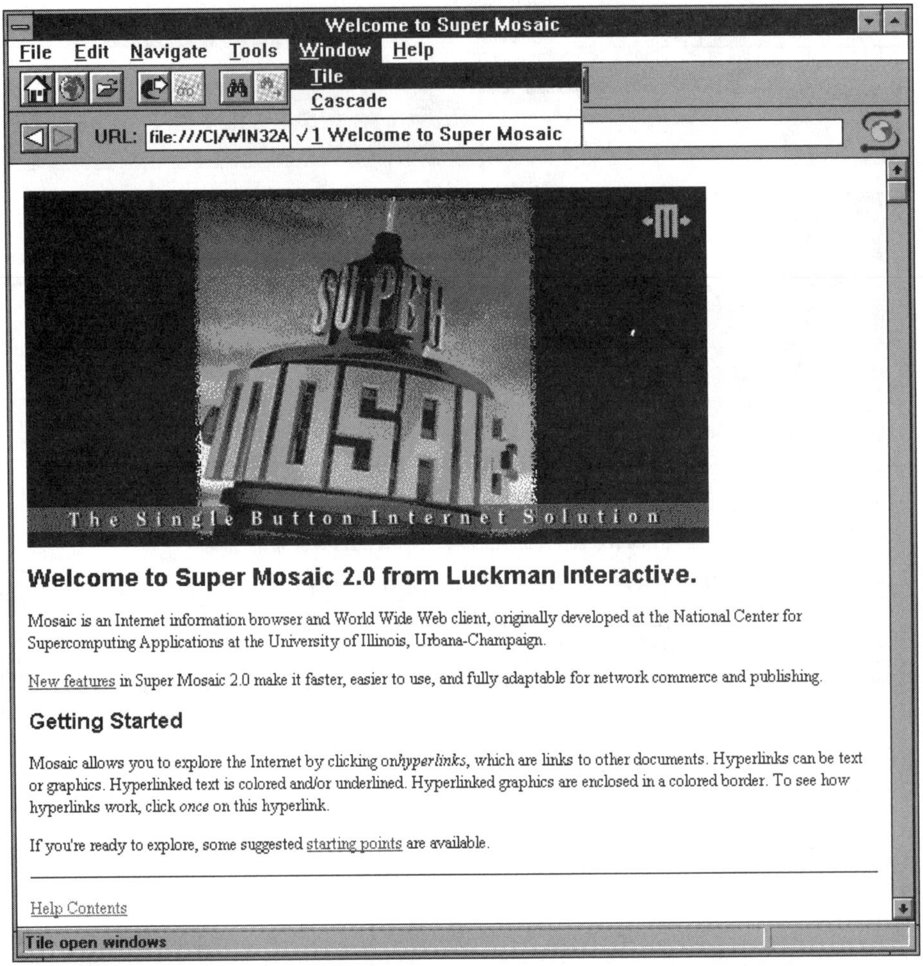

The Window menu

Tile	Arranges open windows side by side, making them all visible.
Cascade	Arranges open windows so that the title bar of each window is visible.
List of Windows	Lists the names of all windows at the bottom of the Window menu. To open a window, select its name from the list.

Help Figure 7-8 shows the Help menu.

Mosaic Help Page	Displays online help.
About Mosaic	Displays copyright, system information, and technical support information.

Figure 7-8

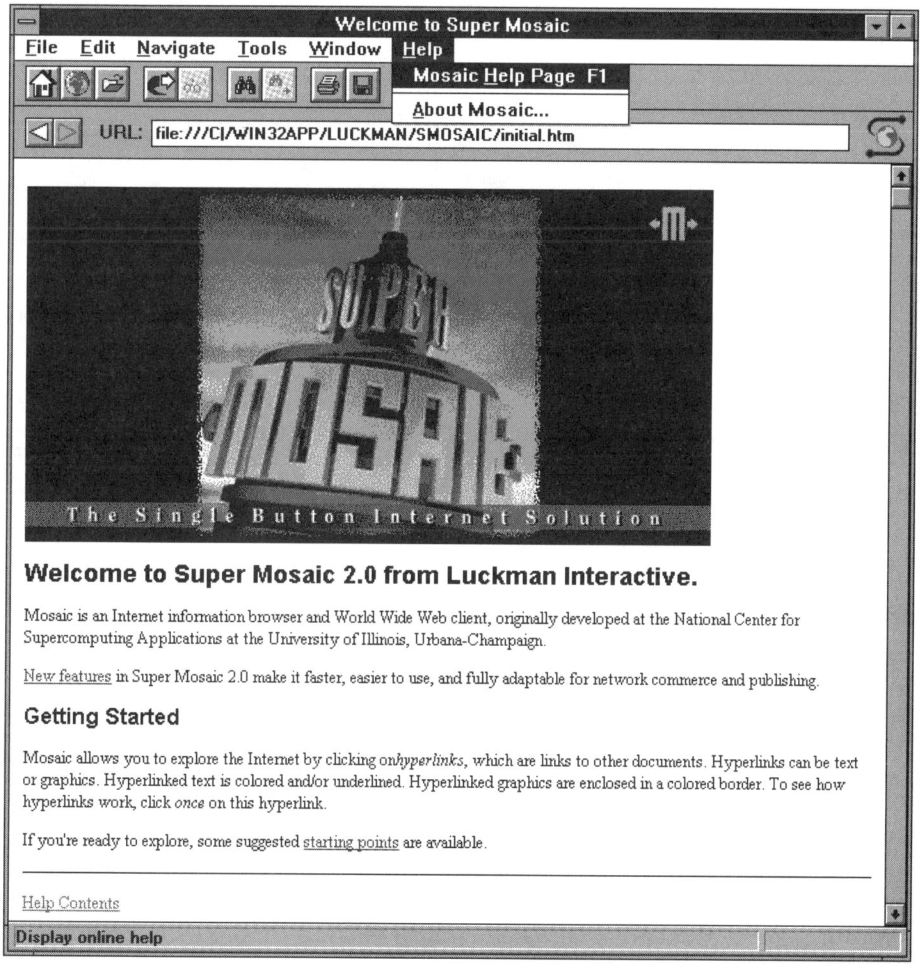

The Help Menu

Toolbar menu

Figure 7-9 shows the Toolbar pulldown menu.

Figure 7-9

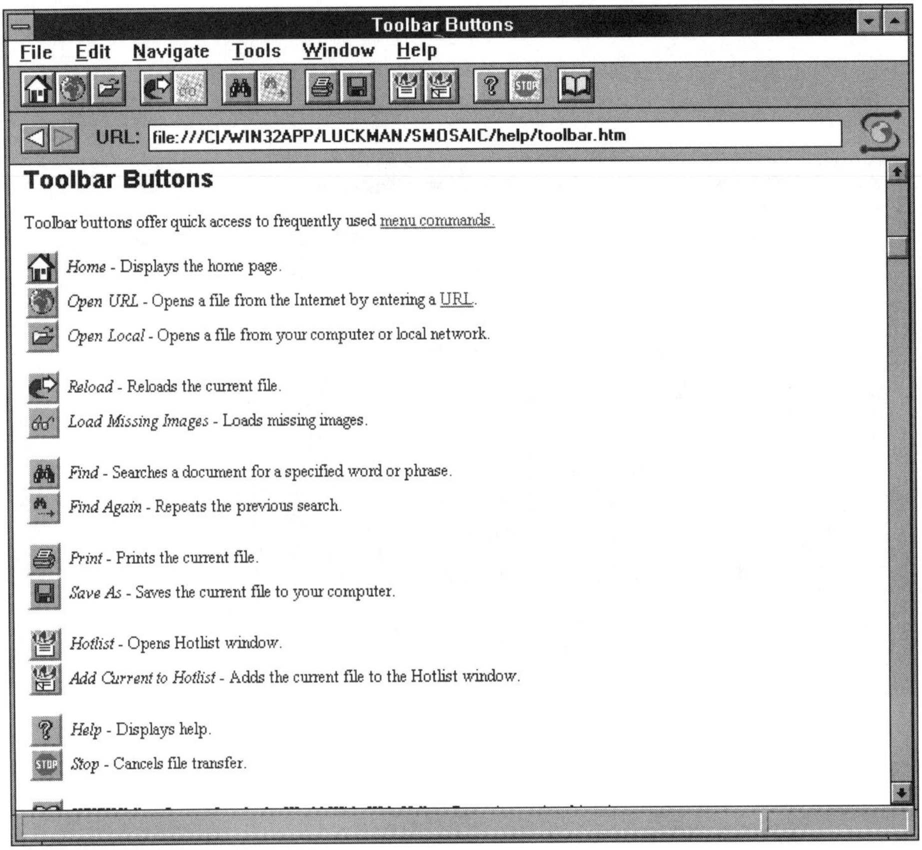

The Toolbar menu

Security

The Security menu is found under the Edit menu in Fig. 7-5.

Security modules are third-party software that allow Mosaic to communicate with secure servers using a variety of security schemes. (See Fig. 7-10.)

First Virtual Supports an Internet payment system from First Virtual, Inc. (See Fig. 7-11.)

Figure 7-10

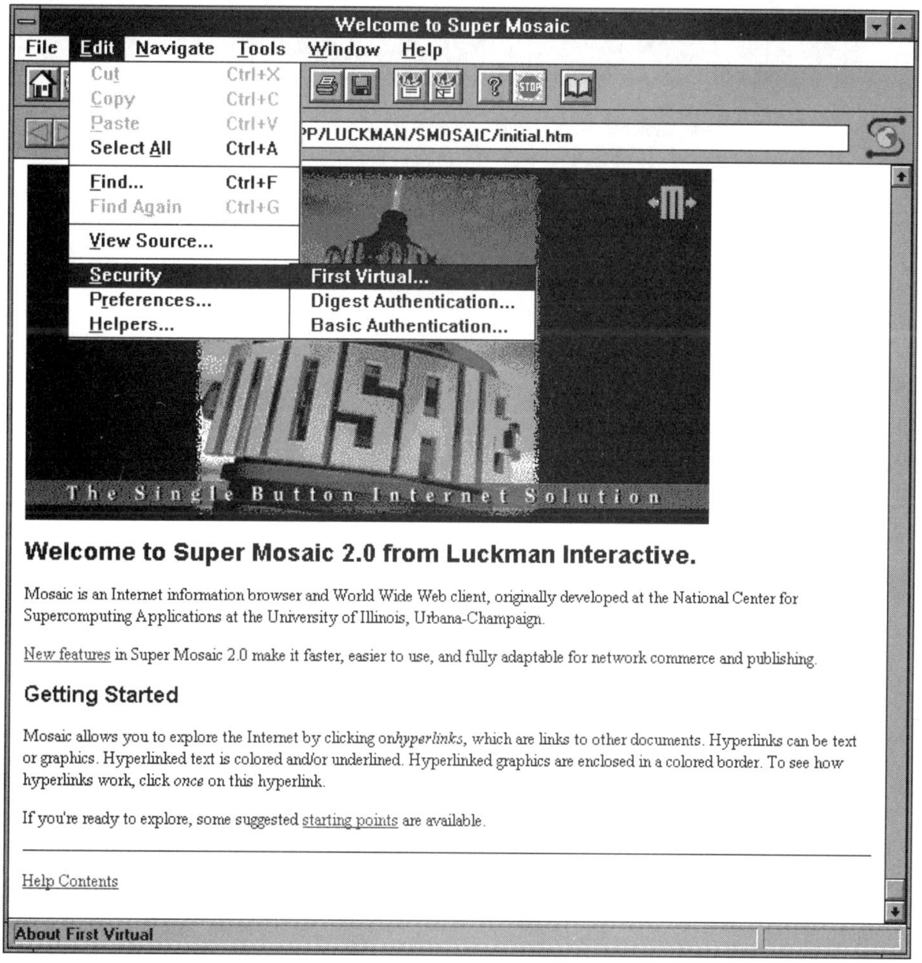

The Security menu

Digest Authentication Uses MD5-encrypted passwords for authorization to receive an HTTP reply. (See Fig. 7-12.)

Basic Authentication A basic, nonsecure protocol where a user name and password are sent to the server in UUENCODED form. (See Fig. 7-13.)

✳ **Preferences** Found under the Edit menu in Fig. 7-5.

Figure 7-11

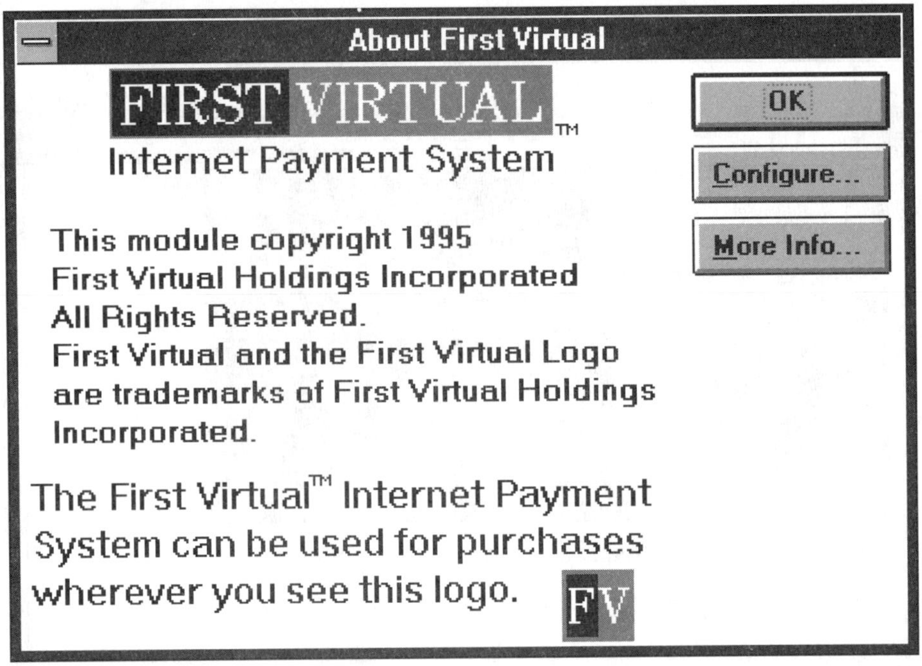

First Virtual

Figure 7-12

Digest Authentication

Figure 7-13

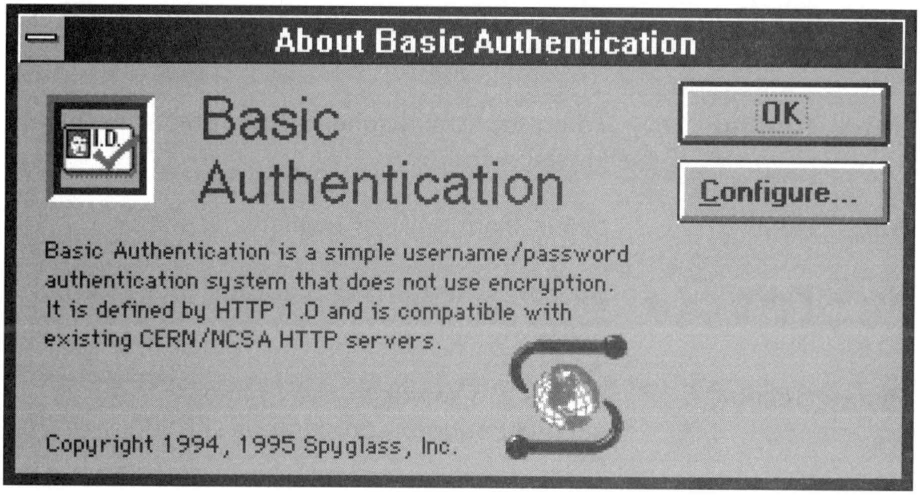

Basic Authentication

Load Images Automatically

To open documents faster by not downloading graphic images, leave this box blank. (See Fig. 7-14.) To load images after the document is loaded, choose the Load Missing Images command from the Navigate Menu.

Figure 7-14

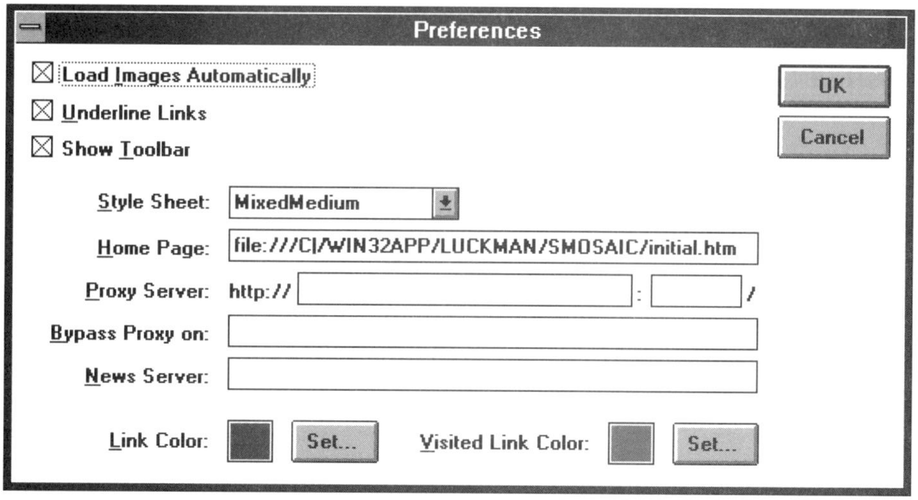

The Preference menu

Underline Links	To have hyperlinks appear underlined, check this box.
Show Toolbar	To control the display of the toolbar in the Mosaic window.
Style Sheet	Select from a list of available fonts.
Home Page	Specifies the starting point for your Internet journey.
Proxy Server	This is the server to use to bypass a secure gateway at your company or site to reach Web sites.
Style Sheet	Select from a list of available fonts.
Bypass Proxy on	A list of systems for which Mosaic should not use the proxy server.
News Server	Specifies the domain name of the news server to which you subscribe.
Link Color	Changes the default link color of hypertext links.
Visited Link Color	Changes the default color of visited (clicked) links.

✳ Helpers

Figure 7-15 shows the Helpers menu, which is found under the Edit Menu (Fig. 7-5).

Add support for other additional file types by configuring helper applications. (See Fig. 7-16 for configure helpers.)

Figure 7-15

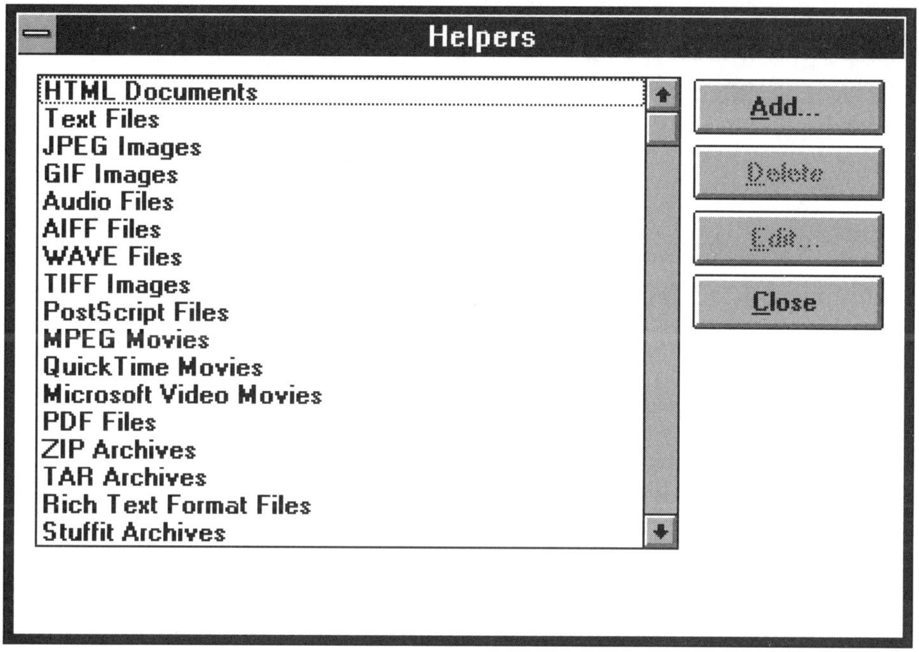

The Helpers menu

Figure 7-16

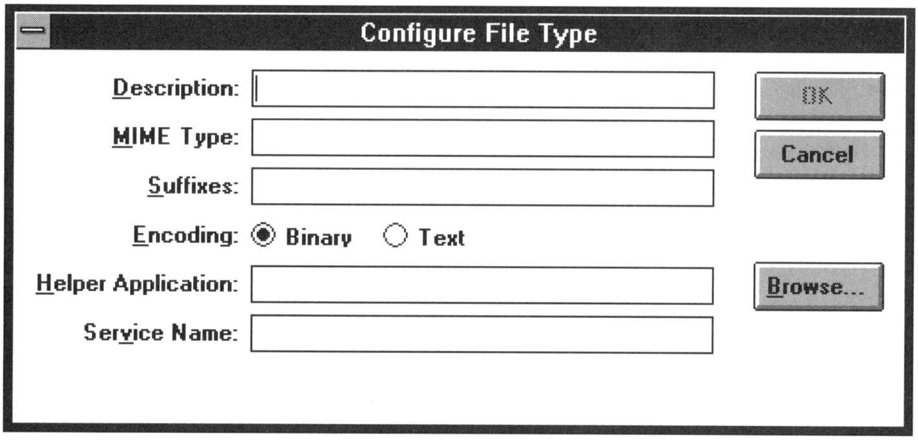

Configure Helpers

Navigation shortcuts

History Found under Navigate menu; lists all the documents you've visited in the current session. (See Fig. 7-17.)

Figure 7-17

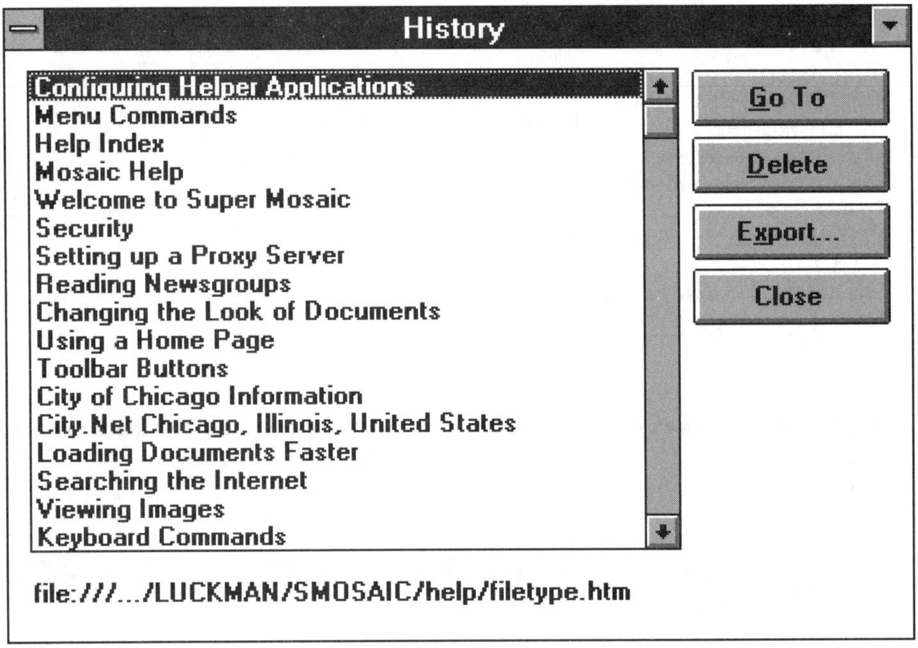

The History window

Hotlist Found under Navigate menu; provides a way for you to save the pointer (URL) to your favorite places on the Internet (add Current to Hotlist) and later use the Hotlist to quickly jump to that reference. (See Fig. 7-18.)

Home Found under Navigate menu; provides a quick method to return to your starting point.

Using URLs Opens URL found under the File menu; allows you to enter the URL of a document you want to see and go directly to it. (See Fig. 7-19.)

Figure 7-18

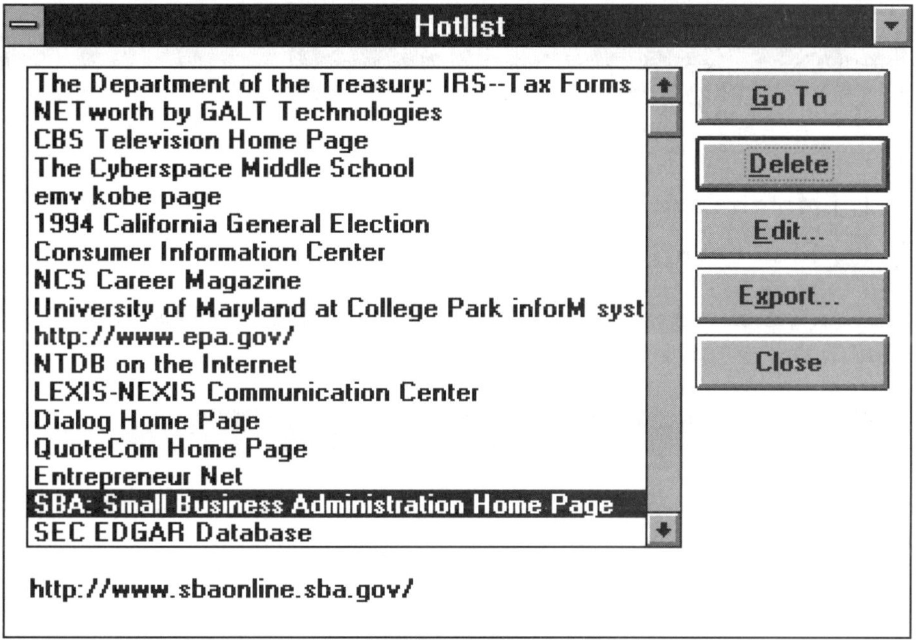

The Hotlist

Figure 7-19

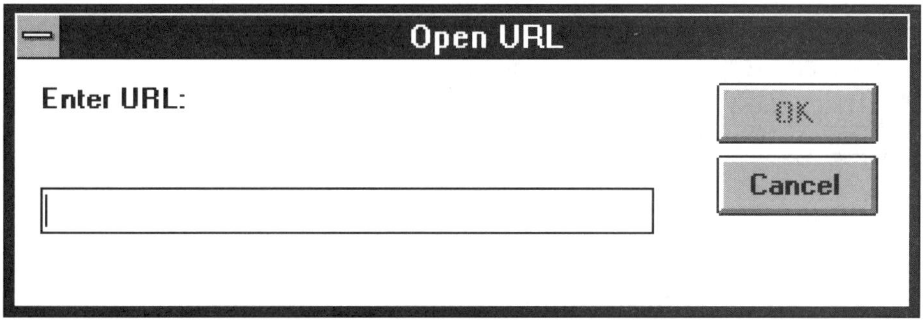

Open URL

Finding Text Found under Edit menu; a quick method to find specific information in the current document. (See Fig. 7-20.)

Saving Files Found under File menu; allows the user to save a copy of interesting documents for later manipulation. (See Fig. 7-21.)

Figure 7-20

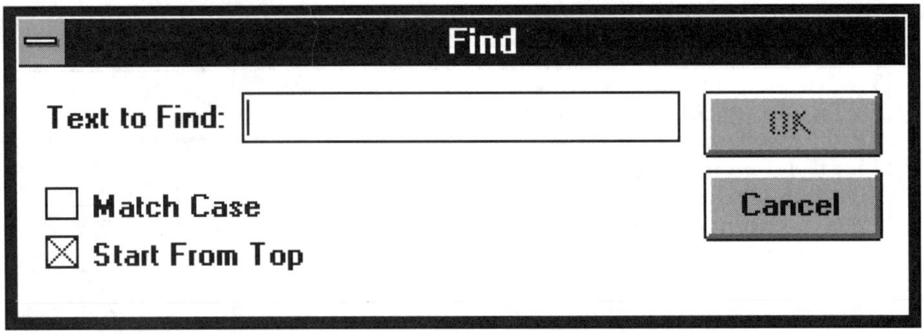

Find Text

Figure 7-21

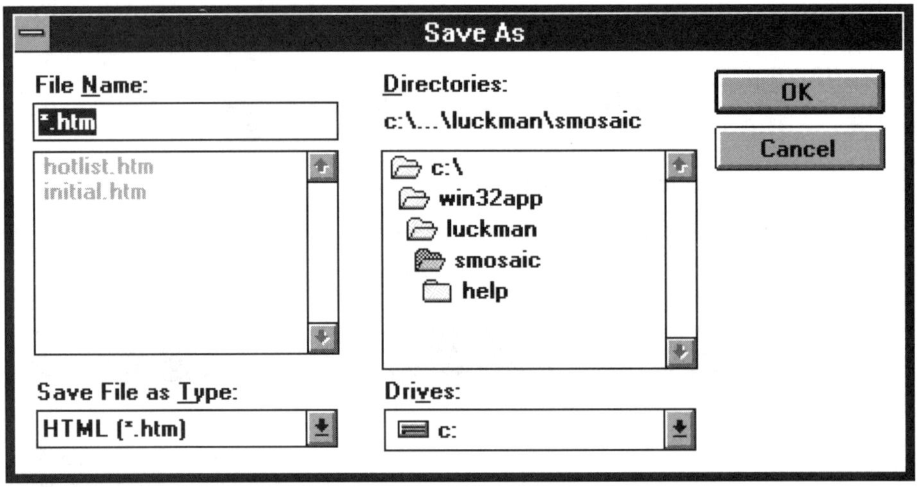

Save As

Keyboard shortcuts

- If loading a document is taking too long, pressing the Escape key or clicking on the stop sign icon in the tool bar cancels document loading.
- To cause a document to appear in a new window, press the Alt key while clicking on link.
- To save a file to disk, hold the Ctrl key while clicking on a link.
- To display link information without displaying a document, place the mouse over the link without clicking on it. The link will be displayed in the status area.

Differences in feel & features of UNIX & PC versions

With this book, we have included software which was based on the Spyglass Enhanced Mosaic version 2.0. The Microsoft Windows version has been enhanced by Luckman Interactive and renamed Super Mosaic 2.0. The UNIX version included on the CD is the Spyglass release. Therefore, while the functionality of the two versions is nearly identical, they will look slightly different. All the figures in this chapter up until this point have shown the Luckman Interactive graphical user interface provided by Super Mosaic 2.0. Figure 7-22 shows the initial screen displayed by Spyglass Enhanced Mosaic for Unix included on the CD with this book.

Figure 7-22

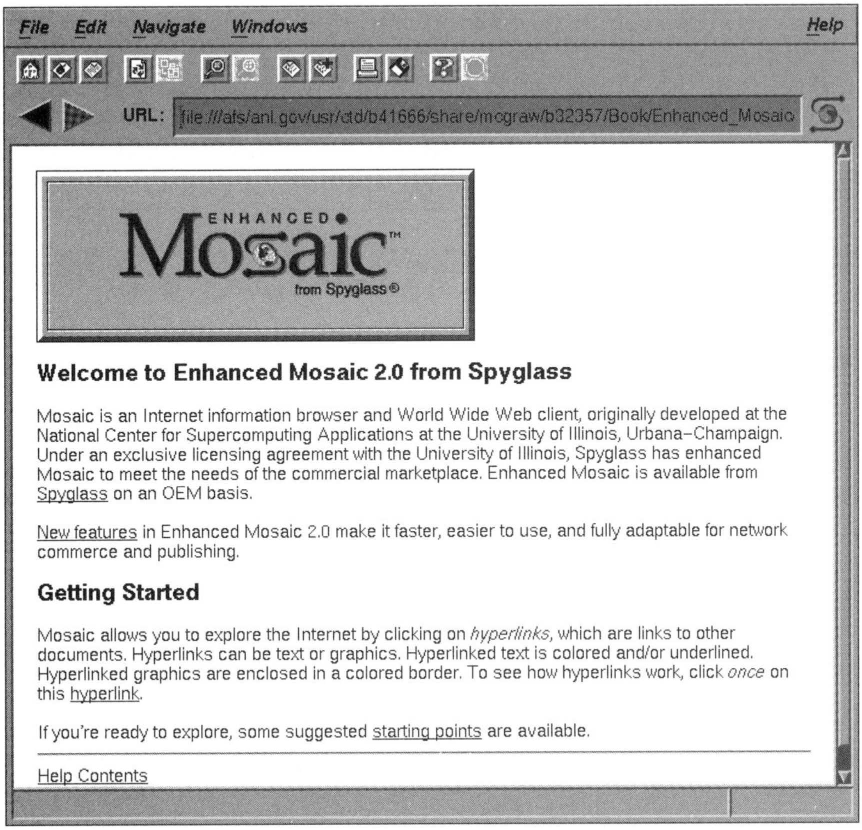

Enhanced Mosaic Interface

You will notice a difference in the Menu bar at the top of the screen as shown in Fig. 7-23.

The Tool bar menu is also slightly different as shown in Fig. 7-24.

Figure 7-23

Menu bar

Figure 7-24

Tool bar

Sharing your newfound treasures

To share your hotlist with your friends and associates, go to the Navigate menu and select Hotlist. Then select Export, which will save your Hotlist as an HTML document, as shown in Fig. 7-25. Give a friend a copy of the HTML document.

Figure 7-25

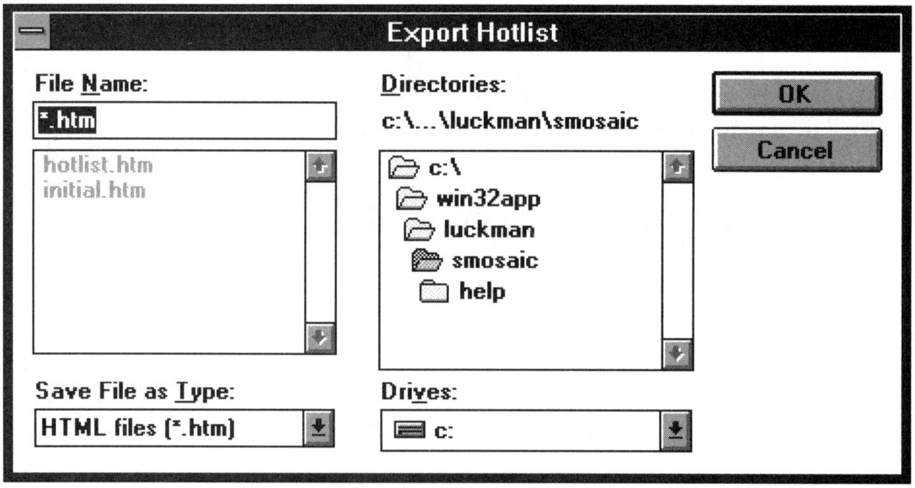

Export Hotlist

To copy links from another HTML document to your hotlist, go to the File menu and select Open Local. Open the document that you want to copy from. If the hotlist was exported as an HTML document you will see a list of links. Open any document that you want to add to your hotlist. After the document is displayed, select Add Current Document from the Navigate menu. Click the Back button to return to the previous document. Repeat the process for each link you want to add.

Viewing multimedia information

To appreciate the full power of Mosaic you must experience using multimedia files on the Internet. Whether you want to play movies, listen to music, look at full-color images, or run scientific models or 3D graphics, the applications are limitless. But Internet multimedia can be somewhat frustrating. The files are usually quite large. Downloading these large files can be quite painful on slow-speed network connections.

Mosaic relies on other programs, called external viewers, that are designed to handle special kinds of files. Different viewers are designed to handle graphics, audio, movies, etc. To configure Mosaic to launch the appropriate viewers refer to the section on Configuring User Options earlier in this chapter. When you click on a link in a document that isn't HTML or plain text, Mosaic tries to launch an external program to display the image or play the sound.

Multimedia support in Mosaic is based on a mechanism originally developed for electronic mail, the Multipurpose Internet Mail Extensions (MIME). MIME defines a set of multimedia content types and subtypes that specify the type of data in the body of an e-mail message. Mosaic makes use of the content types in order to determine the appropriate external viewer to launch. For example, if a hyperlink points to a movie file, the file is downloaded and a program that can play the file is executed. To the user, this means a wide range of data can be made easily accessible. Once launched, the external viewer executes as a separate program, outside the global hypermedia environment. Therefore, external viewers do not recognize hyperlinks of any sort.

Table 7-2 **File Types, Extensions, & Viewers**

File content type	File extension	UNIX viewer	Windows extension	Windows viewer
GIF graphic	.gif	xv	.gif	lview
JPEG graphic	.jpeg	xv	.jpg	lview
MPEG mo	.mpeg	mpegplay	.mpg	mpegplay
PostScript doc	.ps	ghostscript	.ps	ghostview

Appendix B will cover details on how to find new viewer applications on the Internet.

You will notice that Web documents can include inline images in GIF or XBM formats, which can be seen but cannot be manipulated. Still images stored in separate documents, as GIF, JPEG, XBM or JPEG images, can be viewed or downloaded and manipulated.

When things go wrong

Occasionally your trip on the Internet will be unexpectedly interrupted. Many documents and servers are under construction so travelers need to be prepared. Some of the most common roadblocks are listed here.

- **The host is busy**. Wait a few minutes and try again. The most likely cause is that the server or network you must traverse is overloaded.
- **The server is down**. Try again later.
- **The server or home page has moved**. Responsible Webmasters post a forwarding address directing you to their new location.
- **The server or home page has died**. Nothing is forever.

Achieving peak performance

A number of factors will affect how Enhanced Mosaic will perform on your desktop:

- The speed of your Internet connection.
- The traffic load on the Internet between you and the server.
- The load on the server from which you are retrieving the document.
- The size of the document.
- The amount of memory in your local machine.

The downside to multimedia information handling is that it consumes a tremendous amount of space requiring sometimes intolerable amounts of time to download over slow-speed (14.4 Kbps or slower) communication links. As the network speeds to the home improve, this bottleneck will disappear and the associated problems of low-speed network performance will disappear with it.

To speed up your journey, select Preferences from the Edit Menu and disable the automatic loading of images. When you come across an image of interest, select the Load Missing Images selection from the Navigate menu to display the images in the current document.

Mosaic caches documents and inline graphics in your system's memory for reloading instantly when you request them. Mosaic does not, however, cache sound or video files. To enhance the performance of Mosaic over a low-speed link you can set the document caching to a higher number. By default, Mosaic caches the last four documents you have viewed in the memory of your desktop machine. By default, Mosaic will also store 50 images in local memory. When these images are called they will then be brought in from memory instead of the network, thus significantly increasing your performance.

Both of these variables will significantly enhance your Mosaic performance, depending on the types of movement through documents that you are performing. The issue you must be aware of as you increase this number is that you begin to use more and more memory. If you run out of physical memory in Windows you will begin to use virtual memory. While this is relatively expensive in terms of computer resources, it is still better than using the network to pull documents that are viewed multiple times. It is hard to estimate how much memory each image and document will use because no two documents are ever alike. However, it is important to realize that you are using these resources and there is some price to be paid by increasing these variables.

Summary

You now have the basic knowledge to enable your journey through the multimedia resources of the new Internet. As you explore you will become comfortable with many of the shortcuts that make navigation easier. It is likely you will develop your personal list of favorite sites you will want to visit frequently. Remember, this is an evolving and quickly changing environment we have just begun to explore. In the following chapter we will expand your knowledge to allow access to many of the other Internet server types via Mosaic.

8

Mosaic & the rest of the Internet

CHAPTER 8

MOSAIC exists in a piece of the Internet known as the World Wide Web (WWW). This is a relatively new paradigm within the Internet and coexists with many other interfaces to the Internet. While this book focuses on Mosaic and its capabilities within the WWW, it also has the capability to work elegantly with other resources on the Internet, including FTP, WAIS, Gopher, and News. This chapter will describe the Internet, explain how you can access Internet resources from Mosaic, and describe the benefits you receive from services of these types.

The Internet

This book focuses on Mosaic, which is a fundamentally new interface to information on the Internet. Mosaic is built to work with the newest component of the Internet, the World Wide Web (WWW). While Mosaic defaults to the WWW, it will handle the other generic tools of the Internet. Because of this it is important to further your understanding of the Internet and its history and capabilities. This section introduces you to many of the important concepts.

While the Internet has been discussed in earlier chapters, it is important to delve more deeply into the routing and some of the other "old-Internet" issues to ensure that you have the understanding you need to interface Mosaic with some of the older Internet tools. This chapter will present some of this information to help you understand the capabilities and usage of these older Internet tools.

Routing and addressing on the Internet

In essence, the Internet is simply an extension of the phone and leased line infrastructure around the world. There are gateways and routers that connect a large number of disparate networks around the world.

As Fig. 8-1 denotes, you can access the Internet via a variety of components, including modems, routers, and bridges. The Internet uses both the public telephone network and variety of leased lines

Figure 8-1

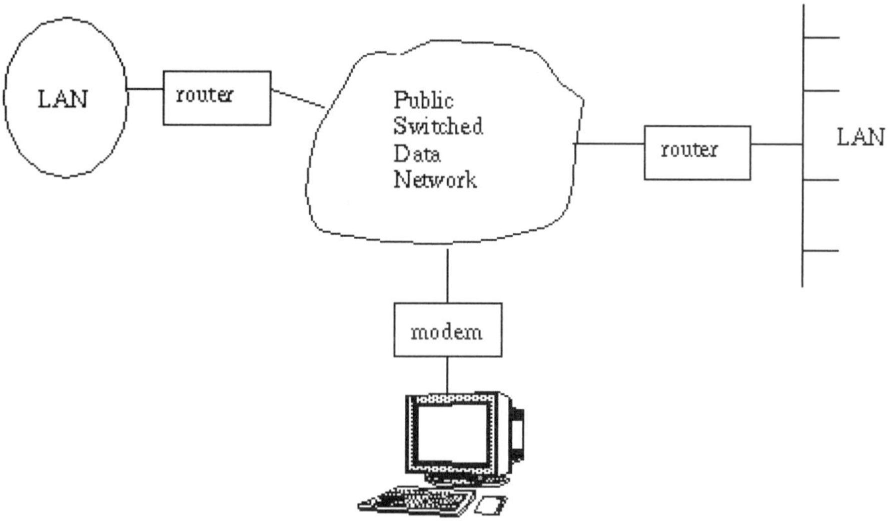

The Internet

from a variety of government organizations and commercial access providers, such as PSI.

Protocols that run between the routers and gateways allow each to understand who they are responsible for, based on a concept called a domain. A domain is established by a place called the Internet Network Information Center (InterNIC). The InterNIC has been responsible for distribution of addresses and domains since the inception of the Internet.

Internet addresses are IP addresses that are represented by four groups of numbers, separated by periods. An example of an IP address is

191.9.200.1

Each number, left to right, represents a subnetwork of the higher level represented to the left. In this example, a large network is represented by 191. Within this network is a subnetwork represented by 191.9. Inside this is 191.9.200, and finally the actual node IP address is 191.9.200.1. The InterNIC is responsible for providing IP (e.g.,

Internet) addresses. These numbers allow routers and gateways to section off certain portions of the Internet to reduce the packet loads on individual segments of the network, similar to the way zip codes enable the US Postal Service to route (direct) your mail.

For example, if you want to send a message to address 192.10.10.10, the initial router you contact through your part of the Internet maintains a table detailing who is responsible for the 192 subnetwork. It then figures out the quickest way to get your information to this subnetwork. It might have to route it through several gateways and routers; however, the algorithm used by the routers will find the most efficient path available at the time.

Figure 8-2 denotes a network that consists of a gateway machine between two networks. If a packet from the 191 network wants to get to the 192 network it must be routed through the gateway. Note that the gateway can be a UNIX computer or a specialized device such as a router. This device contains tables that help to route the packets to the appropriate network based on the IP address. The Internet works very similarly to this. A rough schematic is shown in Fig. 8-3.

Figure 8-3 represents the telecommunication links between the interior gateway routers. Most of these lines are high-speed T1 and T3 lines, but other lines still run at much slower speeds on the Internet network. You must connect to the Internet network, either directly through a router directly connected to the Internet backbone or through an Internet Service Provider such as UUNET, PSINet, or Portal. The Internet itself takes care of routing packets through the network by communicating between all routers on the network. This ensures redundancy and reliability and increases the stability of the entire network.

Internet domain names

Because remembering IP addresses is virtually impossible for people, the InterNIC began to give computers names people could remember. Originally, the InterNIC distributed all IP addresses and names. However, as the Internet began to grow this became impossible. A

Figure 8-2

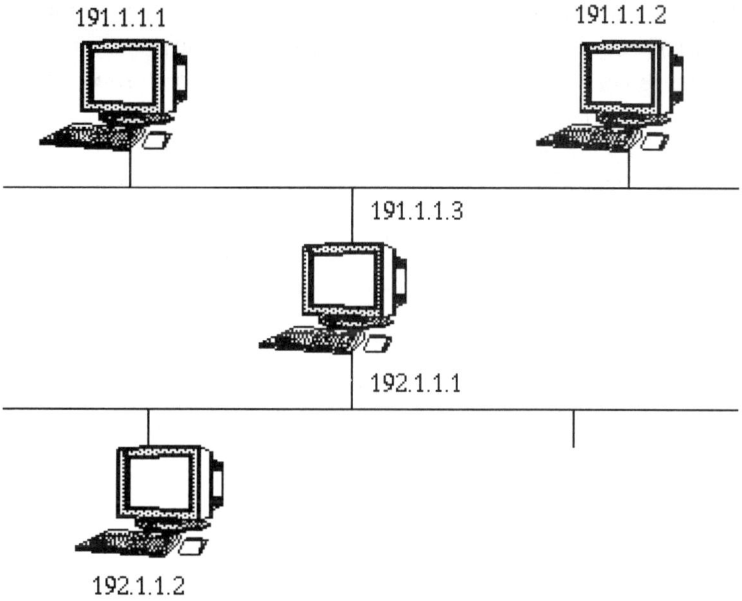

IP gateway

Figure 8-3

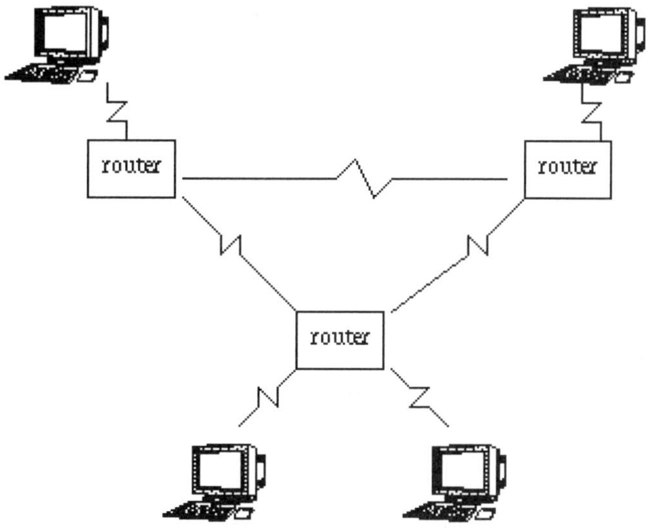

The Internet and its routers

new scheme, known as the Domain Name System (DNS), was developed for resolving name to IP address mapping. This gave each group of users on the Internet the responsibility to manage their own machine names and IP addresses. The naming structure was based on the success of the IP addressing scheme and therefore divided into subgroups, separated by periods. Each level in this system is called a domain. Some examples are:

luckman.com   nic.ddn.mil   fred.csu.upenn.edu

The hierarchy is exactly the opposite as the IP addresses. The major domain is the farthest to the right in this address (known as domain name). There are six main domestic domains: gov (government), mil (military), com (commercial), net (network resources), org (other organizations) and edu (educational institutions). Within a given domain there exist machines and groups of machines. For example, consider the address:

fred.cs.uchi.edu

The machine exists in an educational institution (edu), probably at the University of Chicago (uchi), perhaps in the computer science department (cs), and the actual machine name is fred (who is probably the graduate student who uses the machine). This domain name might translate to an address of 192.9.200.1. There is probably a correlation between the uchi and the subnetwork addresses of 192.9, because the NIC gave the University of Chicago all addresses within 192.9. This correlation is maintained by the NIC and is crucial, because neither IP addresses nor domain names can be duplicated on the Internet. If this occurs major problems result, and therefore duplications must be avoided at all costs.

You can have two machines with the same name, but they must be in different domains. For example, **fred.cs.upenn.edu** would be perfectly fine. Even **fred.bio.uchi.edu** is fine, because the domain names are not exactly the same. Note also that the IP addresses of these machines will be very different, depending on their domains. Most likely, **fred.cs.upenn.edu** has a different major IP address, while **fred.bio.uchi.edu** probably starts with 192.9.

Because of the international nature of the Internet the standards for domain names must encompass the globe. Typically, the domain name ends with a country code (e.g., ca is Canada). The use of this nomenclature is a predominant standard for hostnames on the Internet. For a comprehensive list of International Country Codes refer to Appendix C. As you tour the Internet, it is very intriguing to examine domain names to determine where you have "landed."

Mosaic & the Internet

Mosaic was built to tame an established Internet infrastructure. In the pre-WWW days you needed a variety of tools to use to access all information on the Internet. These included WAIS clients, FTP clients, Telnet, and a variety of other client interfaces. Each had its own interface and commands, and you were forced to use each to access a particular type of resource. Mosaic arrived on the scene with support for a variety of other Internet access methods. Mosaic supports all of these tools from a single interface. In some cases, Mosaic improves upon the functionality of the native tools; in other cases, Mosaic's functionality limits the function of the other tools. Each of these access methods (FTP, WAIS, and Gopher) are discussed at greater length in the following sections.

Mosaic does provide, however, a uniform, standard interface to all tools on the Internet, including these old paradigm tools. You must decide whether Mosaic gives you all the functionality you need. Do the benefits of a single, uniform interface outweigh the advantages of using several different interface tools to access all tools on the Internet? We believe that the benefits of Mosaic far outweigh the costs associated with limitations related to non-Mosaic tools.

Mosaic & FTP

The original paradigm of the Internet was a large number of machines existing on a common IP network backbone. Communications between these machines consisted of FTP file transfers and Telnet log-ins. There was usually a standard account, known as **guest** or **anonymous**, which was established without password protection. You could log-in to these machines and perform tasks such as browsing for public files and downloading them for your own use. You discovered these files and machines largely through word of mouth. This capability came to be known as Anonymous FTP.

FTP stands for File Transfer Protocol and is the core utility that works with TCP/IP to provide file transfer capabilities between nodes on a network. By utilizing log-in security checks, users can transfer files based on the existence of their accounts on each machine. FTP is available on virtually all types of computers.

The general syntax of the FTP command is

```
$ ftp remote-machine-name
```

Remote-machine-name is the name of any other machine that you can access independent of where the machine is or what operating system it runs. As long as it supports the FTP protocol you can use FTP to transfer files.

When a connection is established you are prompted for a username and a password for the remote machine. After typing these in, you are placed at the interactive FTP prompt ftp>. Once you are at the interactive FTP prompt, you are ready to begin transferring files. An example of a file transfer from your current machine named dumpy to another machine named dopey:

```
dumpy>$ ftp dopey
Connected to dopey.
220 dopey FTP server (UNIX(r) System V Release 4.0) ready.
username: kevin
Password required for dopey.
passwd: password
User kevin logged in.
ftp> put /tmp/stuff
200 PORT command successful.
150 ASCII data connection for stuff (55 bytes).
226 ASCII Transfer complete.
83 bytes sent in .02 seconds (4k bytes/sec)
ftp> quit
221 Goodbye.
dumpy> $
```

This example transfers a file named /TMP/STUFF from a machine named DUMPY to a file in your home directory named STUFF on a remote machine named DOPEY. FTP allows for file transfer in both directions. To transfer a file from a remote machine named DOPEY to the local machine named DUMPY use the get command. For example:

```
dumpy>$ ftp dopey
Connected to dopey.
220 dopey FTP server (UNIX(r) System V Release 4.0) ready.
username: kevin
Password required for dopey.
passwd: password
User kevin logged in.
ftp> get /tmp/stuff
200 PORT command successful.
150 ASCII data connection for stuff (55 bytes).
226 ASCII Transfer complete.
83 bytes sent in .02 seconds (4k bytes/sec)
ftp> quit
221 Goodbye.
dumpy> $
```

A variety of commands within FTP might be of some use:

binary	Transfer a file in binary mode and perform no translation.
ascii	Transfer a file in ASCII mode. Perform any necessary translation to maintain an accurate representation.
put local-file-name remote-file-name	Put file from your local machine to the remote machine.
mput filelist	Multiple file put.
get remote-file-name local-file-name	Get a file from the remote machine to your local machine.
mget filelist	Multiple file get.
user username	Log in to remote machine.

help	Print list of all FTP commands.
lcd dir	Change directory on the local disk.
cd remote-dir	Change directory on the remote disk.
close	Close current FTP session on remote machine and return to FTP mode.
delete remote-file-name	Delete remote-file-name on the remote machine.
dir filename	Show remote filename listing (wildcards supported).
open machine	Open a connection to a remote machine.
pwd	Print the name of the current working directory.
quit	Close any open connections and exit FTP.

If you use the mput and mget commands to transfer multiple files you will be prompted for each file before the transfer, unless you issue a "prompt" command first. Keep this in mind before you invoke FTP for file transfer. Also, to interrupt file transfer you can use the Ctrl-C sequence. This will halt file transfer after the server has had time to process the interrupt. It usually takes some time before the data will stop flowing into or out of the local machine, based on network load and file server performance and load. Be patient!

You will note the lack of a cat or type command in the FTP subcommand listing above. If you want to examine a file before transfer you must get a little clever and remember UNIX and its standard input/output structure as described earlier in this book. To examine a file on the screen before transferring it:

```
ftp> get file1 -
```

where the - represents standard out. If this doesn't work, try

```
ftp> get file1 /dev/tty
```

which uses the standard terminal device name for the output file. Remember, everything in UNIX is a file and, as such, redirection is as simple as that shown above.

Anonymous FTP

The FTP utility relies on usernames and passwords for ensuring the integrity of file systems and machines. However, there is a de facto standard in the UNIX and Internet work for using FTP for general-purpose file sharing and transfer. It is known as Anonymous FTP. This means that when you connect to the remote machine and are prompted for your username, you type `anonymous`. The password can be anything; however, it is generally accepted that you will type your mail address so you can be tracked and notified if a problem comes up. Some Anonymous FTP sites do force you to do this.

After logging on, you typically have access only to a small area of files that are explicitly permitted to you. This is how almost all Internet software is shared and propagated. All FTP commands are available; the only difference is that now you don't have to have an account on a machine to access its files. This allows millions of users to share ideas and software without requiring any maintenance and overhead associated with managing large groups of users and software systems.

Given the rather cryptic nature of FTP as described above, it is not surprising that many people have not used FTP and, therefore, have underutilized much of the power of the Internet. However, several newer tools, including Mosaic, will provide a more user-friendly interface to FTP. This is one of the key reasons that many users are moving from old Internet tools, such as FTP command line interfaces, to Mosaic.

Mosaic & Anonymous FTP

While the standard FTP methodology seems fairly primitive by WWW standards, it is still very useful for many more standard activities such as downloading files and viewing general text information on a particular machine on the Internet. In fact, many machines on the Internet do not support WWW, and you will therefore not be able to access them with Mosaic's standard communication protocol known as http. This is not to say that you won't be able to access these non-WWW machines from within Mosaic because, as noted earlier, Mosaic supports Anonymous FTP through a non-WWW interface and specifying a URL of the type:

ftp://ftp.ncsa.uiuc.edu/Web/Mosaic/Unix/binaries/2.4

However, because of the benefits of using a single system interface to the entire Internet, Mosaic supports a variety of services, including FTP transparently. Because of its powerful basic function, FTP is still widely used and is one of the most heavily used services from within Mosaic.

Through the use of the URL you can specify several different types of services, including FTP. Instead of using the standard http protocol specify, you can instead use the FTP string to specify that you want to connect to an FTP server. For example, specify a URL specifier, such as:

ftp://sunsite.unc.edu/pub/sun-info/white-papers

This tells Mosaic to establish an Anonymous FTP connection to the machine **sunsite.unc.edu**. Note that this means that Mosaic is going to establish an FTP session with **sunsite.unc.edu** and log you in with a username of anonymous. If you need to use FTP on a machine where you have a log-in other than anonymous, you will not be able to use Mosaic.

Unlike FTP, Mosaic will automatically determine what type of file download should occur, whether it is ASCII mode or binary mode. Once you have connected to this machine, an initial screen will appear as shown in Fig. 8-4.

Figure 8-4

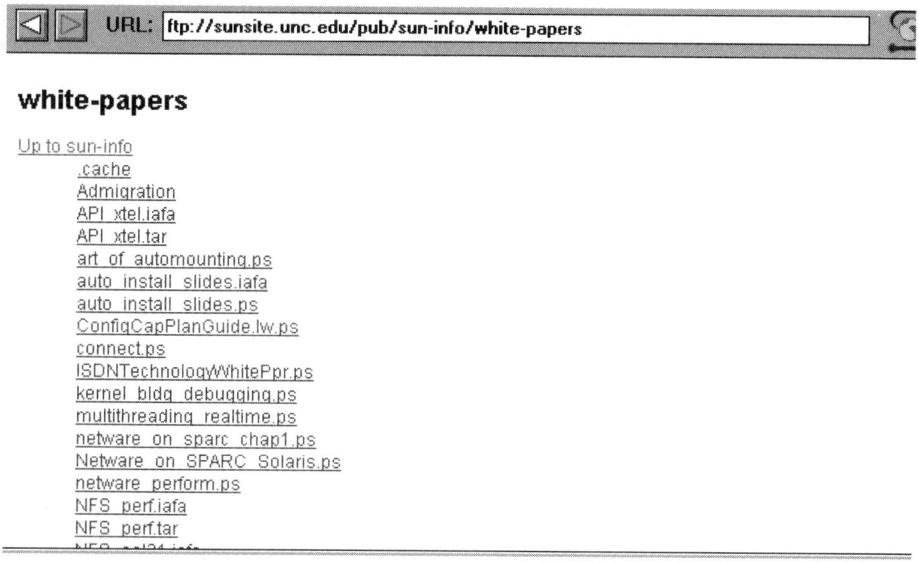

Anonymous FTP screen in Mosaic

Note on this screen that you see a listing of files underlined to indicate that they are hypertext links. Mosaic has very little knowledge of the types of files and their characteristics, and therefore you must be careful in the links that you choose. However, Mosaic does make decisions based on the filetype it is operating on. A simple list of the filetypes and transfer modes is shown below.

File	Mode
Backup file	binary
Compressed file	binary
Database file	binary
Email	ASCII
Executable file	binary
Graphics file	binary
Hypertext file	ASCII
Postscript file	ASCII
Shell archives	ASCII
Source code	ASCII

File	Mode
Spreadsheet	binary
Tar files	binary
Text file	ASCII
uuencoded file	ASCII
Word processor file	binary

For example, the first line on the screen is Up to sun-info. This is the link you can use to move up a directory on the FTP server. Click on this. Now you see a similar listing of the /pub/sun-info directory as shown in Fig. 8-5.

Figure 8-5

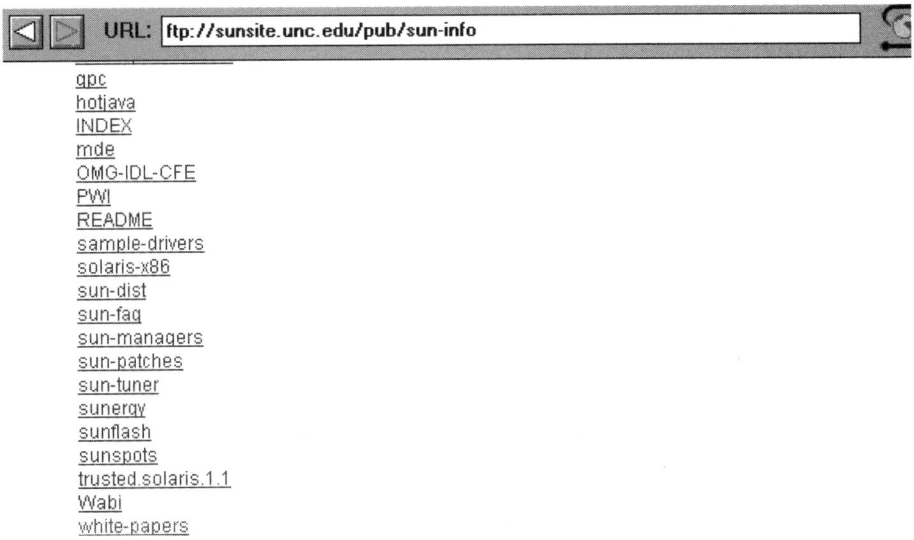

Another Anonymous FTP screen in Mosaic

Note that there are again a large number of links that represent both files and directories. Mosaic does have some basic knowledge of the filetype and will display certain files. For example, click on the INDEX link and watch what happens. By default, Mosaic will display this text file instead of downloading it. If you want to save this file select *File, Save As...* and select a filename on your local machine in which you want to save the file. Next, click the back button to go back to the previous screen.

Next, you can select the white-papers link to again move you into this directory. Now you need to select a file to download. You can do this by simply clicking on the link to begin the download. Mosaic might create a new window and ask you for a new filename if it cannot map the current filename to the desktop operating system you are using (for example, if you are downloading some UNIX files to a Windows computer). Once you select a filename, the download will begin.

Be careful of one thing. When you are downloading files, Mosaic might try to display them automatically depending on their filetype. You might need to download three basic types of files: text, graphics, and binary. Each has its own default Mosaic behavior upon download.

Text files will be automatically displayed in a text editor upon completion of the download. If you want to save the text file to your local disk select *File, Save As...* and give the text file a name. This behavior is consistent across UNIX and Windows versions of Mosaic.

Finally, binary files can be downloaded with FTP and Mosaic. Both the UNIX and Windows versions behave slightly differently due to different types of tools that exist on each machine. On UNIX, you simply click on the filename and the download begins. If the file is compressed with a UNIX compression utility, Mosaic will attempt to automatically uncompress the file with the appropriate compression utility. The most common are compress (.Z) and gzip (.gz) files. If you notice these extensions on the filename and you are running the UNIX Mosaic, it will probably be uncompressed on download. Once the file has been uncompressed, a Save As box will appear and give you a chance to save the file with a particular filename.

Note that UNIX Mosaic makes certain assumptions about the filetype based on the file extensions. Files with extensions such as .tar and .bin will work correctly. However, if you have a filename such as Mosaic.Z, Mosaic will first uncompress the file and then attempt to invoke a text editor to display the file. The Windows version will simply download the file when you click on it and prompt you for a filename. Much of the functionality of the UNIX version is not contained in this version of Mosaic. However, it is easier to use.

Mosaic & disadvantages of Anonymous FTP

One of the disadvantages of the Mosaic system and its FTP capabilities is the lack of information during the download. The only time Mosaic notifies you is when the file transfer is completed. There is no progress reports or status reports during the download, as there are in many other FTP utilities.

You might also experience some difficulties based on the types of files you download. As discussed in the previous section, Mosaic makes certain assumptions about a file based on its filename. If it makes incorrect assumptions it might perform incorrect behaviors on a file, such as attempting to view an executable or invoking the wrong external viewer on a downloaded file.

These and other issues might cause some difficulties. However, overall FTP usage through Mosaic is not difficult and might allow you to be more productive when working within your Mosaic environment.

Hypertext, Mosaic, & FTP

There are other ways to use the FTP interface with Mosaic, as some documents give you the capability to specifically select a hypertext link and move directly to an FTP connection. For example, select the URL **http://gnn.com/wic/visart.16.html**. This will take you to the Smithsonian Institution's image server, as shown in Fig. 8-6.

As you can see, there is a button labeled GO that will take you to an Anonymous FTP server named photo1.si.edu. Simply click on GO to connect and begin the entire FTP process as described above. Note the URL is now **ftp://photo1.si.edu/**. This tells us that we are on the photo1.si.edu machine in the top Anonymous FTP directory.

There are a variety of filetypes on this machine that we can download, including several types of graphics files. If you download a GIF file, for example, and you have configured an external viewer, Mosaic will

Figure 8-6

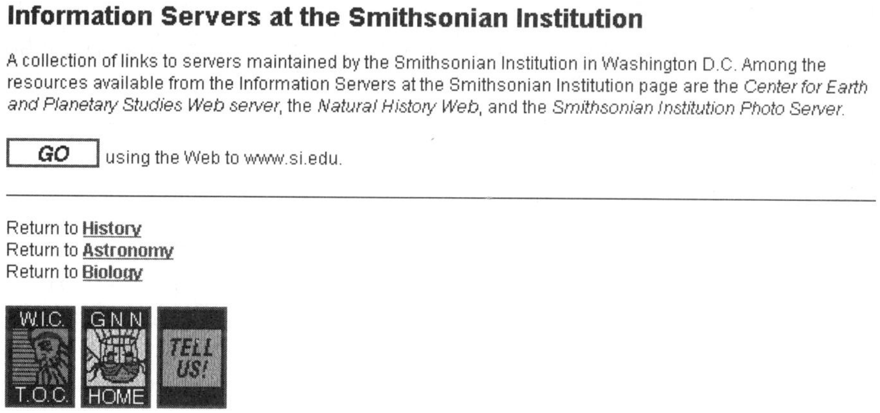

Smithsonian image server screen

automatically invoke the appropriate external viewer and display the graphics image on your desktop.

Finally, some servers provide a transparent interface to FTP through the hypertext link. By clicking on a hypertext link, the server might automatically connect you to an FTP server, log you in, and transfer the file to your local desktop. This allows you to avoid all the previous activities related to using FTP as documented above.

Mosaic & FTP—conclusion

As we have seen in this chapter, can access the Web servers a variety of ways, including Mosaic. You can also use a number of other tools to access the Internet servers, such as FTP, WAIS, Archie, and Gopher. With respect to Anonymous FTP, you must decide that the benefits of using a single, uniform interface such as Mosaic outweigh those offered by a specific FTP tool. You will find more information on tools such as WAIS and Archie later in this book.

Mosaic & Netnews

Mosaic also supports basic Netnews capabilities through its native interface. This means you don't need an external viewer to support

Netnews. Because of this, it is important to have a basic understanding of News and its capabilities. This section will outline those capabilities, as well as Mosaic's capabilities within this environment.

Network News

News is the Internet bulletin board system. News consists of groups of information and exchange based on a topic known as newsgroups. Newsgroups consist of readers that present a menu-like interface to newsgroups and allow you to browse and interact with any newsgroups of your choice. You get information on *newsfeeds* that consist of many megabytes of information per day, depending on which newsgroups you intend to read. The full newsfeed daily traffic is in the hundreds of megabytes per day and requires a tremendous effort to manage. Most users subscribe to a small subset of newsgroups in an effort to minimize the traffic as well as management aspects of the newsfeeds.

News groups are hierarchical in nature, consisting of what look very similar to domain names. For example, in **comp.os.aix**, the largest group is the comp (computer) group, followed by the os (operating system) group, and finally by the aix operating system division of this newsgroup. By far the largest set of newsgroups and information comes from the USENET. The USENET consists of seven primary newsgroup categories:

- comp—Computer science and related topics
- misc—Miscellaneous
- news—Questions relating to the news network itself
- rec—Recreational activities
- sci—Scientific and research activities
- soc—Social activities
- talk—Controversial topics, such as religion, politics, and the like.

There are other sources for newsgroup feeds, but they are beyond the scope of this book. In addition to the core USENET news groups, there are several alternative news groups, including alt, bit, biz, ieee, gnu, k12, and vmsnet. These and other newsgroups like them contain much lively discussion and information on an almost infinite variety of topics. The alt group deserves special mention, as it is the only group in which you can start a newsgroup without following a voting procedure. Lots of inconsequential and bizarre groups are contained in this larger group; however, there are many others that you might find interesting. You can also start your own newsgroup on any subject you would like.

Finally, other sources such as Clarinet, which is run by United Press International (UPI) and contains up-to-the-minute news, information, and broadcasts, are available on a fee basis. You should carefully choose which newsgroups you would like to Receive, as you will quickly be overwhelmed by information if you aren't careful.

To get a better understanding of the Netnews network you must examine its origins. When the USENET began, it consisted primarily of people using early UNIX computers connected with modems. They would periodically dial each other up and trade information. As the group grew, they developed methodologies for sharing information that involved known locations and flows for the shared information. A person or persons agreed to be the distributor of certain types of information by allowing others to dial into their computers and download information that they required. This became known as a news feed. As this matured and the number of news feeds grew, a large network consisting of a complex and confusing architecture evolved. With the adoption of high-speed WAN technology, much of this transfer is now occurring over leased lines. However, there are still many informal news feeds occurring around the world.

Figure 8-7 is from *The Whole Internet User's Guide & Catalog*, by Ed Krol. It is representative of the kind of network that News typically travels through. News servers originally used the base telephone network to transfer information. Today, many news feeds move across the Internet at T1 and T3 speeds for faster transfer.

Different news servers provide different news feeds based on the needs and usage of that particular node's users. Administrators must choose which news feeds they wish to accept and those they wish to distribute. If administrators choose to distribute a news feed, they

Figure 8-7

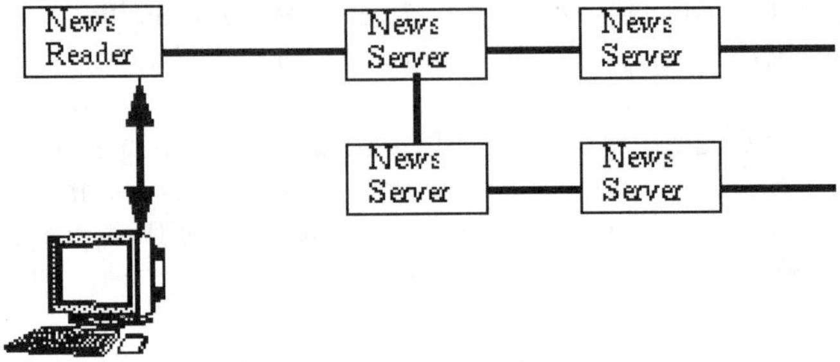

Typical interconnection of news servers

accept the responsibility that others might call and wish to connect to them and they need to be responsive and provide access to those requesters.

By providing transparent network access to users on the network, the news reader can access news groups transparently. The news reader has the responsibility not only to act as the menu-like front end but also to attach to the news server and download articles lists, as well as actual articles selected. It acts as the router to control access to news group information. There are several prominent readers available via Anonymous FTP for all popular types of computers.

Reader choice is like religion; each person prefers one or the other. Each reader has disadvantages and advantages. You can change readers at any time, so feel free to experiment with each of the readers you can get.

Mosaic's interface to Netnews

Mosaic has an interface to the Netnews system consisting of a basic capability to view News articles. You need to first configure the news server using Preferences under the Edit menu.

If your Internet Service Provider has a Netnews server you should substitute the name they give you for their News server. If they don't have one you can use the machine listed above (news.ora.com) to establish a link to a well-known News server. You can change this to a different News server at any time, if you so desire.

Once you have configured your connection to the News server you can access the News groups by manipulating the URL. The syntax for the URL is:

news:newsgroupname

where:

news is the text string that specifies the News protocol as the communications mechanism.

newsgroupname specifies the individual newsgroup to which you want to connect.

For example, to read the postings in the comp.unix.sunos Newsgroup you would use the URL:

news:comp.unix.sunos

This will present you with a screen that looks Fig. 8-8:

Figure 8-8

(Earlier articles...) Articles in comp.unix.aix

- "Novice Q: reducing /usr & rootvg filesystems" - Ken Simler
- "Re: ANNOUNCE: asWedit - text & HTML 3 editor for X/Motif" - Peter da Silva
- "2nd attempt: How to set default value for TZ in Aix 3.2.5?" - Arup Mukherjee
- "Re: Epoch time" - Goran Svensson
- "Re: POP3 and AIX 3.2.5" - Goran Svensson
- "AIX 3.2.5 SLIP support for dynamic address allocation?" - Steve Lee
- "Re: POP3 and AIX 3.2.5" - Lynn Wheeler
- "Re: Spy monitoring software" - Varouj Vosquian
- "Re: firewall for AIX" - JAY LYALL
- "Re: CUT&PASTE with mouse broken after fix installation" - Steven M. Cooper
- "Re: Problems with AIX 4.1.2 install from CDROM" - Connie L. Graff
- "message notification" - BinhDo
- "root logon" - BinhDo
- "Multiple Print Copies" - NGL@nglipq.connect.net
- "WANTED: Foolproof job killing technique." - Mark Peskin
- "Re: RS/6000 320" -
- "Re: ANNOUNCE: asWedit - text & HTML 3 editor for Xšáj/" - Bela Gazdy
- "580 and 3151 310/410?" - Tom G. Poole
- "Kernel (wait) processes eating CPU time" - Manish Desai
- "Re: ANNOUNCE: asWedit - text & HTML 3 editor for Xšáj/" - David C

Mosaic News screen

You can simply click on a message to read the posting. There are a number of disadvantages in using Mosaic to read News articles, including:

- No ability to post articles
- No ability to respond to articles
- No article history
- You can only download text files. You can't download graphics or any other special type or file
- You can only access one group at a time

The Mosaic interface provides a uniform look and feel to all applications including News. However, its function with respect to News is relatively limited. Therefore, if you want to perform more sophisticated types of manipulation within News you should get a more powerful News reader for your particular platform.

Mosaic & Gopher

Gopher was the second wave for access to the Internet. It provided a much more organized and structured way to use the Internet. Mosaic has full support for Gopher and provides virtually all the functionality of Gopher within the Mosaic interface. It is important to understand the fundamentals of Gopher before you begin to use it from Mosaic. The next section outlines basic Gopher capabilities.

Gopher

Gopher is a menu-based system which provides a hierarchical view of the Internet and its resources. The menus consist of lines that represent both files and directories. Gopher replaced previous random tools for Internet access with a well-defined, structured view of the Internet.

Gopher was written at the University of Minnesota and consists of over 5000 servers storing information on virtually any topic. To communicate with the Gopher servers you need a Gopher client. This service provides you with a menu-driven interface to a variety of information servers. It is not necessary for you to know where the information you are looking at actually is, or in what format it is stored—only that you can access it if you can see the menu item in Gopher. There are two public servers from which you can try Gopher before installing it on your machine: **consultant.micro.umn.edu** and **gopher.uiuc.edu**. You can simply Telnet to these machines, log on, and invoke Gopher to see the standard curses UNIX interface to Gopher. Make sure you have defined your terminal type correctly or you might have some strange screen behavior. If you have trouble with this, see your system administrator for more information.

The Gopher server knows the format of any resource available to you on the network and formats the appropriate command based on the type of resource you are interested in. As you continue down into the Gopher menus, you will eventually reach an actual file or piece of information that requires some action. If it is a file, Gopher will automatically invoke an FTP session for you and transfer the file. If it is a log-in resource, Gopher automatically creates a Telnet session, and so on.

A typical first Gopher screen looks like:

```
         $ gopher
         Internet Gopher Information Client v0.9

         Root Directory

---->    1. Welcome to the U of Illinois Gopher
         2. CCSO Documentation/
         3. Computer Reference Manuals/
         4. Frequently Asked Questions/
         5. GUIDE to the U of Illinois/
         6. Libraries/
         7. National Weather Service/
         8. Other Gopher and Information Servers/
         9. Peruse FTP Sites/
         10. Phone Books/

 Press ? for Help, q to Quit, u to go up       Page: 1/1
```

This is the initial Gopher screen. The / at the end of some lines denotes that this is a directory or submenu, while the other lines represent resources. By moving the cursor to the appropriate line you can control the context of your environment. Note that, based on the lines above, you can access many types of information from this one menu. Note also that option 8 provides you with the capability to move to other Gopher servers and sites.

This is a very brief overview of some of the capabilities and functions of Gopher. It is an extremely powerful tool to help you to search and use the Internet more effectively. Mosaic has an interface that supports all of this functionality.

Searching on Gopher

Many Gopher servers are available on the Internet and it is important to find the best Gopher servers based on your particular needs. Searching through Gopher space is as much an art as it is a science. However, there are some tools that you can use to enhance your search capabilities.

Veronica

Veronica is a search tool that you can use to search Gopher servers for matching text strings to documents and directories. To connect to Veronica you need to choose a Search item from a Gopher menu. For example:

```
1. Information about Gopher
2. Computer Information
3. Discussion Groups
4. Fun & Games
5. Internet file server (FTP) sites
6. Libraries
7. News
8. Other Gopher and Information Servers
9. Phone Books
10. Search Gopher titles at the University of Minnesota
11. Search lots of places at the University of Minnesota
12. University of Minnesota Campus Information
```

As you can see, you can select a variety of directories and searches based on which line you select. To use Veronica, select either 8, 10, or 11. If you select 8 you will see the screen:

```
1. All the Gopher Servers in the World
2. Search All the Gopher Servers in the World
3. Search titles in Gopherspace using veronica
4. Africa
5. Asia
6. Europe
7. International Organizations
8. Middle East
9. North America
10. Pacific
11. Russia
12. South America
13. Terminal based Information
14. WAIS-Based Information
15. Gopher Server Registration
```

This menu offers you a variety of capabilities, including selecting a Gopher server based on geography or search services based on Veronica, or on WAIS (to be covered shortly).

If you choose the Veronica service (3) you will get a new screen that has a large number of menu selections, most of them revolving around either the string Find ONLY DIRECTORIES... or Search GopherSpace by Title....

As stated earlier, Gopher menu items consist of either files or directories. Most often the filenames correspond with the directory names, and it is unnecessary to search GopherSpace. Instead, you can search only directories. This will reduce the number of matches and the subsequent time and effort required to find the file you are looking for. For a first search, select one of the menu items Find ONLY DIRECTORIES by ... When you select this you will be prompted for a search string. Enter a string and Veronica will match and present you with a screen of matching menu items. Select from one of these and you will have found the resource you are looking for.

Veronica searches accept not only strings to match but Boolean operators as well. You can use AND, OR and NOT to separate text strings for your search. For example, when Veronica prompts you for your string you can enter:

```
Gopher AND UNIX
Gopher OR UNIX
Gopher NOT UNIX
```

The first of these means that you will match only items that contain both Gopher and UNIX. The second matches items that contain Gopher or UNIX, and the final string matches items that have Gopher and *not* UNIX in the string. Boolean operators are evaluated from right to left. Finally, you can use wildcard characters to ask for combinations of strings. For example, you might specify a string like exec*.

This will match all strings such as executable, exec, execl, and any other string that begins with exec.

Jughead

By default, Veronica searches all Gopher servers in the world. If you don't need to search this many servers and have some idea of where your information resides, you can use a more regionalized search mechanism named Jughead. In many cases you are using Jughead and you don't even know it. When you search for information on a specific machine you are probably using Jughead and not Veronica. It is a good idea first to search for information on a specific machine or geographic area before searching on a wider range of Gopher servers. This helps lower the traffic on the Internet as well as on Gopher servers throughout the Internet.

Occasionally you will see specific Jughead search items, which you should use as a first effort for your search. If you don't find what you are looking for you can either expand your search to a different Jughead service or use Veronica to widen your search. Jughead supports all the operations that are supported by Veronica, including Boolean operators and wildcards.

This section has outlined the basic search capabilities of Veronica and Jughead. The best way to get to Veronica is from Gopher, and a great way to get to Gopher is through Mosaic. The Gopher interface in Mosaic is quite good and will provide all the capabilities documented in this section, and more. The following sections describe how to access Gopher and its associated search services, both Veronica and Jughead.

Mosaic & Gopher

As mentioned earlier, Mosaic supports Gopher in a manner that will be relatively transparent to the traditional Gopher user. In fact, the basic paradigm of selecting a line as either a file or a directory in Gopher is very similar to hypertext selection in Mosaic. Each Gopher line can be either a file or a directory, and these can exist on the same machine you are currently accessing or a different machine. This is completely transparent to you and the resource will be accessed without your ever knowing or caring where the resource resides.

Let's connect to a Gopher server. Use the URL:

gopher://gopher.micro.umn.edu

This takes you to the default Gopher screen for all Gopher servers. This machine contains a large amount of information about other Gopher servers, as well as information about services and data available on **gopher.micro.umn.edu** itself. The initial Gopher screen is shown in Fig. 8-9.

Figure 8-9

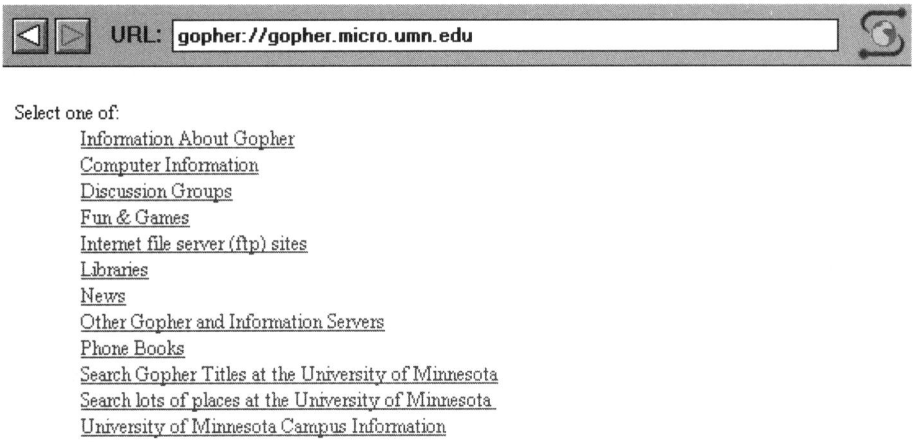

Gopher screen in Mosaic

As you can see, you can select from a variety of links. Select the Information About Gopher link. This presents a new screen as shown in Fig. 8-10.

Figure 8-10

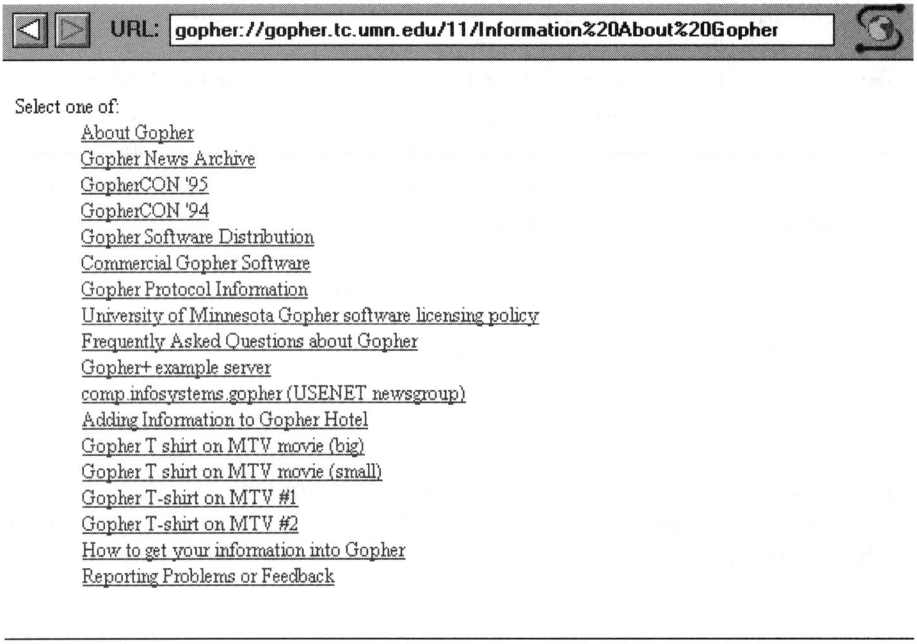

Next Gopher screen

This presents you with another list to choose from. Choose the About Gopher link. This is a text file and will be displayed in a text window for you to read. You can move back and forth between the menus by simply clicking the back and forward arrows in the upper left-hand corner of the Mosaic window. You can also use the hypertext links to move up and down within the menu system of Gopher.

This demonstrates the basic power of Mosaic's interface to Gopher. There are several disadvantages of using Gopher, including the nesting of the menus and the potential for searching a large number of submenus before you find what you are looking for. This is not a feature of Mosaic but of Gopher itself. You can avoid some of this by specifying a URL that takes you directly to that menu within a Gopher server. For example, to get immediately to the last Gopher screen show above, use the URL:

gopher://gopher.tc.umn.edu/00/Information%20About %20Gopher

Unfortunately, this URL doesn't directly correspond to the menus in the Gopher system. Therefore, you will have to go through the menu systems manually to get the exact URL. However, once you find a Gopher menu that you will use frequently you should save the URL in your Hotlist and can simply reference it from your Hotlist when you want to get to this Gopher location.

You can access the search services of Veronica and Jughead exactly as you would access them from the standard Gopher clients as described earlier in this chapter. More detail on this searching process is provided in Chapter 9.

Mosaic & WAIS

WAIS stands for *Wide-Area Information Servers*. The WAIS system consists of a variety of WAIS database servers that provide text-search capabilities to anyone running a WAIS client. Currently there are over 600 WAIS servers on the Internet. WAIS is based on an ANSI draft standard known as Z39.50, which has been under development for some time in the library community. Z39.50 specifies an architecture consisting of information servers that provide text-search services to clients. WAIS clients are available in a variety of formats, including the X Window System, Windows, and curses. These clients can be found in the Thinking Machines Corporation Anonymous FTP site—try the URL:

ftp://think.com/wais/

WAIS specifies a way to search for things on the Internet. Volunteers index documents and graphics files on machines around the Internet and provide an indexed database against which you can search. WAIS is the tool that allows you to search these indexed databases. Through WAIS you can specify any text string and find appropriate documents and image files that you can then access through Mosaic. Most often, WAIS is hidden inside Mosaic so you don't directly access it.

There are a variety of WAIS clients, based on machine type, which you can download. You can also access WAIS directly from Mosaic, either directly through an appropriately structured Mosaic document or through the Gopher interface. The discussion in this section applies to all interfaces to WAIS, including those found within Mosaic.

When you issue a search request from a WAIS client, WAIS queries a list of servers for possible matches. Each server then sends a matching listing back to the client and the client normalizes the response matches and displays them. The system with the most relevant matches has a value of 1000, while the others have proportionally less. This allows you to move immediately to the document and system that is most likely to be a good match.

This system is not flawless by any stretch of the imagination, and it contains many strange characteristics and quirks. However, it does provide a relatively simple querying means for documented text files on the Internet.

There are several examples of WAIS clients you can telnet to on the network, including ones at quake.think.com and nnsc.nsf.net. You simply log in as WAIS and proceed from there. This is a good way to see how a real live WAIS client works before you download your WAIS client. As mentioned earlier, you can also use the Mosaic system to interface with WAIS transparently.

WAIS has a relatively stupid interface that will not understand complex queries and relational operations, such as OR or AND. You must simply specify words you would like to match as a query, and then issue the query to the known list of WAIS servers. Each WAIS client contains a listing of known WAIS servers; from this you can generate a larger list of servers if you so desire.

The best way to learn more about WAIS is to log into one of the example WAIS client machines as mentioned above and try it for yourself. If you find it useful, simply download the appropriate client and have at it. The first and clearly the easiest way to access WAIS is directly through the Mosaic interface. By referencing a document that has a searchable index, you will most likely be using WAIS to perform the search within the context of the Mosaic document.

The best example of this is *The Whole Internet Catalog* at **http://nearnet.gnn.com/gnn/wic/**. Within this document, you will find several searchable indexes against which you can search for specific things. This uses WAIS behind the scenes to search WAIS databases for matches. This is a simple and elegant way to use WAIS with Mosaic.

The other way to use WAIS with Mosaic is through Gopher. By specifying a Gopher server you can access a WAIS interface through the standard Gopher interface. Try the URL:

gopher://gopher.micro.umn.edu

Next you will want to select Other Gopher and Information Servers. This is the standard way within Gopher to non-Gopher services. Once you select this, you will see a screen containing various other choices. Select WAIS-Based Information. This places you in a window that specifies a variety of WAIS databases including one called WAIS Databases by Letter. This allows you to select the WAIS databases by their first letter and not by their subject. Because of the seemingly random nature of WAIS server names, it is best to choose Directory of WAIS Databases from the next list, as this will allow you to search all databases for possible keyword matches. Finally, you must enter keywords to search on in the boxed area.

The result of this search is a list of possible WAIS servers that match your search criteria. You can select on any of these databases that appear to match your criteria the best. You will then be asked to re-enter your search criteria, and that particular database will be searched. The result of this search will be a list of documents that match your search string. You can then select from this list and view the text file or image. Once you have selected the file by clicking on it, Mosaic will download the file to your local desktop and view it as it would any other downloaded file.

WAIS is a very powerful tool but is dependent on volunteers to maintain their databases and keep them current. These frequently get out of date, so you should use the WAIS system as just one source of information and not your only source.

Summary

This chapter outlined the major Internet services that are available through Mosaic. By providing access to these tools, Mosaic ensures that you can access virtually all information available on the Internet, including information that is not directly stored on the Web. Each service described above has its strengths and weaknesses, but each will provide you with basic capability that you need to fully utilize the power of the Internet through Mosaic.

9

How to use Mosaic effectively

CHAPTER 9

HAVING reached this chapter, you should have a good idea by now how Mosaic and the New Internet could enhance your home or professional life, and how you can get connected to the Internet and get Mosaic up and running in your own environment. So far, so good. But how do you make Mosaic and all its associated technology truly work for you? If you still find yourself asking, "But how can I find what I'm looking for?" then this chapter is for you.

Information about virtually every subject known to man or woman can be found somewhere on the Internet. And most experts agree that the ultimate usefulness of the Internet will depend on how quickly and easily users can find the information they're looking for.

However, the search is complicated by many factors. First is the sheer size of the Internet. Nobody knows just how large it really is, much less where all of the servers are. New information servers go online every day, with only recommended registration procedures. And there are several different types of servers—HTTP (World Wide Web), Gopher, Anonymous FTP, WAIS, and so on.

Second, there is no hierarchical structure to the Internet. The web-like nature of information on the Internet virtually guarantees that several possible paths can be traversed to reach the same resource. Finally, most resources are added to the Internet without particular regard for indexing and searching protocols. The Internet is not a relational database.

So much for the bad news. But take heart—several factors are working in your favor as well:

- Mosaic itself has features that can help you manage the problem, such as the hotlist and the global history.
- Conventions are emerging and, generally speaking, Internet server administrators (like good computer system administrators in general) understand the benefits of sticking to them. A prime example is server names, which nowadays routinely begin with www, gopher, ftp, and other recognizable letter sequences.

- Countless "scouts" are out there collecting the Internet locations of resources in their areas of interest. These folks usually find benefit in also making their findings known—they attract "birds of a feather" that way.
- Internet curators who think they possess information of value want their sites to be known, and there are places where they know to "advertise."
- The network protocols used to reach Internet servers are known and understood. As a result, many exploring and indexing functions can be and are being automated.
- Finally, you have this book to help you get started.

In this chapter we'll tackle the question, "How can I find what I'm looking for?"

We address the question in three stages. First, we ask what kinds of resources are out there and how can Mosaic help to manage their access. Second, we ask who is out on the Internet trying to help you, and how. And third, we ask how you should look for some of the most common types of information, such as companies, topics of interest, people, or software.

The Mosaic view of the Internet

You could say that what we've been calling the New Internet all this time is essentially the Internet as seen through Mosaic. It's "new" because there never used to be any one view of more than just a fraction of the Internet (see Fig. 9-1). Mosaic in part has fueled the Internet revolution, and World Wide Web servers and HTTP traffic have accounted for the bulk of its recent growth. But very large bodies of information still, and will, continue to live on servers that deal in other protocols such as Anonymous FTP, Gopher, Netnews, and WAIS. Much of Mosaic's impact comes from the way it gracefully handles all these other resource types, as depicted in Fig. 9-2.

Figure 9-1

The Internet before Mosaic

Figure 9-2

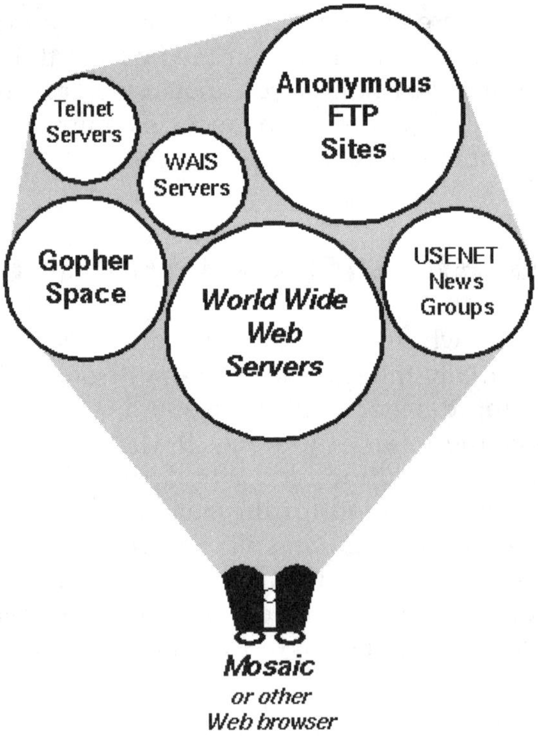

The New Internet

Being able to reach virtually all of the Internet through Mosaic offers you several benefits:

- You now have a single tool to learn and understand, and in the case of Mosaic this is especially easy.
- You can access many of the resources built for access via FTP, Gopher, and other tools more easily and intuitively by using Mosaic (see Chapter 8).
- Mosaic lets you keep track of all of your important "finds" (and everywhere else you've visited) in one place, no matter what types of resources they are. This is worth a closer look.

Using the Mosaic hotlist

As we mentioned in Chapter 7, you manage your hotlist from within the Navigate menu. You can always add a pointer to the document you are currently viewing to your hotlist by dragging down from Navigate and selecting Add Current To Hotlist. It's the quick and easy way to save pointers to important resources, whether they are from the Web, Gopherspace, Anonymous FTP sites, or wherever.

Here are three important tips for managing your hotlist:

- Try to be selective. If your motto is, "Ooh, this might be useful someday—I'll stick it in my hotlist!" then you can expect your hotlist to become unwieldy before long. In that case, the following tips will be especially important.
- Don't be afraid to edit titles in your hotlist. Many times the title of a useful resource does not reflect why it's useful to you in particular. So change the title to whatever will clue you in to its benefits. (Of course, when a document has no title at all, this becomes essential.) To edit a title, bring up the hotlist, click once on the title you wish to change, and select Edit Title.
- Export your hotlist to an HTML file. This might sound intimidating but it's really not. Follow the steps in Chapter 7 to save the hotlist to a file. Then use the information in Chapter 10 to edit the file and create a custom-tailored, well-organized Web page you can access via Open Local File. Add this page to your hotlist in place of the others and you're all set.

One type of Web page you *cannot* save in your hotlist is a page generated by means of a keyword search. Such pages are transient—the search engine creates a temporary URL for a limited period of time only. A hotlist pointer to this URL is useless in the long run, yet this is likely to be just the sort of reference you'd like to have handy.

The solution is to save the page in a local file—select *Save As...* under the *File* menu and name the file with the extension .html in UNIX, or .htm on a PC. Then open the local file and add it to your hotlist, as explained in the third hotlist tip above.

Using the Mosaic global history

When you start navigating the Internet with Mosaic, before long you'll notice that Mosaic remembers when you have already traversed a hyperlink. Such links appear more purple than blue, and are underdashed rather than underlined. Mosaic will remember this information session after session, as part of your global history.

This feature is much more useful than it might seem at first. Remember the factors that complicate searching the Internet? Suppose you're looking up information about mutual funds. You find a Web page that contains a link called *How to select a mutual fund,* click on the link, and voila—there's a lengthy document entitled *Ten Tips For Selecting A Mutual Fund* (note that the link text and the document title were not the same). You print the document to read later, step back to the Web page, and see that the link is now underdashed, as you would expect.

Two weeks later, you're navigating an entirely different section of the Internet, when you come upon another Web page about mutual funds. This page contains a link that reads, *Mutual fund selection made easy.* You're about to click on the link when you notice that it's underdashed. Mosaic is telling you that you can jump there if you wish, but *you have been there before.* Aha!

Eventually you will have logged enough Mosaic time, and pursued enough topics, so that the information in your growing global history will become less and less useful. Then it's probably time to pull down the Navigate menu, select History, and Delete unwanted entries.

So Mosaic does its best to help you keep track of where you've been. But the big question remains—how do you find what you want in the first place?

Where on Earth to begin?

People to whom we explain the Internet often ask, "Where's the beginning?" You've probably guessed by now that the Internet begins anywhere you want it to. The Internet is widely distributed in virtually every sense—the types of resources, who runs the networks, who manages the servers, where addresses are resolved, and so on. And besides—if there really *were* a single beginning to the Internet it would become hopelessly bogged down with traffic.

So various *doorways* to the Internet have sprung up around the world on a volunteer basis, in various forms. Having pooled our navigational experience, we will be devoting the next several sections to describing the most popular and useful of these sites. We've grouped them into five categories:

- Registries and billboards
- Internet atlases
- Subject catalogs
- Robotic search engines
- Other specialized search tools

Read through the sections to understand the different ways organizations and individuals have approached the challenge of facilitating Internet resource discovery. When we're done we will explain the best ways to use these tools to locate whatever you might be looking for.

(Want to get a sense for just how fast the Internet is evolving and changing? Here's an exercise for you. This chapter was completed in

May 1995. Count how many of the home page screens and instructions are already out of date!)

Registries & billboards

These are the places in which maintainers of Internet resources can advertise themselves to the world. They tend to be run by key organizations in the New Internet, such as CERN, InterNIC, and NCSA. You'll see that, while they are all accessible using Mosaic, some were originally set up to serve different audiences.

NCSA/GNN What's New

NCSA/GNN What's New URL:
http://www.ncsa.uiuc.edu/SDG/Software/Mosaic/Docs/whats-new.html

The What's New With NCSA Mosaic Home Page (see Fig. 9-3) has evolved into one of the most popular sites on the World Wide Web. NCSA established the page as a place where Web maintainers could

Figure 9-3

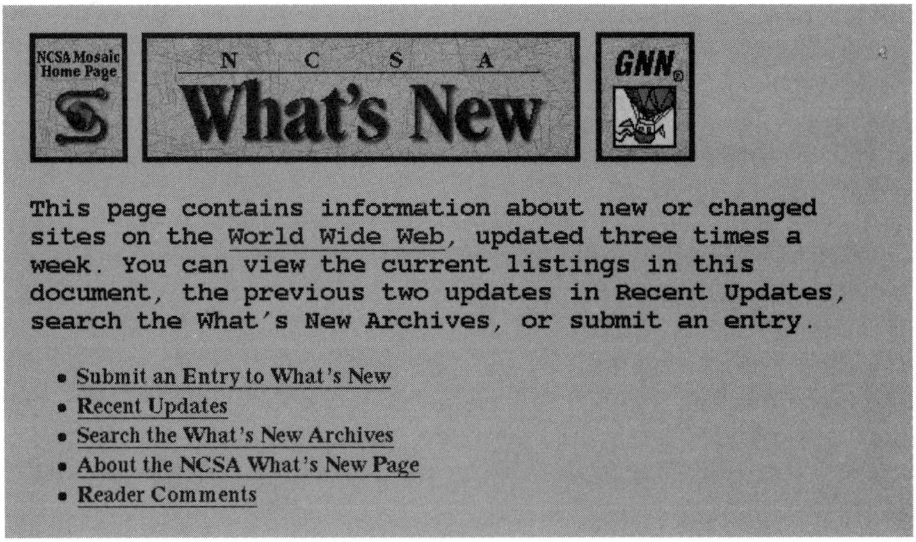

NCSA/GNN What's New Home Page—***http://www.ncsa.uiuc.edu/SDG/Software/Mosaic/Docs/whats-new.html***

announce new or updated Web services. Perhaps due to the growing number of submissions (currently running around 300 per week), What's New is now a joint production of NCSA and GNN, the Global Network Navigator, from O'Reilly and Associates. Submitters can send electronic mail to GNN or fill out a form through Mosaic, providing a paragraph of description and the pertinent URLs.

Updated three times a week, What's New is a fascinating place to visit. Here's a sampling (in the seemingly random order they were listed in) of announced services posted on January 25, 1995:

- National Career Search, Inc.
- New England Culinary Institute
- Curious Pictures Corporation
- Mansfield University Libraries
- The NASA/JPL Imaging Radar Home Page
- PennState Young Americans for Freedom
- Institute for Astrophysics of Paris
- The Rhombus Interactive Gallery
- Charleston Beer Works
- Nationwide Nannies
- The Cyrano Server
- Volksmarch and Walking Event Index
- Doctor Bob's $5 Internet Guides
- Fellowship for Intentional Community
- KUGS 89.3 FM (Bellingham, WA, US)
- America's Cup On-Line
- Manchester Business School
- Association of America's Public Television Stations
- Underwater Video Systems
- Mount Wilson Observatory

- P-Law Legal Resource Locator
- Calypso Party Cruises

Because What's New is arranged chronologically it's not a good place to browse for anything in particular. However, it's a great place to learn about the evolving Internet community and to see something new. What's New is archived back into 1993, and it's all searchable using the CUI W3 Catalog described later in this chapter.

CERN Web Server Registry & The Virtual Tourist World Map

CERN Web Server Registry URL:
http://www.w3.org/hypertext/DataSources/WWW/Servers.html

Virtual Tourist World Map URL: **http://wings.buffalo.edu/world/**

Organizations are encouraged to register their World Wide Web servers with CERN, where the Web was invented, as a means of making their presence known to the world. The CERN Web Server Registry is now maintained by the W3 Consortium. You can visit the CERN Web Server Registry (shown in Fig. 9-4) and zero in on any registered server in the world by traversing menus of continents, then countries, and so on.

Figure 9-4

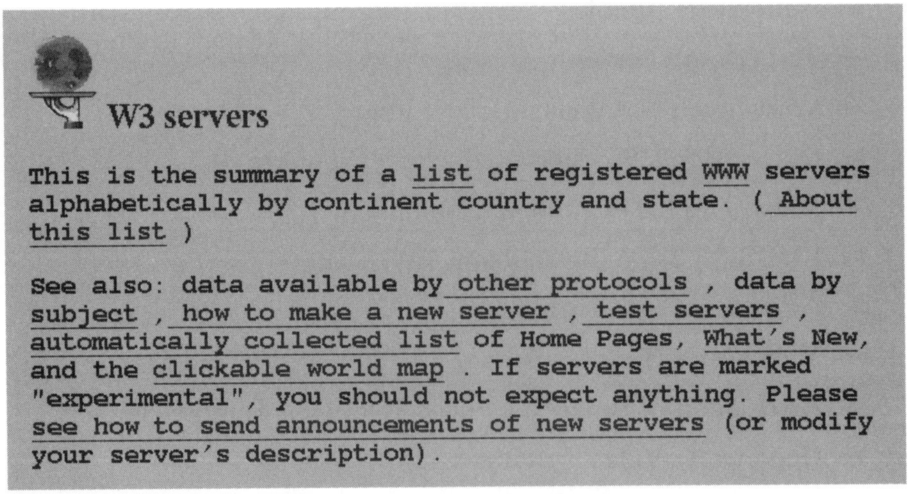

*CERN Web Server Registry Home Page—**http://www.w3.org/hypertext/DataSources/WWW/Servers.html***

Of course, you might find it useful to visualize where you are headed right from the start. The Virtual Tourist was developed by Brandon Plewe at the State University of New York at Buffalo, and presents the CERN registry starting with a click-sensitive image of the world (see Fig. 9-5). Regional maps are maintained in various locations on the Internet.

Figure 9-5

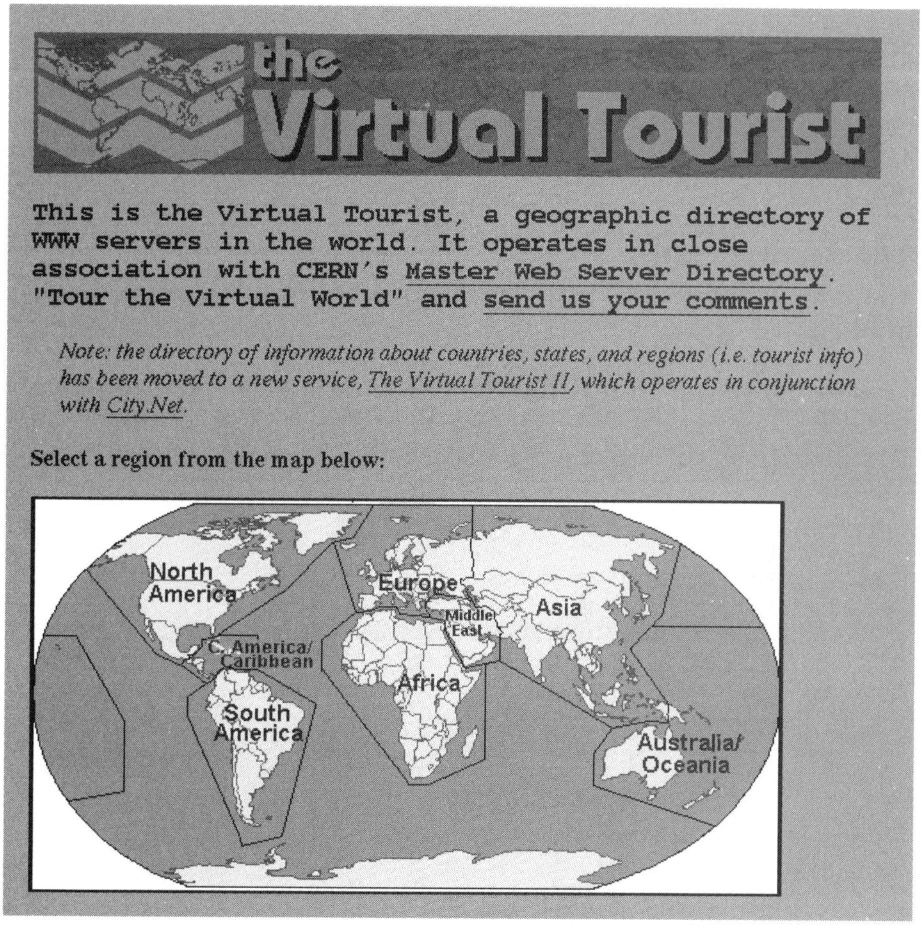

Virtual Tourist Home Page—**http://wings.buffalo.edu/world/**

Net-Happenings
Net-Happenings URL: **http://www.mid.net/NET/**

Net-Happenings (Fig. 9-6) is an electronic-mail discussion group moderated by Gleason Sackman of North Dakota's SENDIT Network for K-12 (Kindergarten through 12th grade) educators. MIDnet, a regional network provider based in Lincoln, Nebraska, makes Net-Happenings available with hyperlinks to the Mosaic community. The 20 or so daily submissions to Net-Happenings announce new Internet resources, as well as calls for papers, newsletters, conference announcements, and other items of interest for network administrators and users. You can browse the daily postings using Mosaic, or you can search the archives by title, subject, keyword, or all three.

The Scout Report
The Scout Report URL: **http://rs.internic.net/scout_report-index.html**

Figure 9-6

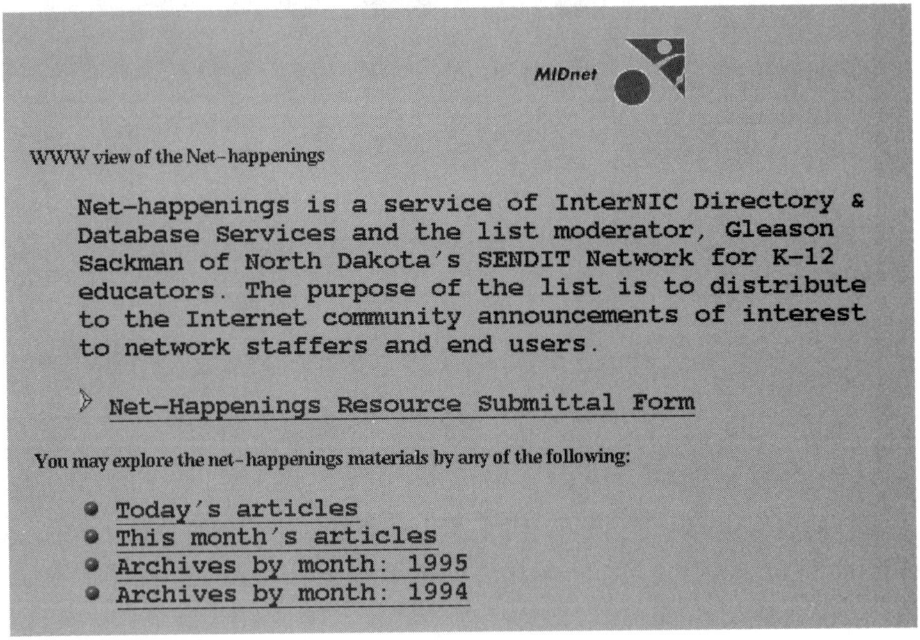

*Net-Happenings Home Page—**http://www.mid.net/NET/*** Net-happenings is a service of InterNIC Directory & Database Services and the list moderator, Gleason Sackman of North Dakota's SENDIT Network for K-12 educators.

The Scout Report is published weekly by InterNIC, to keep Internet users abreast of new resource announcements and other news on the Net. The Scout Report Home Page (shown in Fig. 9-7) contains links to the last 4 issues, plus a link to the archives of older issues. All references in the Web version of the Scout Report are active links, so navigation through the Scout Report is quick and easy.

Figure 9-7

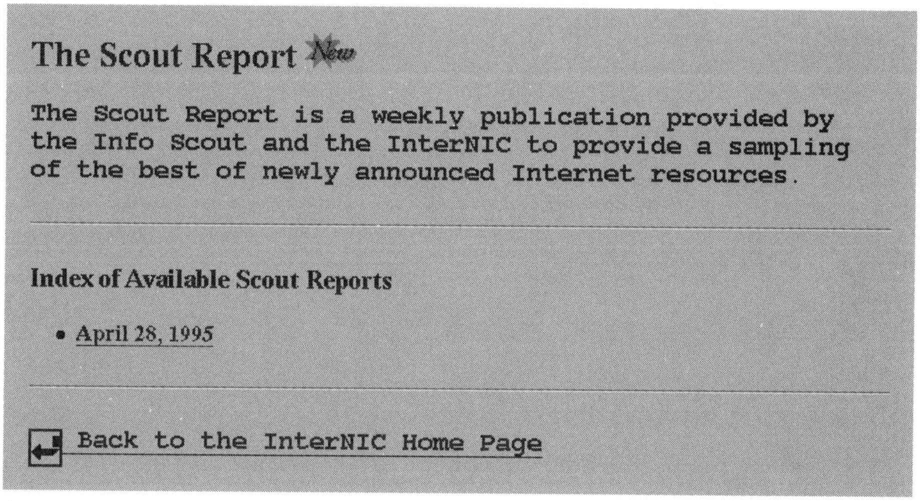

Scout Report Home Page— ***http://rs.internic.net/scout_report-index.html***

Internet atlases

Organizers of Internet atlases seek out sites on the Internet where information about local government, culture, and institutions are presented, and build a geographically organized browsing capability around them. Many of the sites reachable through these tools are run by universities or by local public access networks, called *Freenets* (pay attention to the URLs as you travel).

The USA CityLink Project

USA CityLink URL: **http://www.neosoft.com/citylink/**

NeoSoft of Houston, Texas, manages the USA CityLink project. USA CityLink regards itself as the Internet's most comprehensive listing of

World Wide Web pages featuring U.S. states and cities, pulling together state and municipal home pages, freenet home pages, and pages created by CityLink itself. From the CityLink Home Page (see Fig. 9-8), choose from the alphabetical list of states and follow along to the locality of your choice.

Figure 9-8

USA CityLink Project Home Page—**http://www.neosoft.com/citylink/**

✻ Virtual Tourist II

Virtual Tourist II URL: **http://wings.buffalo.edu/world/vt2/**

Virtual Tourist II was spun off of the original Virtual Tourist described above, and is now run in conjunction with City Net Express of Portland, OR. Whereas the original Tourist deals with server registry data, Virtual Tourist II (Fig. 9-9) actually leads you to tourist and geographic data and pictures of thousands of places, often maintained at local universities. It's a wonderful tool for cultural exploration, and for learning about governments around the world.

If your connection is relatively slow you can select *text only version* to bypass the graphics. Virtual Tourist II is also searchable—select *City.Net Search* and type in your destination.

Figure 9-9

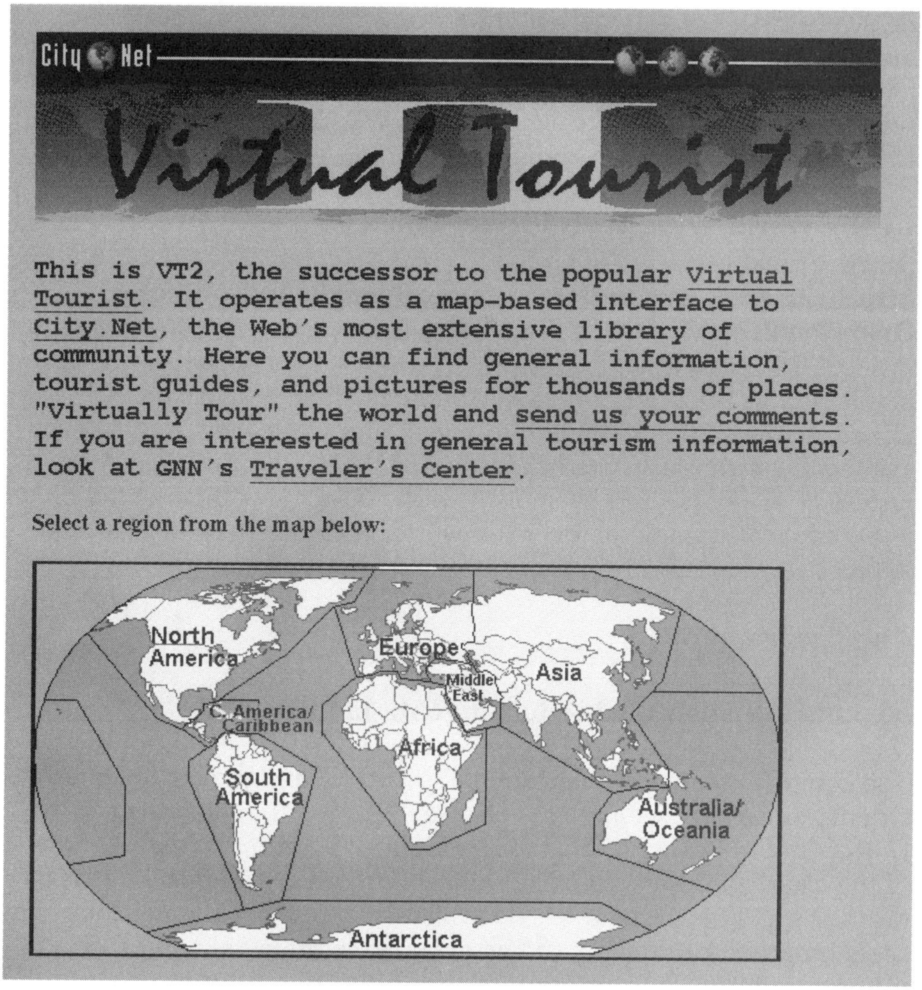

*City.Net Home Page—**http://wings.buffalo.edu/world/vt2/***

Subject catalogs

Here are the key sites on the New Internet where you can browse subject areas in a hierarchical way. These subject-oriented lists are usually maintained by guest editors, or grow from the submissions of users, or both. In a few cases one person maintains the list, and through his or her efforts becomes a recognized name on the Internet. In general, the more manpower contributed the larger the resource.

Be aware that, even though all these tools are arranged by subject, the subjects covered might differ greatly. About half of these tools provide their own search interfaces. Others are indexed for keyword search at a separate site, called the CUI W3 Catalog (see the heading, *Other specialized search tools*).

✻ CERN World Wide Web Virtual Library

CERN Virtual Library URL:
http://www.w3.org/hypertext/DataSources/bySubject/Overview2.html

In addition to the Web Server Registry described above, the W3 Consortium also maintains the top level of a worldwide Web subject catalogue called the *Virtual Library* (Fig. 9-10). World Wide Web resources are organized by subject, with subject lists maintained by knowledgeable people all over the world. Many of these lists are quite impressive.

✻ The Clearinghouse

The Clearinghouse URL:
http://http2.sils.umich.edu/~lou/chhome.html

The complete name of this resource is The Clearinghouse for Subject-Oriented Internet Resource Guides (see Fig. 9-11), maintained at the University of Michigan. Originally a Gopher-based resource, the goal of the clearinghouse is to collect subject-oriented guides to Internet resources and make them widely available. Select HTML Versions and see a broad list of subjects and associated maintainers' names. Scan the list carefully. Click on one and land most anywhere on the Internet. (*Buddhism,* for example, points to the Buddhist Studies Web server at the Australian National University.)

Only some of the Clearinghouse is directly available in HTML, but the entire Clearinghouse in text-only form is searchable from the Web. Click on Search the Full Text of these Guides to reach a search screen.

✻ John December's CMC Information Sources

John December's CMC Information Sources URL:
http://www.rpi.edu/Internet/Guides/decemj/icmc/top.html

Figure 9-10

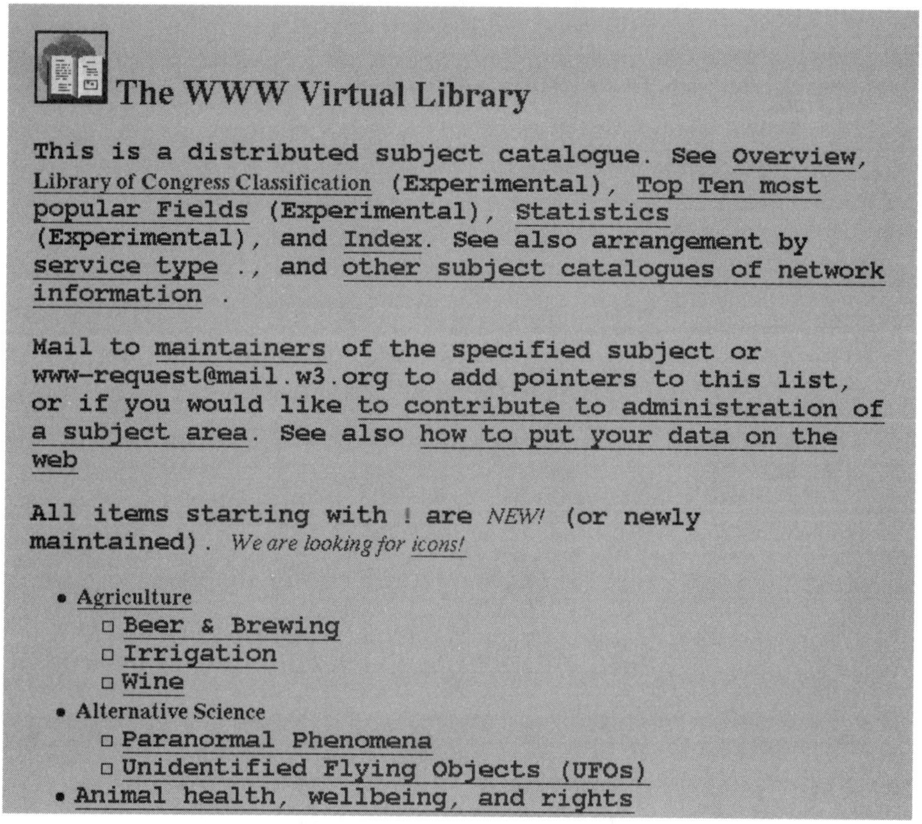

The World Wide Web Virtual Library: Subject Catalogue—**http://www.w3.org/hypertext/DataSources/bySubject/Overview2.html**

John December, at Rensselaer Polytechnic Institute, is the editor of the Web-based Computer Mediated Communications Magazine, and maintains this list of Computer-Mediated Communication Information Sources (see Fig. 9-12). It covers multiple resource types and is aimed toward "technical, social, rhetorical, cognitive, and psychological aspects of networked communication and information." For our purposes, though, it's a fine subject-organized collection of resources that is also searchable.

Click on 2-level to start out and quickly see the topics covered. Selecting 3-level shows more detail.

Figure 9-11

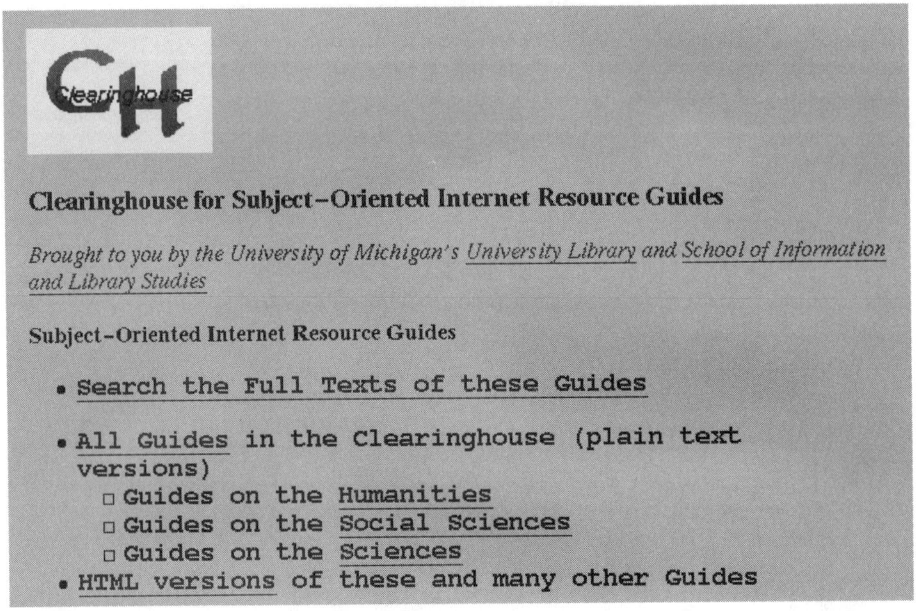

Clearinghouse

Clearinghouse for Subject-Oriented Internet Resource Guides

Brought to you by the University of Michigan's University Library and School of Information and Library Studies

Subject-Oriented Internet Resource Guides

- Search the Full Texts of these Guides
- All Guides in the Clearinghouse (plain text versions)
  - Guides on the Humanities
  - Guides on the Social Sciences
  - Guides on the Sciences
- HTML versions of these and many other Guides

The Clearinghouse for Subject-Oriented Internet Resource Guides (HTML Versions) Home Page—***http://http2.sils.umich.edu/~lou/chhome.html***

Figure 9-12

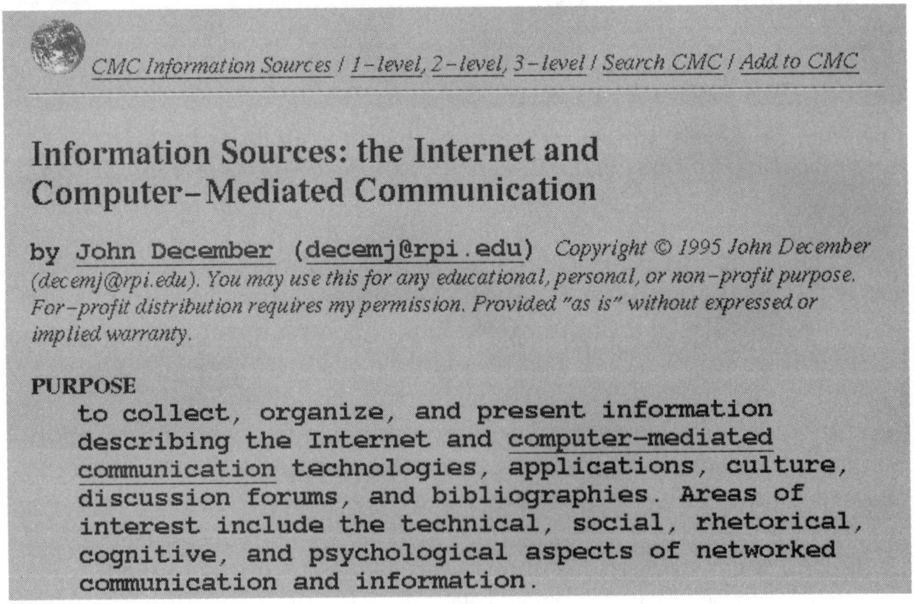

CMC Information Sources / 1-level, 2-level, 3-level / Search CMC / Add to CMC

Information Sources: the Internet and Computer-Mediated Communication

by John December (decemj@rpi.edu) *Copyright © 1995 John December (decemj@rpi.edu). You may use this for any educational, personal, or non-profit purpose. For-profit distribution requires my permission. Provided "as is" without expressed or implied warranty.*

PURPOSE

to collect, organize, and present information describing the Internet and computer-mediated communication technologies, applications, culture, discussion forums, and bibliographies. Areas of interest include the technical, social, rhetorical, cognitive, and psychological aspects of networked communication and information.

John December's CMC Information Sources Home Page—***http://www.rpi.edu/Internet/Guides/decemj/icmc/top.html*** © 1995 John December.

☼ EINet Galaxy

EINet Galaxy URL: **http://galaxy.einet.net/galaxy.html**

The Enterprise Integration Network Group of Austin, TX, maintains the EINet Galaxy, where volunteer guest editors have indexed Internet resources by topic. The first page presents the high-level index of topics as hyperlinks that can be browsed (see Fig. 9-13).

Click on the word *searched* in the introduction to jump to the bottom of the page, where you can set parameters and launch a search. (Actually, you should probably scroll instead, to save an additional

Figure 9-13

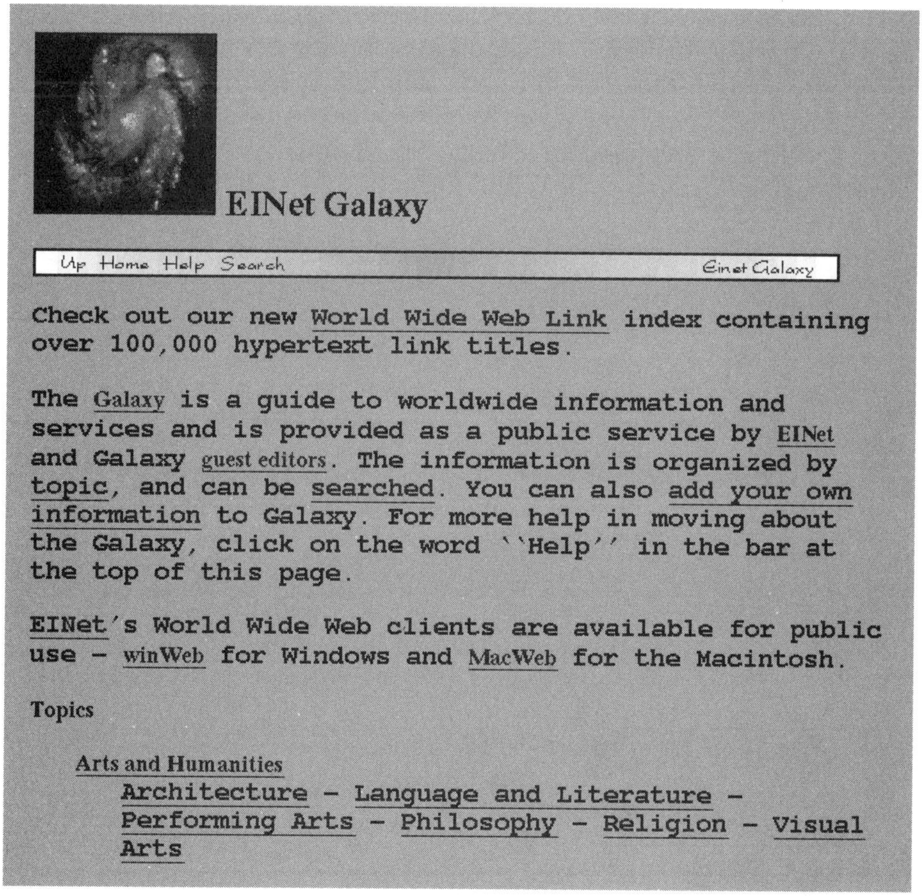

*EINet Galaxy Home Page—**http://galaxy.einet.net/galaxy.html***

connection delay.) The pages for each of the high-level topics are arranged in the same way. This is useful—it lets you zero in on a broad subset of the database and search only in that space.

You might search the pages of the Galaxy itself, or search resources on Web, Gopher, or Telnet servers. A search in the EINet Galaxy returns hyperlinked titles of documents.

✳ FedWorld

FedWorld URL: **http://www.fedworld.gov/**

FedWorld is managed by the National Technical Information Service (NTIS), an agency of the U.S. Department of Commerce. FedWorld was developed to provide a one-stop location for the public to locate U.S. Government information online (see Fig. 9-14). Resources maintained on U.S. Government Web, Gopher, Anonymous FTP, and other servers are arranged by subject. Scroll down, or select U.S. Government Information Servers (Internet) to jump to the alphabetical

Figure 9-14

*FedWorld Home Page—**http://www.fedworld.gov/***

list of subject categories. Even though FedWorld is limited to U.S. Government servers, the sheer volume of information produced by the government makes FedWorld a significant search tool.

✳ The Whole Internet Catalog

The Whole Internet Catalog URL:
http://gnn.com/gnn/wic/index.html

The Whole Internet Catalog first appeared in the book of roughly the same name written by Ed Krol of the University of Illinois. Organized hierarchically by subject, the Catalog (shown in Fig. 9-15) is now provided on the World Wide Web by GNN (see NCSA/GNN What's New). It's a large collection of resources but it has no obvious search capability. It is also often difficult to connect to The Whole Internet Catalog, due to heavy network activity at GNN.

Figure 9-15

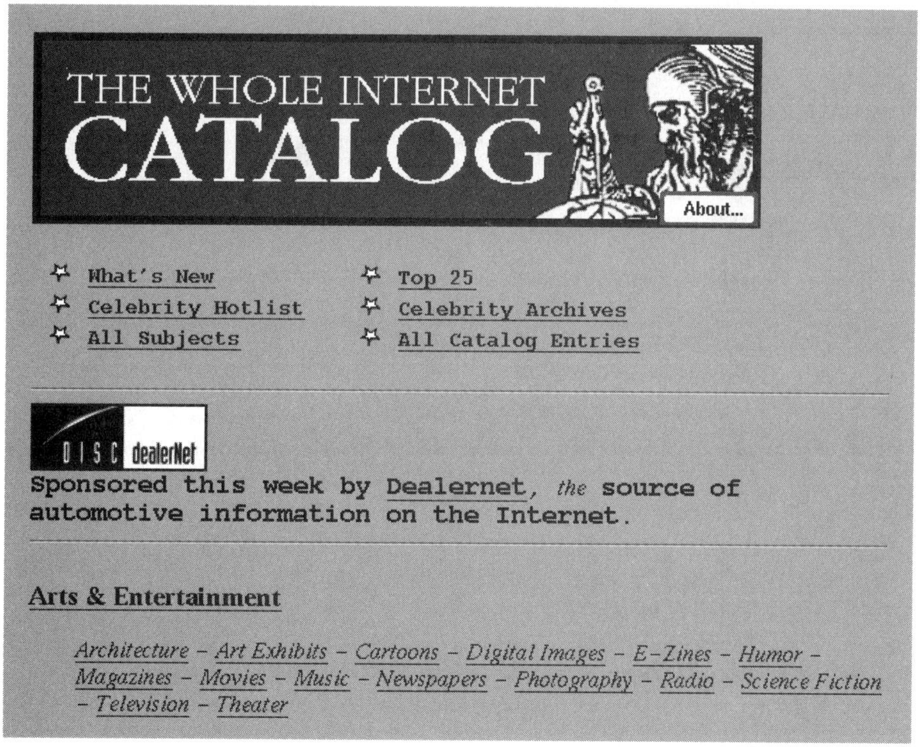

*The Whole Internet Catalog Home Page—**http://gnn.com/gnn/wic/index.html***

※ Yahoo

Yahoo URL: **http://www.yahoo.com/**

Yahoo stands for *Yet Another Hierarchically Organized Oracle* and was originally maintained by David Filo and Jerry Yang at Stanford University. They have since moved it to a commercial site (see Fig. 9-16). Yahoo has over 30,000 browsable and searchable entries as of this writing.

About half of the current additions to Yahoo come from user submissions. The other half are collected by a robot (see the next

Figure 9-16

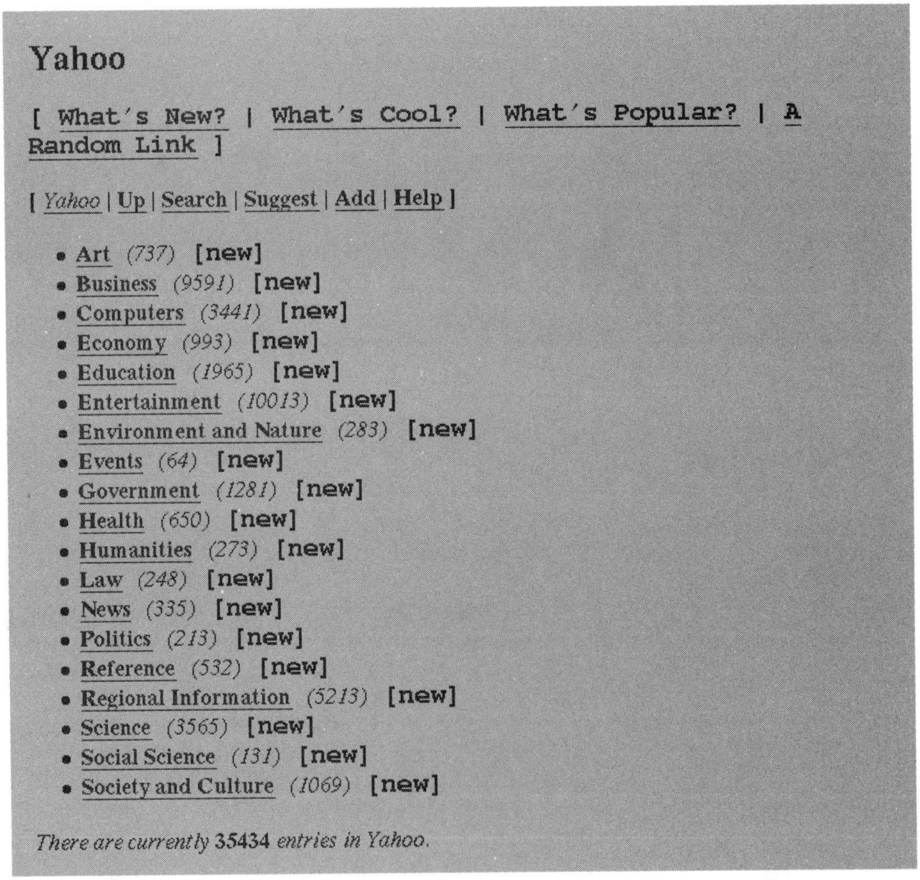
Yahoo

[What's New? | What's Cool? | What's Popular? | A Random Link]

[*Yahoo* | Up | Search | Suggest | Add | Help]

- Art *(737)* [new]
- Business *(9591)* [new]
- Computers *(3441)* [new]
- Economy *(993)* [new]
- Education *(1965)* [new]
- Entertainment *(10013)* [new]
- Environment and Nature *(283)* [new]
- Events *(64)* [new]
- Government *(1281)* [new]
- Health *(650)* [new]
- Humanities *(273)* [new]
- Law *(248)* [new]
- News *(335)* [new]
- Politics *(213)* [new]
- Reference *(532)* [new]
- Regional Information *(5213)* [new]
- Science *(3565)* [new]
- Social Science *(131)* [new]
- Society and Culture *(1069)* [new]

There are currently 35434 *entries in Yahoo.*

Yahoo Home Page—***http://www.yahoo.com/***

section) and categorized by hand. The maintainers even provide graphical keys to identify newly added resources and ones with especially strong presentation or content.

- **Scott Yanoff's Special Internet Connections**
  Scott Yanoff's Special Internet Connections URL:
  http://www.uwm.edu/Mirror/inet.services.html

Scott Yanoff of the University of Wisconsin, Milwaukee, is the author and maintainer of one of the more popular subject-oriented resource lists on the Internet. Special Internet Connections, shown in Fig. 9-17, includes all types of resources and can be searched using the CUI W3 Catalog (see below).

Figure 9-17

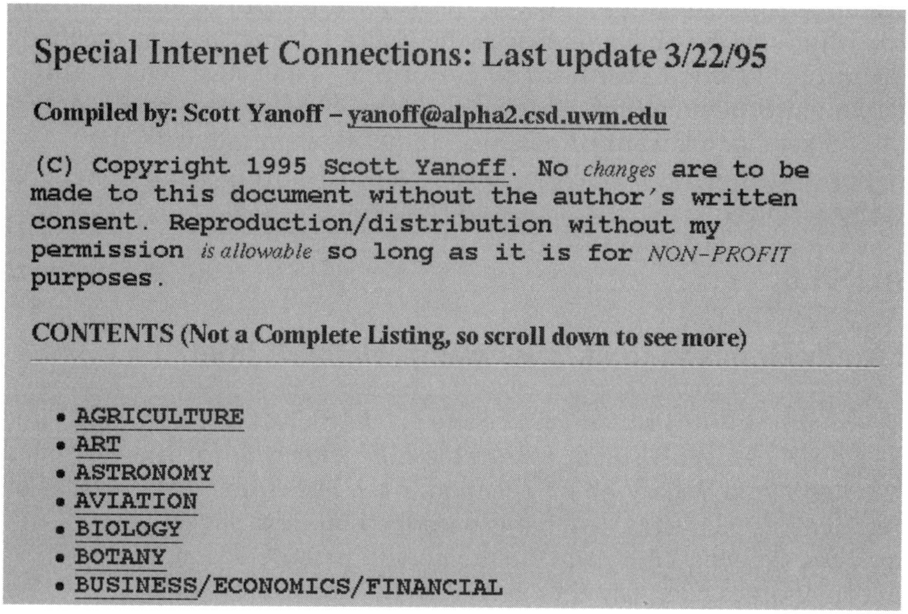
Special Internet Connections: Last update 3/22/95

Compiled by: Scott Yanoff – yanoff@alpha2.csd.uwm.edu

(C) Copyright 1995 Scott Yanoff. No *changes* are to be made to this document without the author's written consent. Reproduction/distribution without my permission *is allowable* so long as it is for *NON-PROFIT* purposes.

CONTENTS (Not a Complete Listing, so scroll down to see more)

- AGRICULTURE
- ART
- ASTRONOMY
- AVIATION
- BIOLOGY
- BOTANY
- BUSINESS/ECONOMICS/FINANCIAL

*Scott Yanoff's Special Internet Connections Home Page—**http://www.uwm.edu/Mirror/inet.services.html*** © 1995 Scott Yanoff.

Robotic search engines

Often called robots, spiders, worms, or crawlers, these tools routinely travel subsets of the Internet, collecting information about resources that can then be indexed for search. They differ in the subsets of the Internet searched, the information gathered for indexing, and the types of search queries they support.

So how do *robot-fed* indexes compare to *human-fed* resource lists? Robots can gather data more quickly than people can, so robot-fed tools tend to know about more resources. At the same time, knowledgeable people can judge the value of a resource subjectively, whereas robots cannot discriminate between the wheat and the chaff. Humans can also organize information in ways that robots cannot. Therefore, while robot-fed tools are usually keyword searchable only, human-fed tools can also present resources hierarchically, by subject or geographic location.

We already understand, however, that no search tool of either variety can offer you the ability to search the entire Internet. But in reality, you probably won't ever need to perform an exhaustive search, the way an attorney might need to search legal files for case precedents. More likely, you'll want some "hits" to get you started, with the option over time of building a collection of sites from there if you are really serious.

ALIWEB

ALIWEB URL:
http://web.nexor.co.uk/public/aliweb/aliweb.html

The main ALIWEB server (shown in Fig. 9-18) lives at NEXOR Limited in the UK. ALIWEB stands for *Archie-Like Indexing for the Web*, and handles World Wide Web information much like Archie handles files at Anonymous FTP sites. (Archie is described on next page.) This includes allowing Web page maintainers to provide descriptive information to complement what ALIWEB finds automatically.

Mirrors of the NEXOR ALIWEB are accessible from the NEXOR Server Home Page; select a server that is operating outside midday hours for the best response time. Like Archie, ALIWEB gives you plenty of control—you choose the search type, fields to search, domains to include, and the maximum number of matches to report.

Figure 9-18

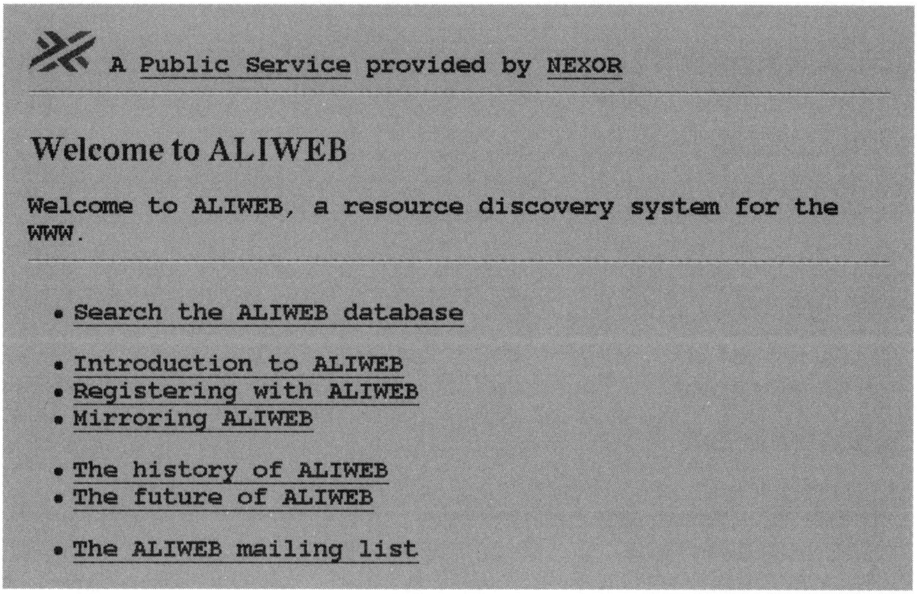

Nexor ALIWEB Home Page—***http://web.nexor.co.uk/public/aliweb/aliweb.html***

ArchiePlex

ArchiePlex URL: **http://web.nexor.co.uk/archie.html**

An ArchiePlex server is a World Wide Web interface to the collection of machines known as Archie servers. ArchiePlex (shown in Fig. 9-19) is a wonderfully straightforward and powerful way to find software and other files at Anonymous FTP sites (described in Chapter 8). To clarify the benefits of ArchiePlex we first need to explain what Archie is.

There are 20 or so public Archie servers around the world. Each one periodically visits several thousand Anonymous FTP sites, traverses their directories, and collects and indexes all directory and file names. You can then query the Archie server's database to pinpoint the locations of files—Archie reports the site's domain name, the actual name of the file (you usually search on substrings of the file names), and the directory it resides in.

Figure 9-19

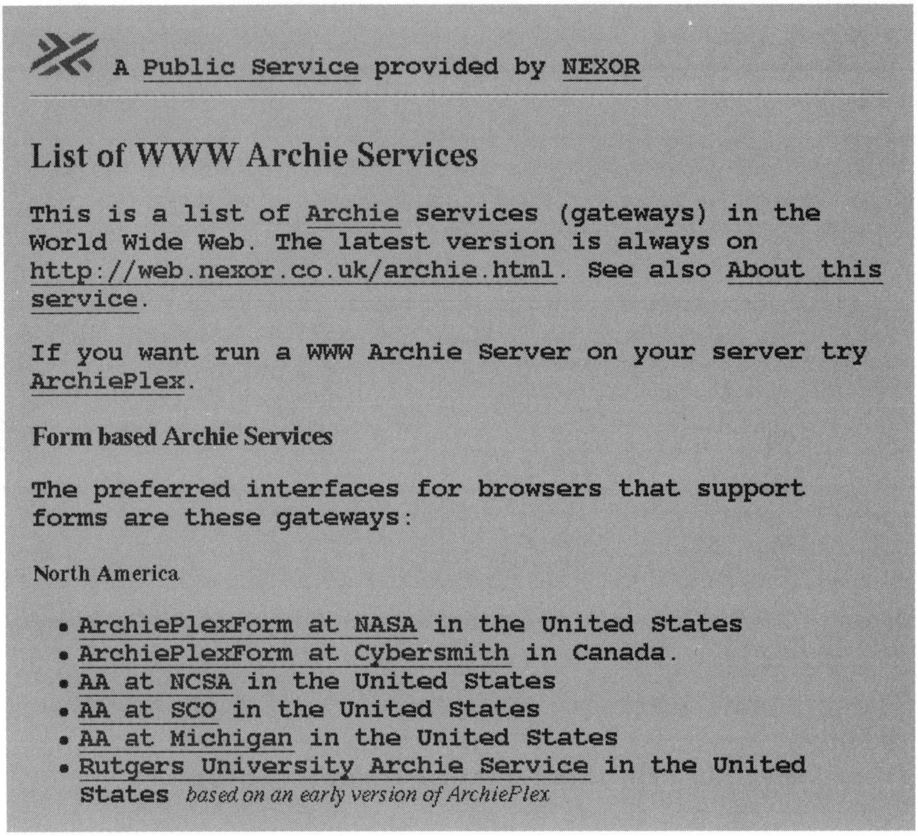

A Public Service provided by NEXOR

List of WWW Archie Services

This is a list of Archie services (gateways) in the World Wide Web. The latest version is always on http://web.nexor.co.uk/archie.html. See also About this service.

If you want run a WWW Archie Server on your server try ArchiePlex.

Form based Archie Services

The preferred interfaces for browsers that support forms are these gateways:

North America

- ArchiePlexForm at NASA in the United States
- ArchiePlexForm at Cybersmith in Canada.
- AA at NCSA in the United States
- AA at SCO in the United States
- AA at Michigan in the United States
- Rutgers University Archie Service in the United States *based on an early version of ArchiePlex*

ArchiePlex Home Page—***http://web.nexor.co.uk/archie.html***

Before Mosaic, that was the end of the line. You then had to copy down (or perhaps cut and paste) the information, make an FTP connection to the site or sites identified, and manually retrieve the file.

With ArchiePlex, however, the search results are presented as a page in Mosaic, with live links to the files and servers. Retrieving a file is as easy as clicking on a hyperlink, and Mosaic lets you either save the file to your disk or go ahead and display it with an appropriate viewer. (There's more to using ArchiePlex effectively, as we'll see later in this chapter.)

✳ Harvest

WWW Home Pages Harvest Broker URL:
http://harvest.cs.colorado.edu/brokers/www-home-pages/query.html

The Harvest Information Discovery and Access System is a set of advanced robotic Internet search tools under development at the University of Colorado, in Boulder. The search interface of Harvest is called the Broker. The project coordinators manage a WWW Home Pages Harvest Broker, which by early February 1995 had indexed over 25,000 documents from over 11,000 Internet servers.

The query interface (shown in Fig. 9-20) is very powerful—scroll down to Example Queries to better understand how to harness the power of the search interface.

By the way, along with the WWW Home Pages broker, University of Colorado, at Boulder also maintains several demonstration brokers. You might find some of these useful as well.

Figure 9-20

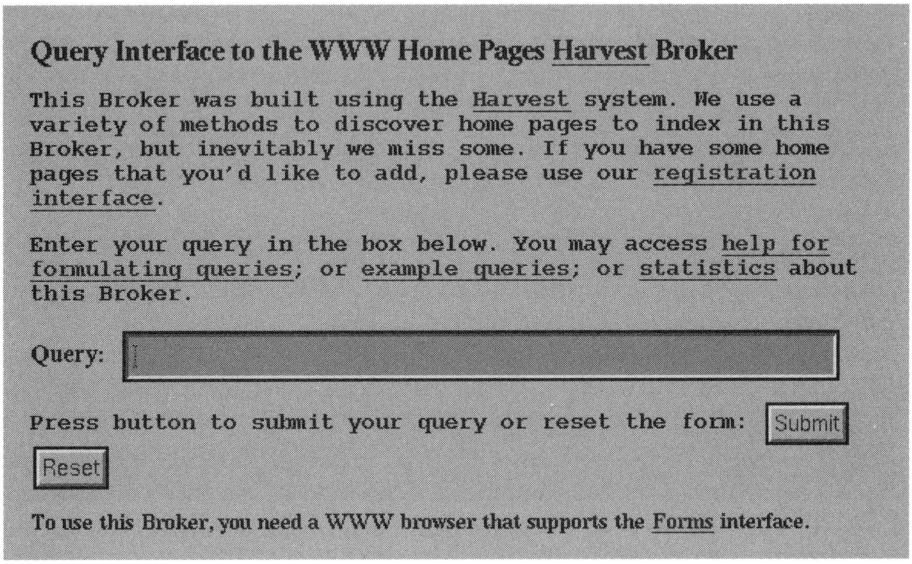

*WWW Home Pages Harvest Broker Home Page—**http://harvest.cs.colorado.edu/brokers/www-home-pages/query.html***

✳ JumpStation II

JumpStation II URL: **http://www.stir.ac.uk/jsbin/jsii**

As the name suggests, JumpStation II is the second generation of a tool developed by Jonathon Fletcher at the University of Stirling in Scotland. JumpStation II (Fig. 9-21) searches each Web document it encounters for its title and header information (as identified by the HTML tags discussed in Chapter 10). It also indexes the full text of the document and, through word frequencies, determines (as best it can) the subject(s) of the document. You might search in any or all of these indexes—select The Document Search and scroll down for instructions.

JumpStation II also provides *The Server Scanner*, which allows you to type (perhaps guess at) a partial URL and see all URLs in the database that contain what you've typed.

Figure 9-21

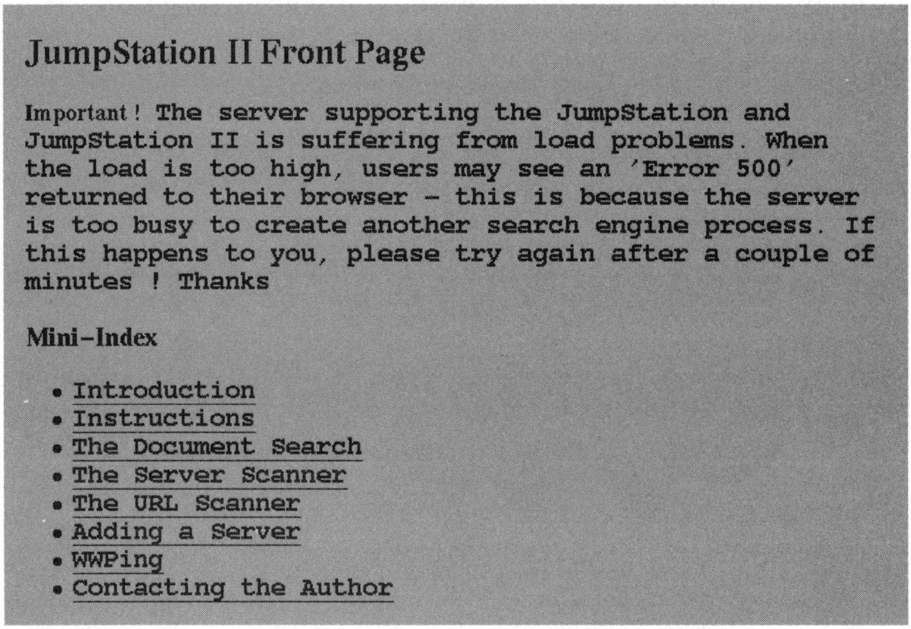

JumpStation II Front Page

Important ! The server supporting the JumpStation and JumpStation II is suffering from load problems. When the load is too high, users may see an 'Error 500' returned to their browser - this is because the server is too busy to create another search engine process. If this happens to you, please try again after a couple of minutes ! Thanks

Mini-Index

- Introduction
- Instructions
- The Document Search
- The Server Scanner
- The URL Scanner
- Adding a Server
- WWPing
- Contacting the Author

*JumpStation II Home Page—**http://www.stir.ac.uk/jsbin/jsii***

❊ Lycos

Lycos URL: **http://lycos.cs.cmu.edu/**

Lycos (see Fig. 9-22) was developed at Carnegie Mellon University in Pittsburgh. As of mid-February 1995 the collection of Lycos servers at CMU had collected over 1.75 million unique URLs with descriptions, and had indexed over 250,000 complete documents.

The Lycos search engine is called Pursuit, and uses what's called *fuzzy logic* to locate not only the keywords you type but similar words as well. You control which of the servers to query (though your rationale for choice seems arbitrary), and how many references Lycos should return. Results come in the form of live URLs, titles of the server pages, and excerpts from the pages. Lycos is large and very popular (over 100,000 users per week)—they recommend visiting before 11 AM or after 6 PM Eastern Time.

Figure 9-22

*Lycos Home Page—**http://lycos.cs.cmu.edu/***

NIKOS

NIKOS URL: **http://www.rns.com/cgi-bin/nikos**

NIKOS is an acronym for the New Internet Knowledge System, a joint project of Rockwell Network Systems and Cal Poly, San Luis Obispo, California. In early January 1995 NIKOS had indexed over 100,000 Internet documents, with a goal of over 1 million by the time this book is published. NIKOS (shown in Fig. 9-23) accepts a Boolean search string (keywords separated by AND, NOT, and OR) and returns a simple list of document titles that are linked to the documents themselves.

Figure 9-23

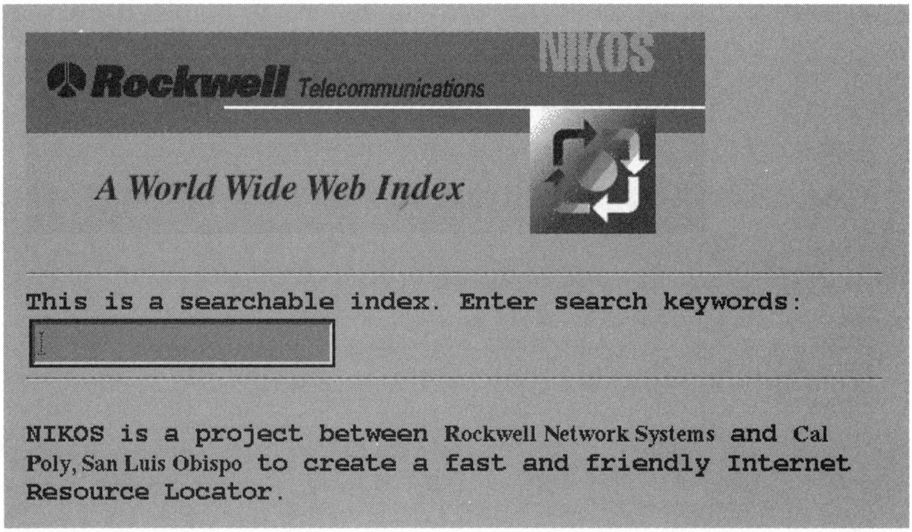

*NIKOS Home Page—**http://www.rns.com/cgi-bin/nikos***

Veronica

Veronica URL:

gopher://futique.scs.unr.edu/hh/veronica/About/veronica-homepage%28html%29

Veronica is your key to Gopherspace, the collection of over 5000 Gopher servers worldwide that have been registered with (or are otherwise reachable from) the "Mother Gopher" at the University of Minnesota. There are ten public Veronica servers worldwide as of this writing. Each one traverses all of Gopherspace about once a month, and builds a keyword index from all of the menu items encountered. Through these menu items Veronica servers also reach documents and other objects from another 5000 World Wide Web and Telnet servers.

There's a nice Veronica access page for Mosaic users at the University of Nevada, Reno (shown in Fig. 9-24). You can see which Veronica servers are presently operational to choose from. But it probably makes more sense to select Simplified Search. The Nevada SCS server will then select the server with the lightest perceived load, which still might be very busy, and send your query there.

Figure 9-24

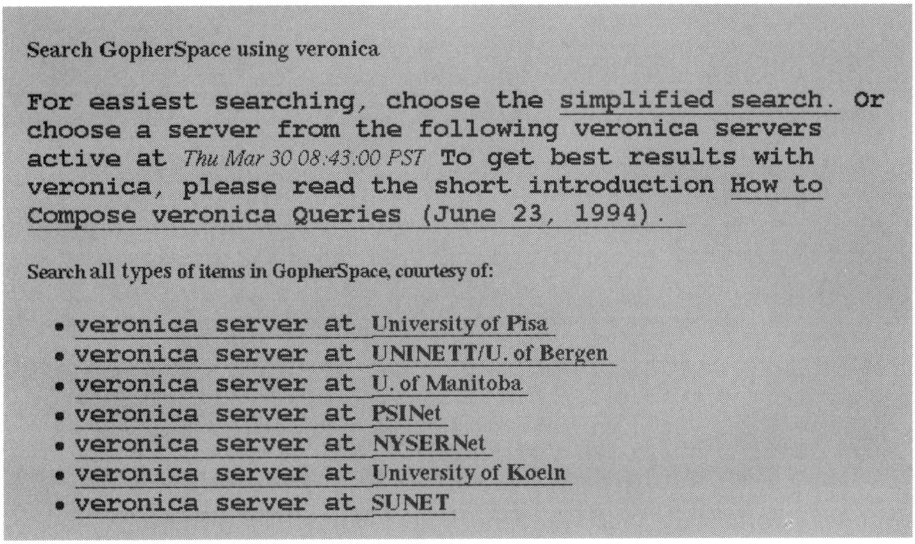

Search GopherSpace using veronica

For easiest searching, choose the simplified search. Or choose a server from the following veronica servers active at *Thu Mar 30 08:43:00 PST* To get best results with veronica, please read the short introduction How to Compose veronica Queries (June 23, 1994).

Search all types of items in GopherSpace, courtesy of:

- veronica server at University of Pisa
- veronica server at UNINETT/U. of Bergen
- veronica server at U. of Manitoba
- veronica server at PSINet
- veronica server at NYSERNet
- veronica server at University of Koeln
- veronica server at SUNET

Veronica Access Page From Nevada SCS—
gopher://futique.scs.unr.edu/hh/veronica/About/veronica-homepage%28html%29

If Veronica reports that it's too busy to handle your request, keep on trying. Be advised, too, that during peak times a successful Veronica search can take several minutes to complete.

※ Wandex

Wandex URL: **http://www.netgen.com/cgi/wandex**

Wandex (see Fig. 9-25) is The World Wide Web Wanderer Index, created by Matthew Gray at MIT. Gray brought Wandex along to a local startup company called net.Genesis. Compared to some of the other robotic search tools we are discussing, Wandex is small—approximately 6000 home pages and 27,000 documents indexed as of this writing.

Figure 9-25

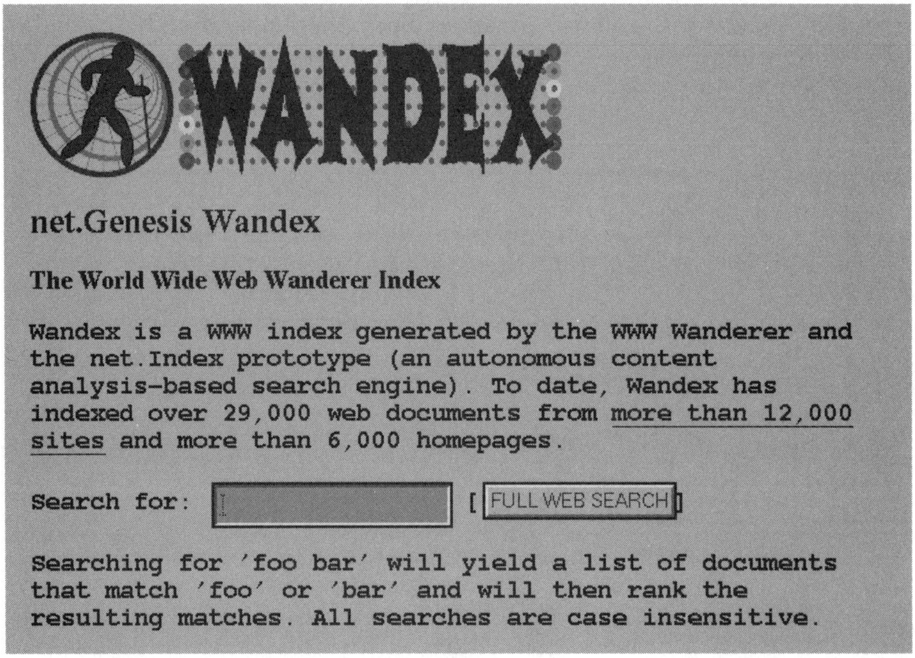

*Wandex (World Wide Web Wanderer Index) Home Page—**http://www.netgen.com/cgi/wandex*** © 1995 net.Genesis.

⁂ WebCrawler

WebCrawler URL:

http://webcrawler.cs.washington.edu/WebCrawler/Home.html

The WebCrawler was developed by Brian Pinkerton at the University of Washington. WebCrawler (Fig. 9-26) indexes the full text of each document it finds, which is a time-consuming task. As of January 1995 the WebCrawler had indexed 70,000 documents but knew of

Figure 9-26

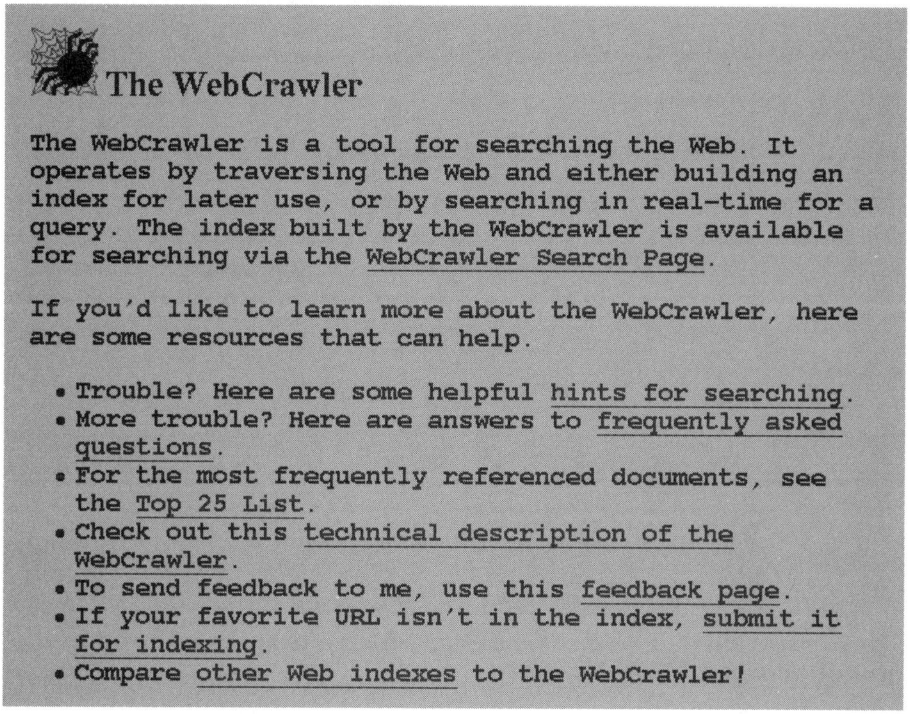

*WebCrawler Home Page—**http://webcrawler.cs.washington.edu/WebCrawler/Home.html***

700,000 more to process! Developers of WebCrawler are also experimenting with new search strategies. You can currently search on multiple words, with a crude Boolean capability.

✲ World Wide Web Worm

World Wide Web Worm URL:
http://www.cs.colorado.edu/home/mcbryan/WWWW.html

The World Wide Web Worm, or WWWW, comes from Oliver McBryan at the University of Colorado. WWWW (shown in Fig. 9-27) has indexed over 300,000 multimedia objects as of September 1994. In addition to search capabilities on document titles, names, and text, you can also search on citations—the text used to identify the hyperlinks to the document from other documents. You can select your search space and type your keywords on the main search page, or jump to a page of Search Examples that you can modify as you wish.

Figure 9-27

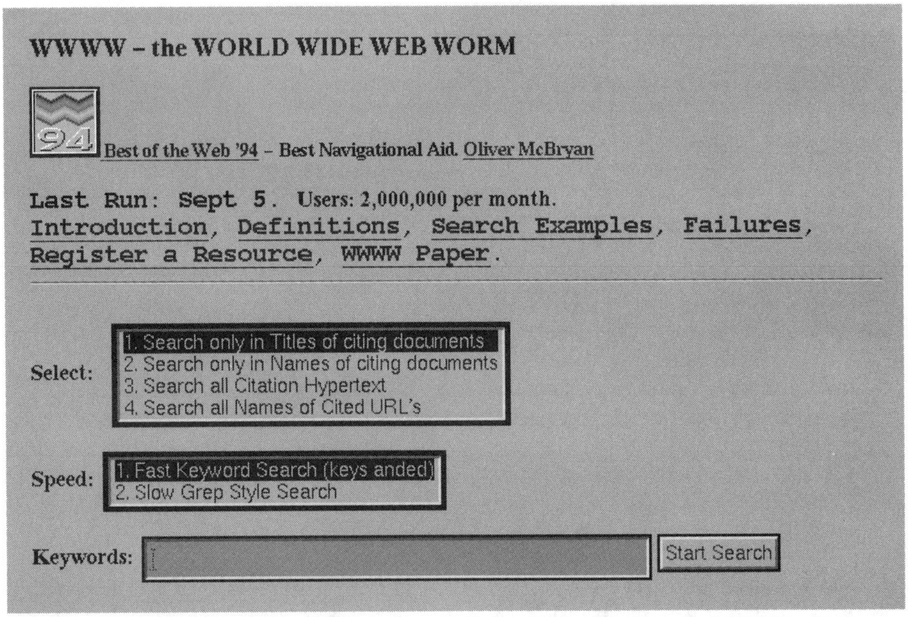

*The World Wide Web Worm Home Page—**http://www.cs.colorado.edu/home/mcbryan/WWWW.html***

Other specialized search tools

This category is somewhat of a catchall for other sites you can visit to perform searches on defined portions of the Internet. Such a site might be a searchable index over several sites we have already described (CUI W3 Catalog), a collection of electronic mail *white pages* tools (InterNIC), or a window into managed subject-oriented databases (WAISGATE).

CUI W3 Catalog

CUI W3 Catalog URL:
http://cuiwww.unige.ch/w3catalog

The CUI W3 Catalog (see Fig. 9-28) is maintained at the University of Geneva, Switzerland. Here lives a searchable index into several of the sites we've already described, including NCSA/GNN What's New, CERN Virtual Library, Scott Yanoff's Special Internet Connections,

Figure 9-28

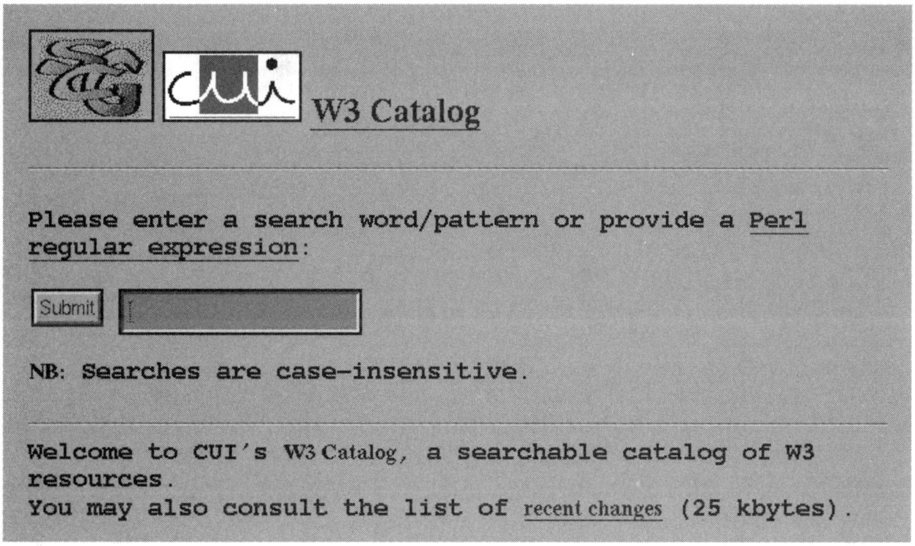

*CUI W3 Catalog Home Page—**http://cuiwww.unige.ch/w3catalog***

John December's CMC Information Sources, and ALIWEB. It has over 11,000 entries in all.

InterNIC Directory Services

InterNIC Directory Services URL:
http://ds.internic.net/ds/dspgwp.html

Within the Directory of Database Servers arm of the InterNIC (the part managed by AT&T) there exist gateways to three separate directories of users and organizations on the Internet. All three directories are accessible from the InterNIC Directory Services Web page, shown in Fig. 9-29.

The worldwide X.500 Directory is distributed over approximately 500 sites that hold the public personnel data of nearly 3000 organizations. The X.500 hierarchy can be browsed starting with countries, or searched. You must browse to the lower levels of the directory before you can search for a person, however, and you must know the organization the person belongs to. The X.500 Directory Web page is shown in Fig. 9-30. The hand appearing on your screen and pointing to the right reveals more countries to browse.

Figure 9-29

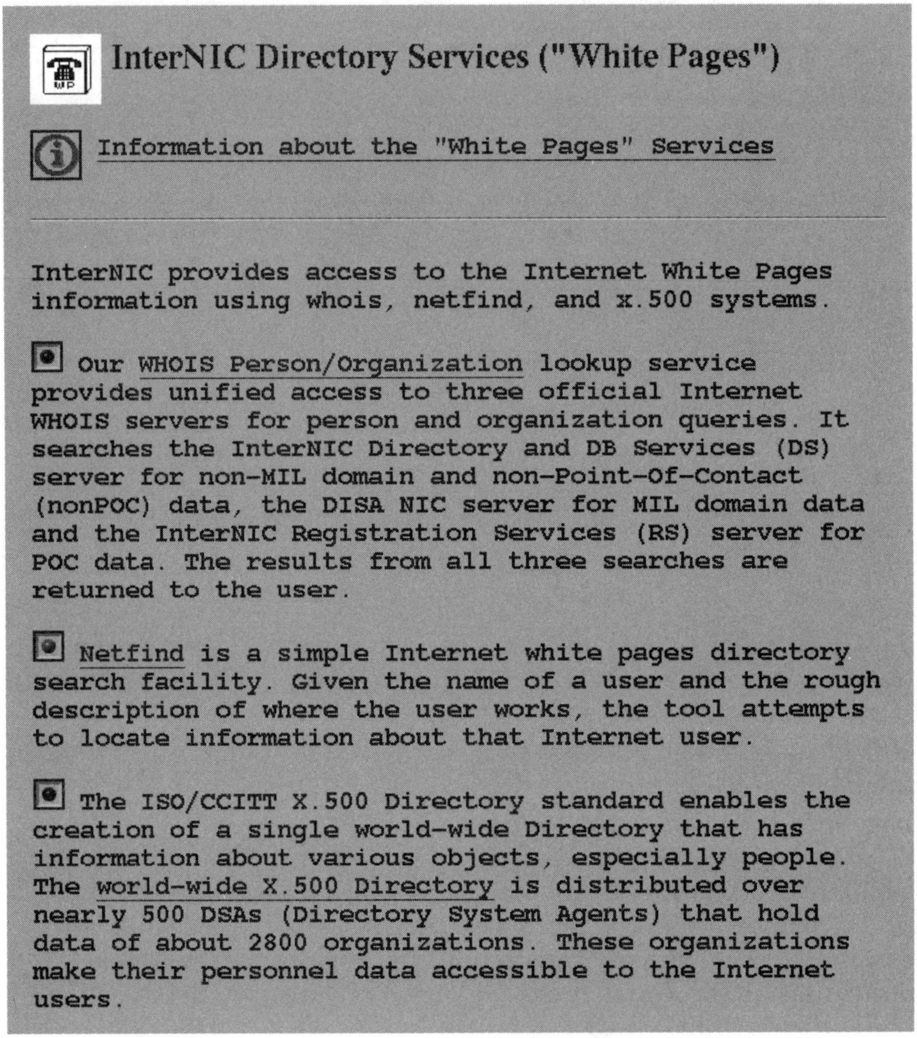

InterNIC Directory Services ("White Pages")

Information about the "White Pages" Services

InterNIC provides access to the Internet White Pages information using whois, netfind, and x.500 systems.

Our WHOIS Person/Organization lookup service provides unified access to three official Internet WHOIS servers for person and organization queries. It searches the InterNIC Directory and DB Services (DS) server for non-MIL domain and non-Point-Of-Contact (nonPOC) data, the DISA NIC server for MIL domain data and the InterNIC Registration Services (RS) server for POC data. The results from all three searches are returned to the user.

Netfind is a simple Internet white pages directory search facility. Given the name of a user and the rough description of where the user works, the tool attempts to locate information about that Internet user.

The ISO/CCITT X.500 Directory standard enables the creation of a single world-wide Directory that has information about various objects, especially people. The world-wide X.500 Directory is distributed over nearly 500 DSAs (Directory System Agents) that hold data of about 2800 organizations. These organizations make their personnel data accessible to the Internet users.

*InterNIC Directory Services Home Page—**http://ds.internic.net/ds/dspgwp.html***

Netfind is a simple Internet white pages search tool. Netfind is accessed through a Gopher gateway—the search screen is not at all elaborate. You must provide a name, followed by a rough description of where the person works.

Figure 9-30

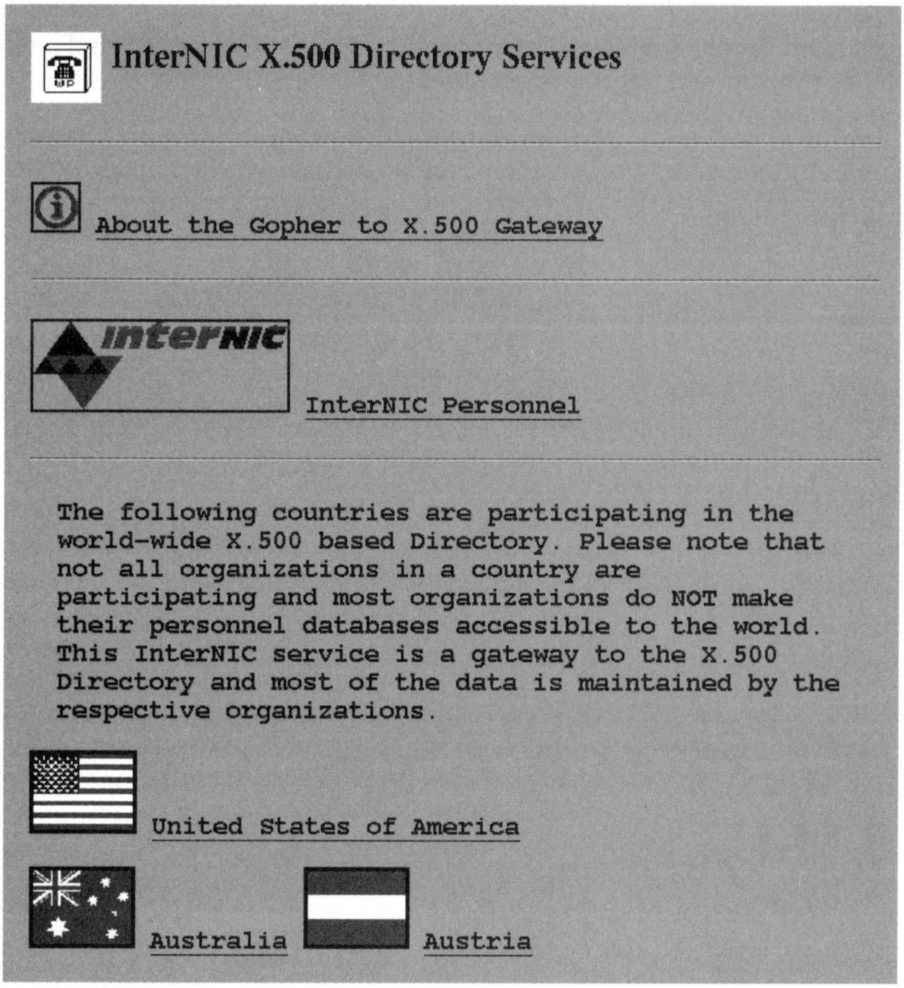

*InterNIC X.500 Directory Services Home Page—**http://ds.internic.net/ds/dspgx500.html***

The WHOIS lookup service gives you unified access to three official Internet WHOIS servers to look up people and organizations. Data comes from InterNIC sources and from the DISA NIC for military domain information.

WAISGATE

WAISGATE URL:
http://www.wais.com/directory-of-servers.html

The Wide Area Information Servers (WAIS) system was developed jointly by Thinking Machines Corporation, Apple Computer, and Dow Jones and Company. The original interest in WAIS was as a means of publishing on the Internet on a fee-paid basis. As the project has evolved to this point, however, WAIS (pronounced *ways*) is better recognized as an indexing and search tool. WAIS indexing and searching happen behind the scenes at sites throughout the Internet—EINet Galaxy, for instance.

Commercial WAIS software is now developed by WAIS Inc., of Menlo Park, California. The legacy of the original WAIS project is the collection of over 500 public (free) WAIS databases sprinkled throughout the Internet. WAIS Inc. maintains WAISGATE (see Fig. 9-31), a WAIS gateway for Mosaic users (and users of other Web browsers) to search and access these databases.

You first search the Directory of Servers, where the public WAIS databases are described at a general level. Broaden your search term to something very general here. WAISGATE will generate a list of hyperlinks to the servers that seem to pertain to your broad topic,

Figure 9-31

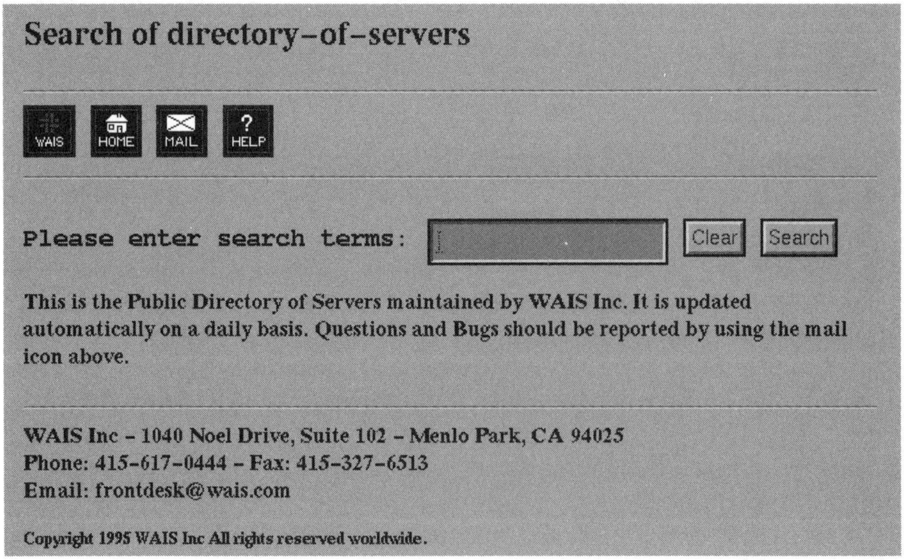

*WAISGATE Home Page—**http://www.wais.com/directory-of-servers.html***

with the most relevant hits at the top of the list. Following a link to a server then allows you to search there for the more specific topic.

Strategies for the perplexed

Critics of the Internet feel it is too big and disorganized to be useful and that you ultimately can't find information when you need it. We believe this opinion is a result of their expectations. So we asked ourselves questions such as, "If someone asked US to find University such-and such on the Internet, using Mosaic, how would we do it?" We offer answers to this type of question in the following section, as applied to seven general types of information:

- What's new on the Internet?
- Information about governments and cultures
- Resources related to a particular topic
- Information about an organization
- Contact information or background information about a person
- Shareware and public domain software
- Multimedia files (image, sound, and movie)

Things change, but Internet things change even faster. By the time you read this, for instance, Lycos might no longer be the largest robotic search tool or some brand new subject catalog might have made one we have listed become obsolete. So be flexible with our suggestions and adjust them based on your own experiences.

It's not our intention to play favorites, beyond selecting what seem to be the most logical places to begin based on the data we've researched, and our own most fruitful experiences. We offer this information in good faith and sincerely apologize if we have inadvertently misrepresented anybody.

Remember that absolutely none of the discovery tools we have described can lead you directly to more than some fraction of the Internet. So start with our recommendations to find some resources relatively quickly, but if you have time, feel free to try them all.

Also, don't feel you have to pigeonhole your specific need into one of the seven approaches. You might benefit from approaching your search from several angles. For example, you might be researching a scientific field—a topic. Who are the foremost researchers in the field? Where can you find them? Where do they work? A serious Internaut can move logically from one approach to the next, and he or she can paint a more complete picture from a wider variety of resources.

How to find what's new

If you're looking for new places to visit on the Internet, the best place to start is NCSA/GNN What's New, introduced on page 162. It's like a favorite meeting place. What's New can keep you busy for hours. If you're still wanting to surf the Net, the Scout Report (page 166) is a good second choice, followed by Net-Happenings (page 166).

On the other hand, if it's recent Internet-related news and announcements you seek, work these in reverse. Start with Net-Happenings which is strong on newsletters, conference announcements, and the like. The Scout Report gets into Internet news as well, so try them next.

How to find governments & cultures

Relatively speaking, locating information about governments and cultures is not difficult. There are three ways to go, depending on where you want to end up—states and cities in the United States, the U.S. Government itself, or locations outside the U.S.

U.S. states & cities

The most direct way we know of to find U.S. states and cities is through USA CityLink, introduced on page 167. Simply scan the alphabetical list of states and you'll be within a few mouse clicks of hundreds of sites explaining state and local governments, tourist attractions, and even restaurant recommendations. Also try the United States section of the Virtual Tourist II (page 168). Then visit the Whole Internet Catalog and select State & Local Government for more leads.

✻ The U.S. government

If you have some sense of how the federal government is organized, a good first avenue into the U.S. government is via The First Family. Tom and his cohorts visited The White House back in Chapter 1. While a virtual visit with the Clintons might interest you as well, the most useful link from The White House home page is through the image area Executive Branch. This leads you to clickable images shown in Fig. 9-32, which in turn can take you to any government office or agency that's on the Net: Executive, Legislative, or Judicial. If the organizational-chart approach doesn't suit you, or if the

Figure 9-32

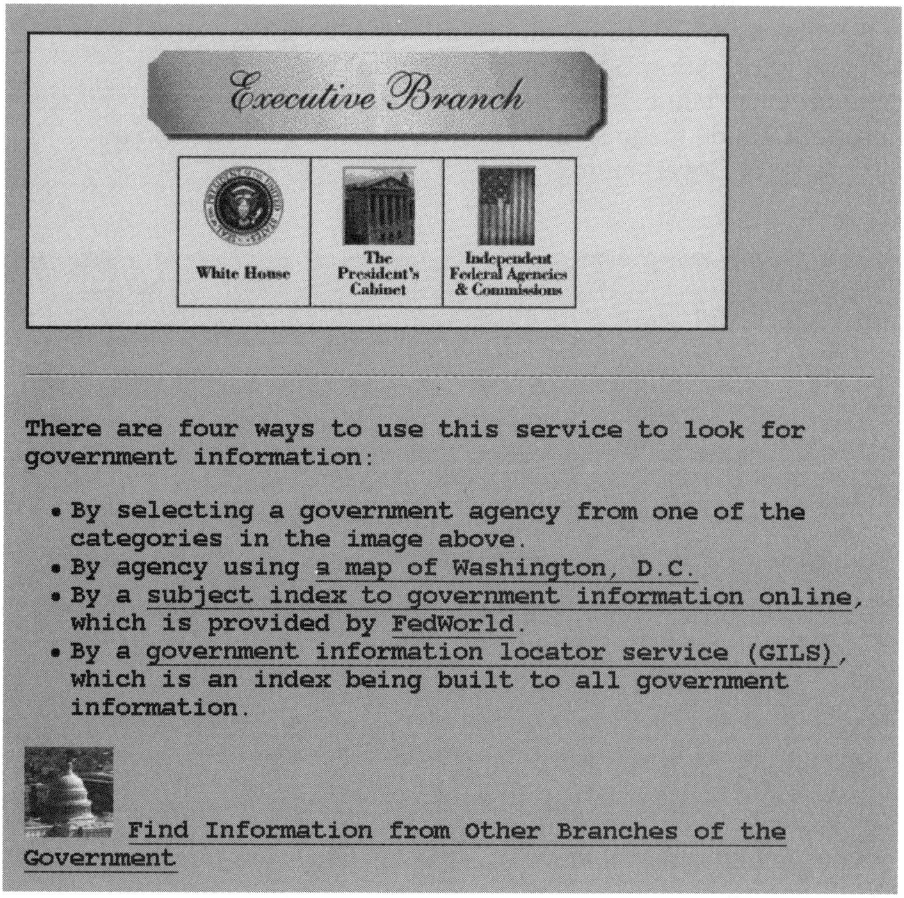

One step beyond the White House Home Page
http://www.whitehouse.gov

clickable images take too long to load across your connection, try FedWorld, introduced on page 174. Navigating FedWorld by subject will take you to most of the same U.S. Government servers.

Outside the United States

The best way to zoom in on worldwide locations outside the U.S. is through the Virtual Tourist II (page 168). Click on the successive maps and select Text-Only Version if your connection is slow. Or, search the Tourist directly. Next, proceed to MARVEL from the U.S. Library of Congress Web server (shown in Fig. 9-33). Select LC MARVEL to reach the MARVEL Gopher server and then choose Government Information. Foreign Government Information (Non-U.S.) then leads you to resources of foreign countries, and then General Information By Country gives you even more room to explore. Once you exhaust these two excellent resources the Whole Internet Catalog (page 175) is worth a look—select Foreign and International Government.

Figure 9-33

Library of Congress Home Page—***http://lcweb.loc.gov/homepage/lchp.html***

How to find topics

First check out the subject catalogs (page 169-177). It only makes sense to see if someone has already done your legwork for you, and the major Internet subject catalogs are really coming into their own. Which one should you peruse first? We seem to have good luck with Yahoo, which has been growing rapidly, but there is no best answer; for example, no way to know exactly how many resource links each catalog contains, except for Yahoo, which tells you right on their home page. Besides, subject catalogs are bound to be stronger in some areas and weaker in others.

Two of the eight catalogs are particularly focused—FedWorld on U.S. Government information sources and John December's CMC list on Internet and technology-related topics. So, if you expect your topic to be covered by one of these catalogs, that catalog should be the first searched.

Each time a catalog leads you to a list of resources on your topic, add that page of pointers to your hotlist and move on to another catalog. The subject catalogs we have discussed are organized no more than three levels deep, so with this approach you can scope out several in a short time.

If it's important that you not overlook resources about your topic that have been added to the Internet recently, be sure to also search for your topic at the CUI W3 Catalog. This will reveal resources that were announced in NCSA/GNN What's New.

If you exhaust all of these options and are still short on leads, then the robotic search tools are all good choices to try (except, perhaps, ArchiePlex, due to its orientation around filenames rather than topics). WAISGATE might also be of help.

A final suggestion. If you found it difficult to collect resources on your topic, consider sharing what you have found with one or more catalogs. It could be a fine contribution to the Internet community.

How to find organizations

Broadly speaking, companies, schools, and nonprofit groups participate on the Internet in one of the following three ways, depending primarily on their size and their goals:

- Some operate their own information servers, usually World Wide Web or Gopher. These are often medium to large organizations, or smaller ones that also happen to be technology-oriented (such as software vendors). They aspire to serve information and give the Internet community a relatively complete picture of who they are.
- Others lease Web home page space in "online malls" or from Internet service providers. These are usually smaller companies wanting to have a presence for the purpose of prospective customers contacting them through other means, or eventually to conduct online sales.
- Still others establish an Internet domain for e-mail communication, but perhaps do not even have a permanent Internet connection. They nonetheless expect to need to communicate with other Internet users.

When trying to reach an organization on the Internet, first assess what you already know. Is the organization commercial or noncommercial? Is it large and established, or smaller? Where is it based—what country, state, or city?

Then ask yourself what you really want. Are you simply seeking directory information—a phone number or an e-mail address? Or would you rather be able to peruse catalogs, press releases, and other public information about the organization?

Once you have taken stock of these questions you can choose an approach that improves your odds of success with a minimum of effort.

Organization directory information

At this time there are only a few tools on the Internet that we might recommend for this specific purpose. One is the worldwide X.500

directory at InterNIC Directory Services, introduced on page 189. If the organization you seek is relatively large and you know in what country it is located, X.500 might be of use. The WHOIS search tool at InterNIC allows you to search for organizations, but the results of such a search tend to mix organizations themselves with people who work there, which might be a little confusing.

If you seek a relatively small company, however, your options are more limited. Our best advice for now is to try to locate a home page for the organization.

✻ Organization home pages

Here we ask, "Does this organization maintain a presence on the Internet?" There are several ways to approach this question:

1 Take a stab at guessing their URL (U.S. organizations only). Let the long-standing and emerging Internet domain-name conventions come to your aid. Think about two things: (1) what type of organization is it in Internet terms (i.e., commercial, educational, government, or military); and (2), how would they distinctively identify themselves with a short name or acronym within that context?

Let's say you want to visit the University of Arizona. Build a World Wide Web URL as illustrated in Fig. 9-34. Remember that Web server URLs always begin with **http://**, and that their domain name tends to begin with **www**. Domain names of educational institutions end with **.edu**, so most of the puzzle is already solved.

This technique is fast and surprisingly effective. More often than not, if the organization you seek has a public Web server you can guess its URL in a minute or less.

The general guidelines for constructing URLs within the U.S. are illustrated in Fig. 9-34. Of course, if you cannot locate an organization's Web server this way, you could fish for a Gopher or Anonymous FTP site using the same naming conventions (Telnet servers tend not to follow these conventions). We would suggest you probably move on to the next steps.

Figure 9-34

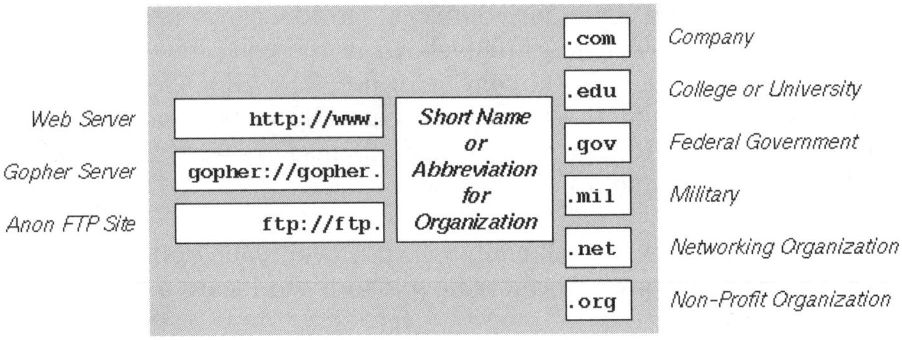

Guidelines for guessing URLs in the U.S.

2 Query the JumpStation II Server Scanner (page 182). Think again about a logical short name or acronym for the organization. Select The Server Scanner from the Front Page, then next to Enter Partial Server Address type the organization's name or acronym between two asterisks, as shown in Fig. 9-35.

Figure 9-35

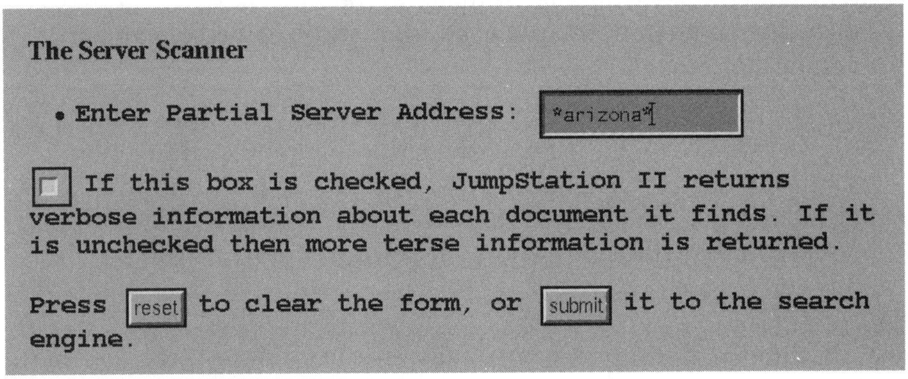

JumpStation II Server Scanner Page (search for Arizona)—
http://www.stir.ac.uk/jsbin/server_scanner

The Server Scanner will probe JumpStation II's index of URLs and return all the URLs containing the entered search string. Scan the results carefully—you might find more than one home page for the same organization.

3 Visit the CERN Web Server Registry (page 164) or the Virtual Tourist World Map (page 164). If the organization operates its own

Web server rather than leasing home page space, and if it has it registered with CERN, you can locate it geographically. This assumes, of course, that you know the whereabouts of the organization.

4 Visit the CUI W3 Catalog. CUI is useful to us here because their searchable index includes all the submissions to NCSA/GNN What's New, where organizations with a Web presence are likely to have announced their services.

5 If the preceding steps have borne no fruit try the robotic search engines. We would begin with Lycos for two reasons: it's the largest of the robots and it's not as Web-centric as many of the others, so you might have a better chance of locating a Gopher or Anonymous FTP site.

How to find people

The approach outlined here is intended to help you locate basic directory information about an individual—their postal, organizational, and e-mail addresses, or just some sense of where the person fits into the electronic world. If you wish to research an individual in more depth (even historical figures), treat their name as a topic and approach the Internet such as outlined above.

We would like to see Internet-based directory information improve dramatically. For now, locating such information is a piecemeal process that is incomplete at best—too much like being a private eye!

A key question is this: Do you know what organization(s) the person you are looking for is affiliated with? If so, you have a big advantage. For example, all three tools at InterNIC Directory Services (page 189) become available to you (only WHOIS allows you to search solely for a person's name without an affiliation). Spend a few minutes there first—you might be successful. Realistically, you'll probably meet with speedy failure, but at least it will be speedy.

At the time of this writing, the best approach from there is to stop searching for the individual and start searching for an affiliated organization. Concentrate on actions that might lead you to a server operated by the organization, which could include a staff or student directory, or pages that otherwise make reference to the person. We outlined how to find organization home pages in the previous section. Follow steps 1 through 4 as applicable.

If you reach step 5 and you're about to begin searching on keywords, launch searches for the person as well as the organization. Here again, try Lycos first, especially because USENET newsgroups are often archived at Anonymous FTP sites, and newsgroup articles often contain signature information for the contributors.

On the other hand, if all you have to go on is the name of the person the situation is trickier but by no means hopeless. Proceed directly to Lycos and then to the rest of the robotic search engines that let you search on the text of a resource. You might either find the information you seek or learn where the person works or studies.

How to find software

When in the need of shareware or public domain software, the logical first places to search are Anonymous FTP sites. Using Mosaic, this means using ArchiePlex (page 179). Here are a few hints for performing effective ArchiePlex searches.

- Archie is a very popular search tool, and both ArchiePlex and Archie servers get very busy during prime time hours (midday, Monday through Friday). If it's not currently prime time where you are, select an ArchiePlex server that's located close to you. If you ARE working during prime time, try to locate an ArchiePlex server where it's roughly the middle of the night. Then choose an Archie server the same way. The default Archie server for that ArchiePlex is likely to suffice.
- Understand Anonymous FTP filename conventions, because Archie tries to match filenames. Software is usually saved in filenames comprising an abbreviation of the application name, then a version number, and then one or more extensions, such as:

  fax_v310.zip (FaxMail, version 3.10)

ghostscript-2.5.2.tar.gx (Ghostscript PostScript file viewer, version 2.5.2)

spells13.zip (a Windows spelling checker, version 1.3)

Think of an abbreviation to use as the search term.

- Choose your search type wisely. For the best chance of finding a file for which you don't know the exact name, always perform a *case-insensitive substring search*.
- Files often exist at multiple Anonymous FTP sites. Ask first for a small number of results (search hits)—select 10, and ArchiePlex will report on the first 10 files found. You might then search for more if necessary.
- When searching for software, how do you know if the file you find is for your platform? Learn to spot the clues. First read the reported pathname—look for msdos, mswin, a UNIX supported platform like SUN or SGI, or some other tipoff. Then look at the filename extension and see if it looks proper for your type of computer. Common PC software filename extensions are .exe (executable), .zip (a PKZIP archived/compressed file), and .zoo (a ZOO archived/compressed file). Common UNIX filename extensions are .tar (TAR archive), .Z (UNIX compressed) and .gz (GNUZIP compressed). Common Macintosh software filename extensions are .hqx (BinHex archived/compressed), .sea (self-extracting archive), and .sit (StuffIt archived/compressed).
- Make use of the naming convention regarding version number. ArchiePlex might report several occurrences of the software you seek for your platform. Compare the version numbers to help identify the most recent revision. However, don't put any stock in the file date stamps reported by ArchiePlex. An application's currency and its storage date often do not correlate.

If Archie fails to locate the software, the other sensible approach is to query a robotic search engine. You might discover a Web home page or USENET archive that discusses the application and where to find it.

How to find multimedia files

While this was not true until recently, searches of the World Wide Web are now your best first approach to locating images, audio clips, and digital movies. Web page authors know that Mosaic is a natural tool for presenting multimedia, and therefore incorporate multimedia into their pages wherever possible. Because they are usually referred to by name or incorporated into topical presentations, they turn up easily in keyword searches. As of this writing, here's a logical progression of searches:

First, try World Wide Web Worm citation search. Links returned by the search might point directly to the multimedia file you seek. (Other types of searches can only locate text-based resources that might, in turn, point to multimedia.) Then search Lycos, simply because it's the largest. Proceed to a few more text-based search tools if necessary.

If keyword searches come up empty, try ArchiePlex as you would locate software (see previous section). Multimedia files are usually named with a representative name (perhaps shortened), followed by the filetype extension (explained in Chapter 11), such as:

William-Jefferson-Clinton.gif, **Clinton.gif**

Both of these files can be found by ArchiePlex by searching for *clinton* with a case-insensitive substring search.

Once you have located and selected the image, audio clip, or digital movie you seek, Mosaic will try to render it for you by launching an external viewer. If you intend to save it in a local file, select Save As from the File menu. Mosaic will prompt you for a local filename.

There is, however, one exception to this approach. If the multimedia element is an image incorporated within a Web page, there is no link to select. If you wish to isolate the image in a local file, you must first determine where the image was *inlined* from—it must, in fact, exist in a file on the computer that served the page. This requires that you locate the URL reference to this multimedia file within the HTML for the page. This process, along with the HTML background you might need, is discussed in Chapters 10 and 11.

10

Building Mosaic-ready multimedia documents

CHAPTER 10

ONE of the most exciting aspects of Mosaic is its ability to display multimedia information in the form of color images, 3D graphics, sound, music, movies, and more. Multimedia methods of communication are likely to enhance comprehension, curiosity, and creativity. If you have had an opportunity to begin your Internet exploration you have seen some examples of multimedia information. Now you might be inspired to begin publishing or providing information to the Web. You might be interested in creating "internal" Webs by linking HTML documents shared on your organization's internal network servers. Whether you are interested in preparing material for internal or external distribution, the authoring tools you need to prepare and maintain documents should take advantage of hyperlinks, buttons, and multimedia.

This chapter and the next will introduce you to some of the available tools you will need to get you started as an Internet multimedia information publisher, capable of transforming various media to effectively convey your message. First we will tell you how to create HTML documents (the container for your multimedia elements), including lots of pointers to various editors and authoring tools. Chapter 11 will dive into the other media types and give you the lowdown on graphics, sound, and movies. While this information might seem overwhelming, the introductory material in each section will give you an idea of how easy it is to incorporate these elements into your documents.

Getting started as a Web publisher

Legal ease—copyright versus public domain

You are about to learn the basics of Internet publishing, but first, let us take a moment to address some legal issues you need to be aware of. A copyright is a right of intellectual property granting authors of original works certain exclusive rights to their works, for a limited time. In the United States, copyright law is federal law and derives from the so-called copyright clause of the Constitution, which provides Congress with the power "to promote science and the useful arts, by securing for limited times to authors the exclusive right to their writings."

In the United States, copyright law recognizes the following seven rights:

- The right to reproduce the work in copies.
- The right to produce derivative works based on the copyrighted work.
- The right to distribute copies of the work.
- The right to perform the copyrighted work publicly.
- The right to display the copyrighted work publicly.
- The right of the author to claim authorship of the work and to prevent the use of his or her name as the author of a work he or she did not create.
- The right of an author to prevent the use of his or her name as the author of a distorted version of the work, to prevent intentional distortion of the work, and to prevent destruction of the work.

Copyright protects "original works of authorship" that are fixed in a tangible form of expression. The fixation need not be directly perceptible as long as it might be communicated with the aid of a machine or device. Works that might be copyrighted fall into the following eight categories:

- Literary works, including computer programs
- Musical works, including any accompanying words
- Dramatic works, including any accompanying music
- Pantomimes and choreographic works
- Pictorial, graphic, and sculptural works
- Motion pictures and other audiovisual works
- Sound recordings
- Architectural works

A work in the public domain can be freely used by anyone, for any purpose. You can do whatever you want with a program in the public domain, including charging whatever you want for it. If the author desires to retain the copyright, he or she might provide a non-exclusive license to copy and distribute the work, with a condition on the license that the cost charged for it not exceed media costs. If there is any restriction upon the use of the work, even the restriction that it cannot be sold, the work is not public domain. Indeed, the work is copyrighted and the restrictions are limitations on a licensee's using one or more of the exclusive rights described above. For example, the restriction that a work might only be given away free is a limitation using the distribution right.

At one time, if a work was published without a copyright notice, it lost all copyright protection and entered the public domain. That is no longer the case. However, use of the copyright notice on original works is still recommended, because such notice informs the public that the work is protected by copyright, identifies the copyright owner, and shows the year of first publication. The use of the copyright notice is the responsibility of the copyright owner and does not require advance permission from, or registration with, the United States Copyright Office. The notice should contain all of the following three elements:

- The symbol (the letter C in a circle) or the word "Copyright," or the abbreviation "Copr."
- The year of first publication of the work.
- The name of the owner of the copyrighted work, or an abbreviation by which the name can be recognized.

For additional information on copyrights, refer to URLs:

gopher://wiretap.spies.com/00/Gov/Copyright/US.Copyright.Basics.txt
http://www.cis.ohio-state.edu/hypertext/faq/usenet/Copyright-FAQ/top.html

Getting started

Creating your own Web document is a snap. First, you will need to learn a little HTML. There are three ways to produce HTML documents:

- Write them yourself, using a text editor such as vi (UNIX) or Notepad (Microsoft Windows).
- Use an HTML editor or document template, which assists in appropriate formatting.
- Use conversion tools to transform documents from other formats to HTML.

Whichever method you choose, you will need a few good references to learn the basics of HTML. Once you create a document, check it out using Mosaic's Open Local selection of the File Menu.

Learn the language of the Web

While Web documents do not have to be written in HTML, HTML provides a standard method for formatting documents plus a mechanism for specifying hypertext links to other resources. Keep in mind that HTML is an evolving standard. It is a derivative of SGML (Standard Generalized Markup Language), simplified to be quickly adopted by the mass market.

HTML Level 1 is the original version. HTML Level 2 is essentially the same as the original, with the addition of forms. HTML Level 3, also known as HTML+, is an enhanced version of HTML designed to address some of the limitations of HTML. The HTML Level 3 specification is expected to be released in the spring of 1995. HTML Level 3 supports true tables, right-justified text, centered text, line breaks that do not double space, and many other desired features. At the time this text was written, however, most clients supported only a handful of HTML Level 3 features. Be aware that if you write documents using HTML Level 3 syntax, and browsers who do not understand HTML 3 attempt to view the documents, the results might be unexpected.

A quick trick to learn more about HTML is to use Mosaic's View Source selection of the Edit Menu or the Save As selection of the File Menu to sneak a peek at the HTML for someone else's page, which you find particularly interesting. You are likely to find the documents to be a great deal simpler than you expected.

HTML basics

HTML documents are plain text and include markup tags to instruct Mosaic (or any browser) how to display the content. A HTML Quick Reference of the information provided below is included in Appendix D.

A simple example of HTML:

```
<HTML><HEAD> <TITLE>A simple example</TITLE> </HEAD><BODY> <H1>This is a
level one heading</H1> Welcome to my world. Let's end this paragraph.<P>
</BODY></HTML>
```

Figure 10-1 shows how Mosaic will display the above html example.

Figure 10-1

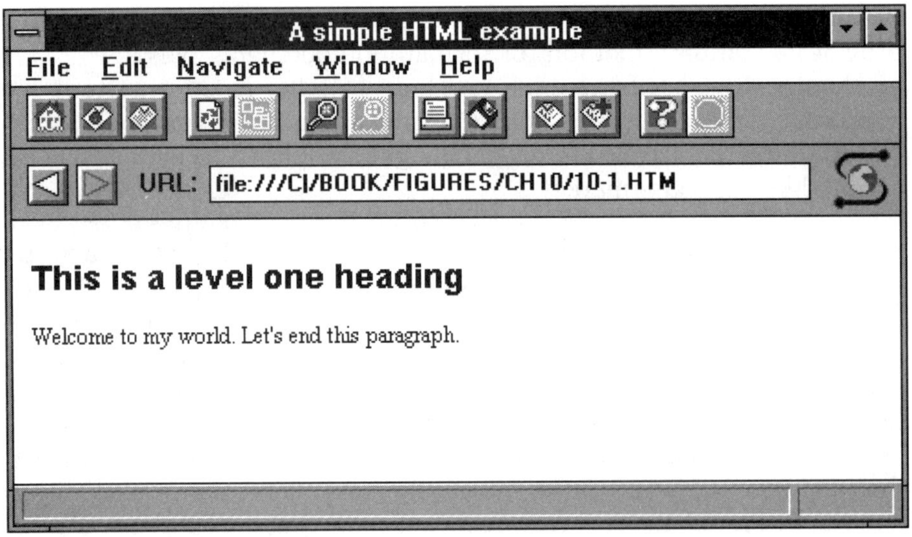

A simple HTML example

HTML formatting is accomplished using tags delimited by angle brackets. Tags begin with a left angle bracket (<), followed by the name of the tag. They are closed by a right angle bracket (>). Tags are generally paired. For example, the beginning tag <TITLE> instructs the browser to begin formatting/displaying the title, while the ending tag </TITLE> informs the browser to terminate the formatting function. HTML tags are case insensitive, thus <title> is equivalent to <TITLE>.

✳ HTML Level 2 basic markup tags

Document Identifier	<HTML> and </HTML>
Header	<HEAD> and </HEAD>
Title	<TITLE> Text of Document Title </TITLE> (The Document Title is displayed at the top of the Mosaic screen.)
Body Identifier	<BODY> and </BODY>
Headings	<H#>Text of heading</H#> (where # is a number between 1 and 6 to specify the heading level).
Paragraph	<P> (The browser separates paragraphs when a <P> tag is read. There is no closing tag associated with the paragraph tag.)
Anchor	<A HREF="filename"> hypertext link </A> (A simple hypertext reference to a file in the same directory as the current file.)
	<A HREF="pathname/filename"> hypertext link </A> (A relative hypertext reference to a file in a different directory than the current file.)
	<A HREF="URL"> hypertext link </A> (A hypertext reference to a file located on another server.) See Chapter 7 for details on URL formatting.
Naming anchor	<A N="younameit">TEXT</A> (This is a useful navigation technique for large documents that allows you to link to named anchors.)
Lists	HTML supports unnumbered, numbered, and definition lists.

An unnumbered list example:

```
<UL>
<LI>lions
<LI>tigers
</UL>
```

The output will look like:

- lions
- tigers

Below a numbered list example:

```
<OL>
<LI>lions
```

<LI>tigers

<LI>bears

</OL>

The output will look like:

1. lions
2. tigers
3. bears

Below a definition list example:

<DL>

<DT>Mosaic

<DD>Mosaic, a World Wide Web browser

<DT>World Wide Web

<DD>WWW (the initiative to create a universal, hypermedia-based method of access to information)

</DL>

The output will look like:

Mosaic

Mosaic, a World Wide Web browser

World Wide Web

WWW (the initiative to create a universal, hypermedia-based method of access to information)

Preformatted Text	<PRE> text to be displayed as-is</PRE> (Used to generate text in a fixed-width font.)
Address	<ADDRESS>whodunit@wherever.com</ADDRESS> (Generally used to specify the author of a document and a means to contact the author [e.g., an e-mail address].)
Inline graphics	<IMG SRC=image_URL ALIGN=direction ALT=alternate_text> (where image_URL is the same format as used in an anchor HREF). ALIGN attribute tells the browser where to align the text. ALT attribute defines alternate text to be displayed if the browser cannot display graphics.
Line Break	 (Forces an immediate line break.)
Rule	<HR> (Produces a horizontal rule line the width of the Mosaic window.)

Text Styles	<B>bold text</B> <I>italic text</I> <TT>typewriter text (fixed-width font)</TT>
Copyright symbol	©

Adding comments to an HTML document

Place the <!-- tag at the beginning of the line you wish to comment out, and close each line with the --> tag. Be aware that comments do not nest, and the sequence "--" should not appear inside a comment except as part of the closing --> tag. This technique should not be used to hide HTML that would otherwise be displayed to the user. Some browsers will pay attention to tags inside the comment and terminate the comment prematurely.

A primer providing an introduction to producing HTML documents is available at URL:

http://www.ncsa.uiuc.edu/General/Internet/WWW/HTMLPrimer.html

A plain text version of the primer is also available at URL:

ftp://ftp.ncsa.uiuc.edu/ncsapubs/WWW/HTMLPrimer.txt

A HTML Quick Reference Guide is available at the URL:

http://kuhttp.cc.ukans.edu/lynx_help/HTML_quick.html

Ian Graham's guide to HTML is available at URL:

http://www.utirc.utoronto.ca/HTMLdocs/NewHTML/htmlindex.html

Another useful HTML resource guide can be found at URL:

http://oneworld.wa.com/htmldev/devpage/dev-page1.html

Gareth Rees' Guide to Publishing on the World-Wide Web is available at URL:

http://www.cl.cam.ac.uk/users/gdr11/publish.html

The Web Developer's Journal covers subjects of interest to those using electronic means to communicate. It is available at URL:

http://www.awa.com/nct/software/eleclead.html

For information about new developments in HTML see the URL:

http://www.w3.org/hypertext/WWW/MarkUp/MarkUp.html

HTML authoring tools

HTML files are text files with an .html extension (or .htm due to PC file naming conventions). While you can use a simple editor to add HTML formatting tags to any text file, the process is tedious, time-consuming, and error-prone. Also, it is difficult to see how the documents you create will actually look when displayed by Mosaic. You might prefer to use a friendlier, graphical editor to create HTML documents. HTML editors can be broadly differentiated by the following features:

- A standalone software editing package.
- A document template that requires other software.
- A rules-checking editor that ensures the HTML you write is valid.
- A WYSIWYG editor that presents documents as they will appear in Mosaic (or close to it).
- A raw text HTML editor.

Standalone editors are self-contained pieces of software, not requiring any other software. Document templates use the template feature of existing software packages (such as Microsoft Word or WordPerfect) to turn the word processor into an HTML editor. You need a copy of the standalone software to make use of the templates.

Rule-based (checked) HTML editors treat HTML as a strict formatting convention. They require that you insert tags in correct places with all the required information. The benefit of such software is that you can be sure to create documents that can be parsed, though minor changes can be slightly more time-consuming. On the other hand, unchecked HTML editors do not make any attempt to verify whether tags are correct. There is nothing to stop you from placing a tag in the wrong place, or invalidating a tag by editing it incorrectly.

WYSIWYG (What You See Is What You Get) editors present the HTML as it will look on a browser. Most WYSIWYG editors assist you in writing HTML by plugging in the desired markup tags for you from a menu. Raw text editors present the HTML as plain text, making no attempt to render it in any way.

Many software filters and converters are available for translating existing documents to HTML from a wide variety of input formats, including mail, FrameMaker, PostScript, troff, LaTeX, Microsoft Word, WordPerfect, and RTF. Your results with these converters might vary. Not all of them are robust or foolproof. Travel these waters at your own risk. The good news, though, is that many commercial products are just beginning to be introduced that hold great promise as supported robust products. Comprehensive lists of tools are available at URLs:

http://www.ncsa.uiuc.edu/SDG/Software/Mosaic/Docs/faq-software.html#editors

http://www.w3.org/hypertext/WWW/Tools/Filters.html

http://www.cis.ohio-state.edu:80/hypertext/about_this_cobweb.html
http://www.nwu.edu/www-authoring.html

http://www.utirc.utoronto.ca/HTMLdocs/intro_tools.html

Also, visit the Yahoo subject catalog at URL http://www.yahoo.com/Computers/World_Wide_Web/Authoring for more pointers to HTML converters and editors.

Figure 10-2

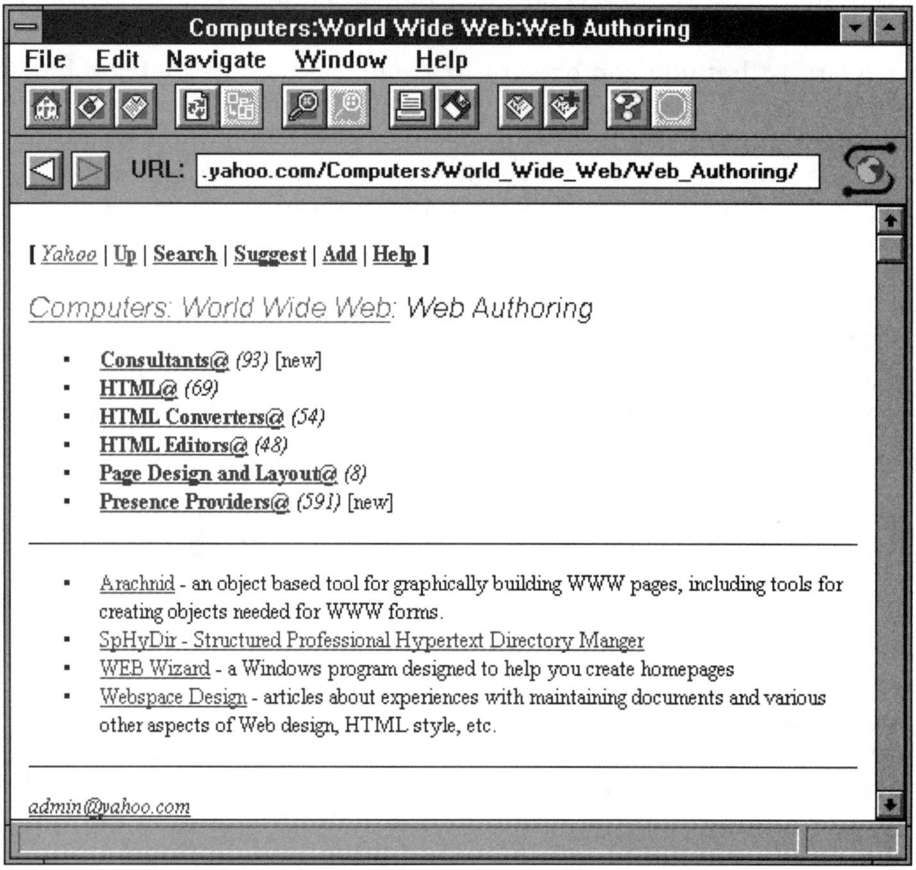

Yahoo's index of web-authoring tools © 1994–95 Yahoo.

Software for Microsoft Windows

HTML standalone editors

HoTMetaL, a checked WYSIWYG editor from SoftQuad, guides you in creating new HTML documents and in cleaning up old ones. HoTMetaL is available for both Microsoft Windows (shown in Fig.

10-3) and Sun SPARC systems. HoTMetaL Pro, a commercially supported version, is available for purchase from SoftQuad and its resellers. Refer to URLs:

http://www.sq.com

http://www.sq.com/sgm/html/html.htm

Figure 10-3

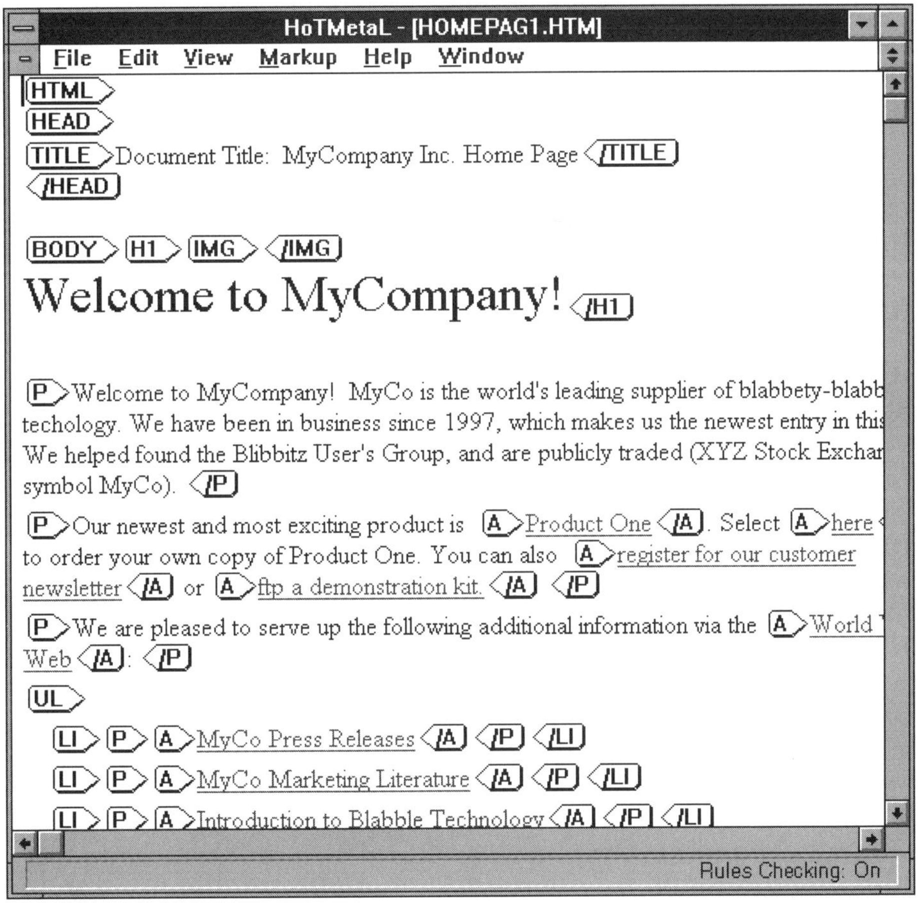

SoftQuad's HoTMetaL © 1995 SoftQuad, Inc.

The freeware version of HoTMetaL is also available for downloading at numerous mirror sites. If you can't get through to one, try another; don't give up! The following URLs are known HoTMetaL mirror sites:

U.S.A.

http://gatekeeper.dec.com/pub/net/infosys/NCSA/Web/html /hotmetal ftp://ftp.ncsa.uiuc.edu/Web/html/hotmetal

Canada

ftp://ftp.cs.concordia.ca/pub/www

Europe

ftp://ftp.ifi.uio.no/pub/SGML/HoTMetaL

ftp://doc.ic.ac.uk/pub/packages/WWW/ncsa/html/hotmetal

ftp://askhp.ask.uni-karlsruhe.de/pub/infosystems/www/ ncsa_mosaic/html/hotmetal

ftp://ftp.sunet.se/pub/www/Mosaic/html/hotmetal

ftp://ftp.uco.es/www ftp://olymp.wu-wien.ac.at/pub/sgml/ exeter/SoftQuad/hotmetal

HTML Assistant is an unchecked hypertext editor for Microsoft Windows for creating and editing HTML documents. In addition to its editing facilities it incorporates features that can help you organize and keep track of the Internet resources that you use. You can use Mosaic to view your documents while you are working on them, without leaving the editor. It minimizes typing and makes it easy to systematically collect and organize URLs. URLs can be saved to files and quickly retrieved for point-and-click insertion into documents. URLs saved in hotlists can be automatically copied and converted for point-and-click insertion into your own documents. Two versions are available. HTML Assistant (see Fig. 10-4) is freeware that is a full working version that will continue to be freely available, and new versions will be released from time to time. It is available at URL:

Figure 10-4

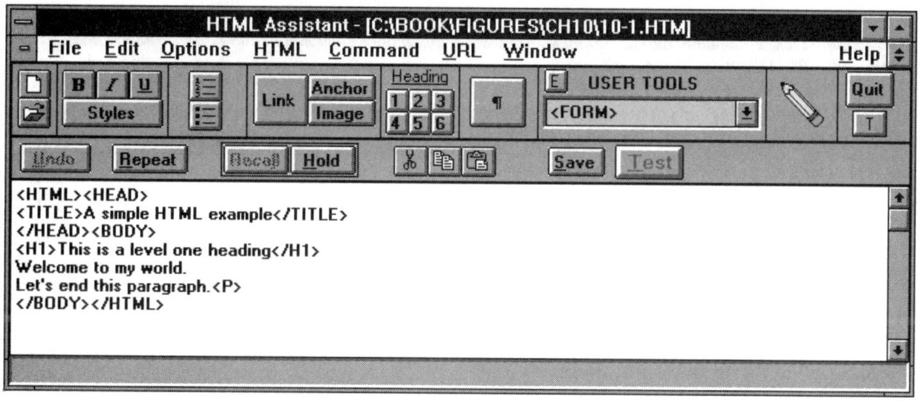

HTML Assistant

ftp://ftp.cs.dal.ca/htmlasst/htmlasst.zip

You will also need to get the file vbrun300.dll available from the same site. The most recent version of the FAQ can be obtained at URL:

ftp://ftp.cs.dal.ca/htmlasst/htmlafaq.txt.

HTML Assistant Pro is the commercially available version with additional features, including a printed manual called *Beginner's Guide to HTML*, an automatic HTML page creator, formatting filters, URL search features, and full support.

HTML HyperEdit (see Fig. 10-5) is an unchecked editor. Two features that make HTML HyperEdit stand out from the others are the background information on hypertext and an introduction to HTML authoring, using HTML HyperEdit. The former is a very brief introduction to the ideas behind hypermedia. The latter is a walk-through tutorial on creating HTML documents using the editor, which is a great idea for first time users and those unfamiliar with HTML. Unfortunately, the brief tutorial doesn't cover enough to be regarded as a basic HTML primer, so other sources will need to be referenced when you first begin creating/editing HTML. HyperEdit is available at URL:

http://www.curtin.edu.au/computing/packages/htmledit/home.htm

Figure 10-5

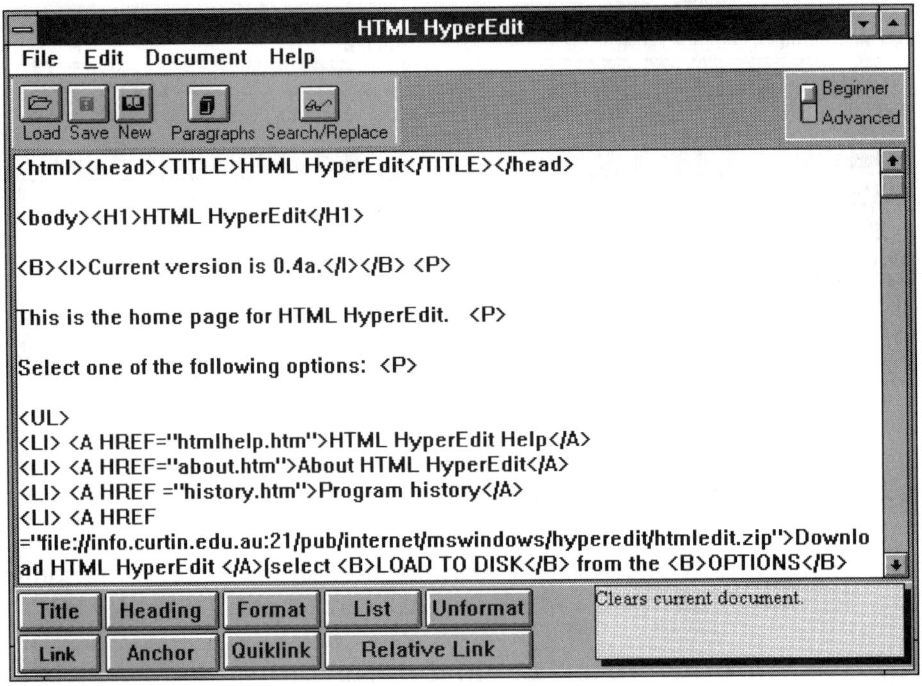

HTML HyperEdit

HTMLed (see Fig. 10-6) is a raw HTML text editor that provides no way of checking to make sure that your HTML fits the specifications. Creating large systems of documents is made easier with the browse function of the link creator, which allows you to easily locate and link to other documents that are stored on the computer. HTMLed provides a testing function that loads your document onto a browser. The package also allows for conversion of Mosaic bookmark files to the HTML format. HTMLed is a well-designed and easy to use piece of software for editing raw HTML. HTMLed is available at URL:

http://src.doc.ic.ac.uk/packages/WWW/tools/editing/ms-windows

HTML Writer is an unchecked HTML editor (shown in Fig. 10-7). A feature that makes HTML Writer stand out from the others is the consistent effort that has been made to ease the difficulty of writing the more complex tags. The URL Builder, which takes you through the steps of creating a URL, is an example. Similarly, the creation of forms,

Figure 10-6

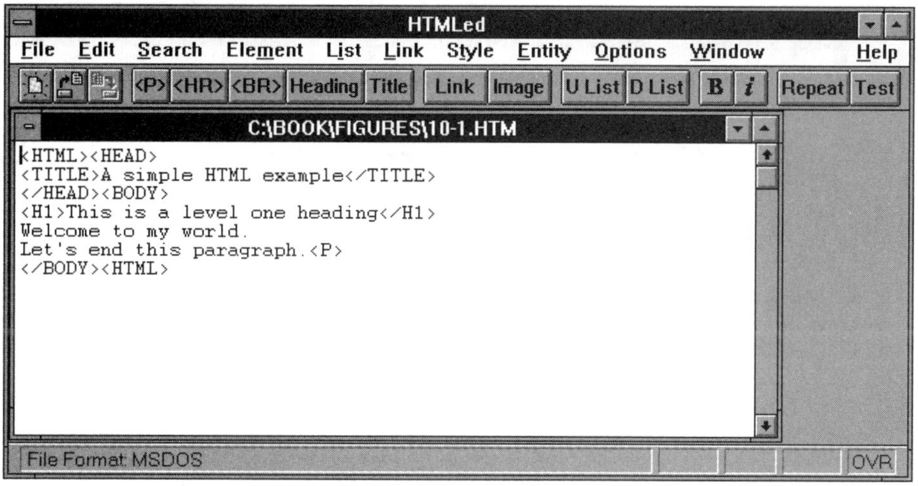

HTMLed

Figure 10-7

HTML Writer

insertion of images, and other tasks are made easy by the use of well-designed dialog boxes. You will also need to get the file vbrun300.dll, available from the same site. HTML Writer is available at URL:

http://lal.cs.byu.edu/people/nosack

WEB Wizard, AKA the Duke of URL, by the Atra Software Group, is a Microsoft Windows program that graphically steps you through building a home page. Screens (such as those shown in Fig. 10-8) prompt you for the important HTML elements. It is available at URL:

http://www.halcyon.com/webwizard/welcome.html

Figure 10-8

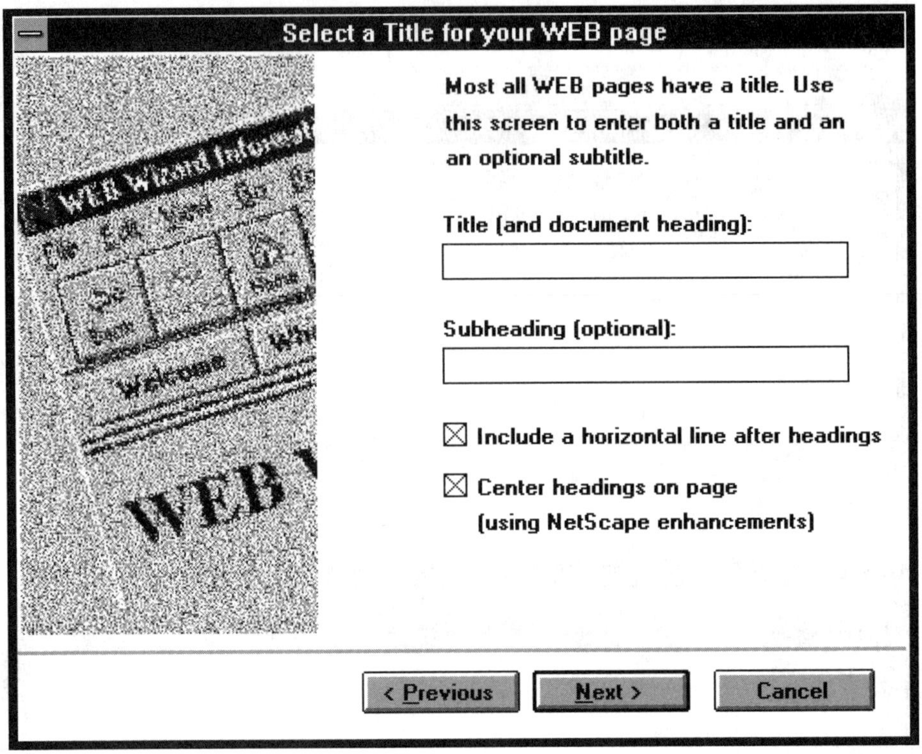

Web Wizard from the Atra Software Group

Word processing templates

Templates are generally implemented as macros for popular word processing packages, such as Microsoft Word or WordPerfect. Each requires that you have a copy of the word processing software to use the template.

ANT_HTML.DOT and **ANT_PLUS.DOT** are Microsoft Word for Windows 6.0 templates designed to convert Word documents into HTML documents in a WYSIWYG environment. ANT templates are available at URL:

ftp://ftp.einet.net/einet/pc/ANT_DEMO.ZIP

CU_HTML.DOT is a Microsoft Word for Windows document template developed by the Computer Services Centre of Chinese

University of Hong Kong. It allows users to create HTML documents in Word and generate an HTML file. You can assign different formatting tags to the paragraphs by simply pointing and clicking. You can also insert inline images and specify hyperlinks by choosing the target file from a dialog box. Inline images in your HTML documents will appear in the Word document. By using the template, you can create HTML documents with little knowledge of the HTML syntax. Existing word processor features, such as spell checking, printing, cut and paste, and macro automation can be used. CU_HTML is available at URL:

http://www.cuhk.hk/csc/cu_html/cu_html.htm

GT_HTML.DOT is a set of Microsoft Word for Windows macros developed by the Georgia Tech Research Institute to facilitate HTML document authoring. The macros are contained in a document template that provides a WYSIWYG authoring environment. GT_HTML is available at URL:

http://www.gatech.edu/word_html/release.htm

Microsoft Internet Assistant (Fig. 10-9) enables anyone familiar with Word to write HTML documents. You create HTML documents in Word's own file format with drag-and-drop ease, creating hyperlinks between Word documents. Microsoft will bundle Internet

Figure 10-9

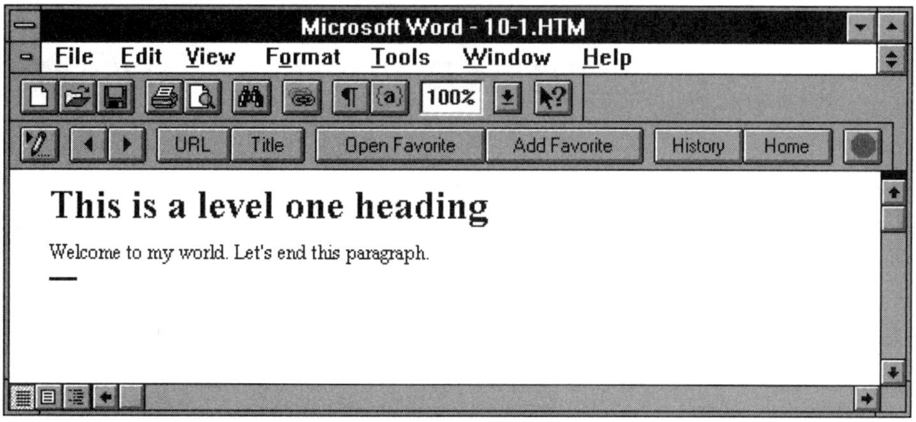

Microsoft Internet Assistant

Assistant with the Windows 95 version of Word. For more information, consult the What's New heading under the URL:

http://www.microsoft.com

WebAuthor, from Quarterdeck Office Systems, is a checked HTML authoring system for Microsoft Word 6.0 for Windows. (See Fig. 10-10.) WebAuthor's features include utilities:

- To review existing HTML documents and prompt users for correction of HTML syntax errors
- To save documents in Word format for easy editing, and then to save them as HTML documents when they are ready to be posted on the Web
- To filter for embedded graphics
- To save documents with the same name when saving as both an HTML and a Word document (i.e., qdeck.htm and qdeck.doc)
- To save documents as ASCII text to support posting to any platform

Figure 10-10

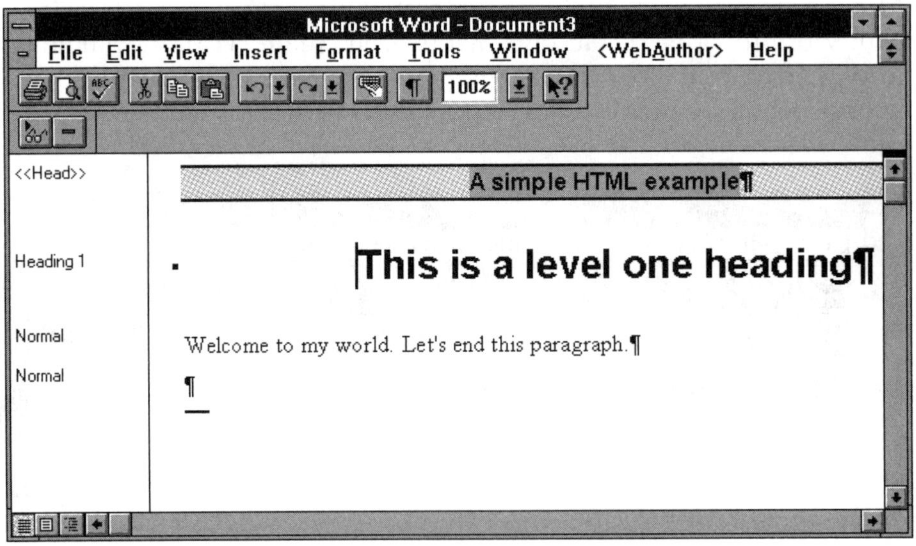

Quarterdeck Office Systems' WebAuthor

Quarterdeck has plans for a WordPerfect version. For more information see URL:

http:///www.qdeck.com

Novell Internet Publisher is a freeware Web browser, and a WordPerfect HTML template for converting and creating documents. The Internet Publisher Pro commercial version will include additional macros to automate document conversion, along with a full TCP/IP protocol stack. For more information on Internet Publisher, refer to URL:

http://www.novell.com/wp/busapps/epub

PC-Write HTML is a package of macros for editing HTML documents with the PC-Write editor. PC-Write is a shareware editor for MS-DOS that will also run in Windows as a DOS task, and is available at URL:

ftp://www.ucc.ie/pub/pcw4.zip

SGML TagWizard, from NICE Technologies, is an HTML authoring system for Microsoft Word 6.0 for Windows. It is a template that adds a handy tool bar and menu extensions to Word. You can paste any graphic into Word, in any format. Simply select the graphic and WebWizard will convert it to GIF format and insert an anchor tag pointing to the new GIF file. You can import existing HTML documents into Word. You can download pages from the Web and use them as guides for your own pages. A fully functional evaluation version of WebWizard is available at URLs:

ftp://ftp.webcom.com/pub/nicetech/Downloads

http://infolane.com/infolane/nice/nice.html

✻ Document conversion tools

Cyberleaf, a product of Interleaf, can be used to convert Microsoft Word, WordPerfect, FrameMaker, and Interleaf to HTML. Use your

Figure 10-11

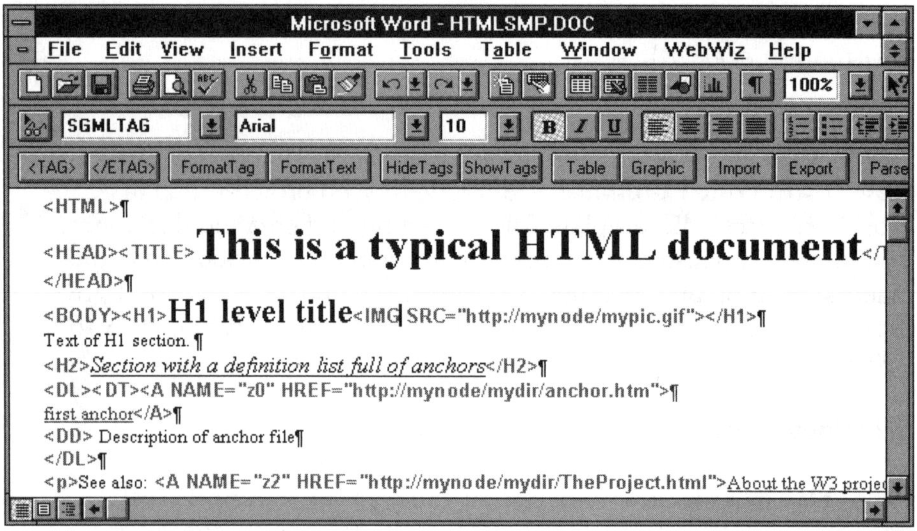

NICE Technologies SGML WebWiz

favorite word processor to create documents as you normally would, then use Cyberleaf to transform those documents to HTML. Cyberleaf is available at URL:

http://www.ileaf.com/ip.html

HTMLCon converts HTML files to text for viewing and printing. HTMLCon operates under DOS or under any program capable of providing a DOS session and using COMMAND.COM as a command interpreter. After processing the input document (.htm), output can be displayed on a viewer or editor of your choice. HTMLCon is available at URL:

ftp://ftp.crl.com/ftp/users/ro/mikekell/ftp/htmlcon.zip

RTFTOHTM is a Microsoft Word for Windows template and conversion tool available at URL:

ftp://oak.oakland.edu/SimTel/win3/winword/htmtl090.zip

TILE (Tool for Internet/Lotus Exchange) converts Lotus Notes databases to HTML documents. It is available at URL:

http://www.shelby.com/pub/tile/home.html

wptohtml is a macro package for converting WordPerfect files to HTML. These macros work with the DOS versions of these programs only. There are two packages available at URLs:

ftp://oak.oakland.edu/SimTel/msdos/wordperf/wpt51d10.zip

ftp://oak.oakland.edu/SimTel/msdos/wordperf/wpt60d10.zip

wp2html is a WordPerfect to HTML translator, available at URL:

ftp://src.doc.ic.ac.uk/computing/information-systems/www/tools/translators/wp2ht ml-macro/html.wpm.gz

Software for UNIX & the X Window System

HTML standalone editors

A.S.H.E. (A Simple HTML Editor) is a WYSIWYG, unchecked editor (see Fig. 10-12) available at URLs:

ftp://ftp.cs.rpi.edu/pub/puninj/ASHE/README.html

http://www.cs.rpi.edu/~puninj/TALK/head.html

GNU Emacs users can use the Emacs editor and html-helper-mode for HTML editing available at URL:

http://goya.ucs.ed.ac.uk/General/epoch.html

HoTMetaL is described fully under the heading *HTML standalone editors* on page 216.

Figure 10-12

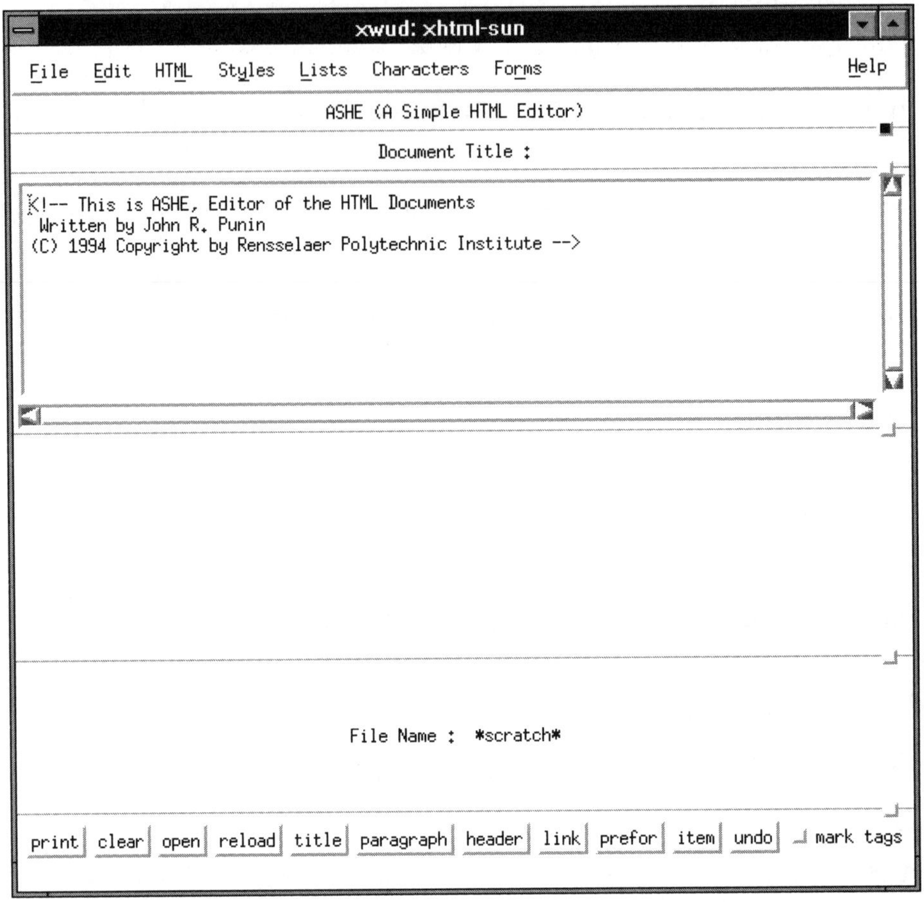

A Simple HTML Editor

htmltext is an HTML rules-checking editor developed at the City University in London, which uses the Andrew toolkit and runs under the X Window System. It provides a WYSIWYG interface for composing HTML documents, including support for inline images (e.g., GIF, JPEG, and XBM). It is available at URL:

http://web.cs.city.ac.uk/homes/njw/htmltext//htmltext.html

Phoenix (Fig. 10-13) is a WYSIWYG rules-checking HTML editor for the X Window System that insulates the user from direct control of

Figure 10-13

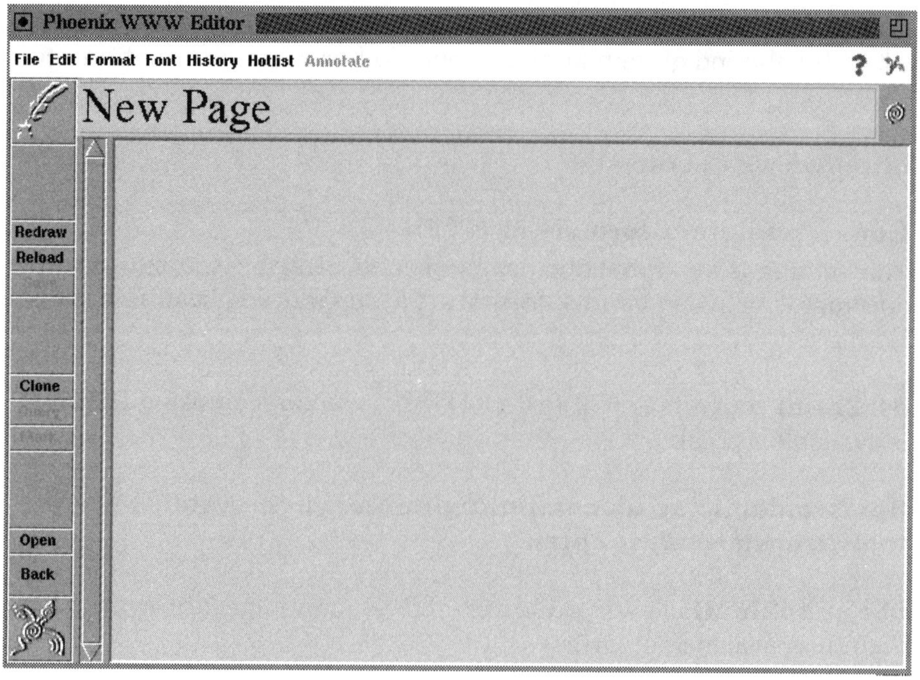

Phoenix

the HTML tags. Phoenix has been tested on Solaris 2.3 and SunOS 4.1.3. It is available at URL:

http://www.bsd.uchicago.edu/ftp/pub/phoenix

tkHTML is a simple unchecked HTML editor based on the Tcl script language and the Tk toolkit for the X Window System. It allows quick composition and editing of HTML documents, as well as a rapid way of converting existing text documents to the HTML format. To get full functionality of tkHTML you must install the wwwish interpreter that has extensions especially for HTML and the HTTP protocol. You will find both tkHTML and wwwish at URLs:

ftp://ftp.u.washington.edu/public/roland/tkHTML

ftp://sunsite.unc.edu/pub/packages/infosystems/WWW/tools/editing/unix/tkhtml

WebMagic Author from Silicon Graphics, Inc. is a powerful HTML editor for the Indigo family of computers. For more information see URL:

http://www.sgi.com

✳ Converting other formats to HTML

This section is an alphabetic listing of tools available to convert documents between various formats. We suggest you scan this section for those formats of interest to you.

asc2html converts ASCII text to HTML, while recognizing URLs. It is available at URL:

ftp://src.doc.ic.ac.uk/computing/information-systems/www/tools/translators/asc2html

bbc_man2html allows you to view UNIX man pages through the Web. It is available at URL:

http://www.stuff.com/~bcutter/home/programs/bbc_man2html.html

Cyberleaf can be used to convert Microsoft Word, WordPerfect, FrameMaker, and Interleaf documents to HTML. You will find a description and its URL on page 225.

edc2html is a Perl script that generates an HTML document to allow navigation through the structure of a FrameMaker (MIF) FrameBuilder Element Catalog. It is available at URL:

http://www.oac.uci.edu/indiv/ehood/edc2html.doc.html

Frame2html, the work of Jon Stephenson von Tetzchner at Telenor Research, converts FrameMaker documents to HTML and is available at URLs:

http://www.w3.org/hypertext/WWW/Tools/fm2html.html

hl2html converts a Mosaic hotlist to HTML. It is available at URLs:

http://www.oac.uci.edu/indiv/ehood/

http://www.cithep.caltech.edu/~kelsey/hl2html.html

hl2Khtml is a HotList-to-Kool HTML generator that allows you to browse your site's hotlists by person or sort hotlists by URL, title or date. It is available at URL:

http://www.unipress.com/cgi-bin/hl2Khtml

HTH (Hotlist To HTML) allows you to put the items in a list, which you can sort or add the dates items were added to the list. It is available at URL:

http://www.cc.wwu.edu/~n9146070/hth.html

html+tables creates pre-formatted text tables from HTML+ Table definitions. It is available at URL:

http://www.stuff.com/~bcutter/home/programs/html_tables.html

htxp is a preprocessor that provides time-saving features for writing HTML files, including user-specified abbreviations and built-in and user-definable macros. It is available at URL:

http://www.mcs.anl.gov/home/kwong/htxp1.html

html-parser is an HTML parser written in Perl. This can be used to convert HTML into other formats. It is available at URL:

http://dri.cornell.edu/pub/davis/html-parser.html

htmltoc is a Perl script to automatically generate a table of contents for HTML documents. It is available at URL:

http://www.oac.uci.edu/indiv/ehood

html2asc is a shell script to strip HTML (and SGML) markup from documents. It is available at URL:

ftp://src.doc.ic.ac.uk/computing/information-systems/www/tools/translators/html2asc.gz

html2ps converts HTML to PostScript and has many options for controlling the layout, size of fonts, margins, and page orientation. It is available at URL:

http://www.tdb.uu.se/~jan/html2ps.html

Hyperlatex is a package that allows you to use a subset of LaTeX to prepare documents in HTML and, at the same time, to describe a fine printed document with all the possibilities of LaTeX. It is available at URL:

http://www.cs.ruu.nl/people/otfried/html/hyperlatex.html

Hypermail is a program that takes a file of mail messages in UNIX mailbox format and generates a set of cross-referenced HTML documents. It is available at URLs:

http://gummo.stanford.edu/html/hypermail/hypermail.html

http://www.eit.com/software/hypermail/hypermail.html

Indexmaker is a Perl script that produces an index for a virtual document consisting of a number of HTML files in a single directory. It is available at URL:

http://hopf.math.nwu.edu/docs/utility.html#indexmaker

LaTeX2HTML, a LaTeX to HTML converter, shows the complex LaTeX formatting, for example for mathematics, and it also has a set of iconic images, which are included for navigation and for marking footnotes and references. It is available at URL:

http://cbl.leeds.ac.uk/nikos/tex2html/doc/latex2html/latex2html.html

l2x parses LaTeX documents and produces HTML. It is available at URL:

http://www.w3.org/hypertext/WWW/Tools/l2x.html

mail2html is a simple mail to HTML converter, available at URL:

http://www.oac.uci.edu/indiv/ehood/mail2html.doc.html

man2html is a Perl script used to convert UNIX-formatted man pages to HTML. It is available from URLs:

file://ftp.vifp.monash.edu.au/pub/src/infosystems/www

http://www.oac.uci.edu/indiv/ehood/man2html.doc.html

mif.pl is a Perl library to parse FrameMaker Interchange Format (MIF), designed to be used by filters. It is available at URL:

http://www.oac.uci.edu/indiv/ehood/

miftran converts from FrameMaker MIF to other formats (including HTML). It is available at URLs:

ftp://ftp.alumni.caltech.edu/pub/mcbeath/web/miftran/miftran.tgz

http://www.w3.org/hypertext/WWW/Tools/miftran.html

mm2html is an nroff mm-to-HTML Perl script based heavily on ms2html and fm2html. It is available at URL:

ftp://cs.ucl.ac.uk/darpa/mm2html

ms2html converts from the Troff MS macro set to HTML. It is available at URL:

ftp://src.doc.ic.ac.uk/computing/information-systems/www/tools/translators/ms2html.pl.gz

PNUTS (pronounced *peanuts*) is an acronym for Previous, Next, Up, Top, and Search. It is a Perl script that takes as an argument the name of a file describing the hierarchical structure of a group of HTML files constituting a single virtual document. It is available at URL:

http://hopf.math.nwu.edu/docs/utility.html#pnuts

ps2html converts PostScript documents to HTML. This is a Perl script package that converts PostScript to plain text. To use this code you will also need a PostScript interpreter, such as Ghostscript. ps2html is available at URL:

http://stasi.bradley.edu/ftp/pub/ps2html/home.html

qt2www is a Perl script to convert QuarkXPress text files to HTML. This is a general-purpose conversion utility; it reads in a map file that lists the Quark Tags used in the source file and shows how they should be translated into HTML. It is available at URL:

http://the-tech.mit.edu/~jeremy/qt2www.html

rosetta-man converts formatted UNIX manual pages to HTML and other formats. It is available at URL:

ftp://src.doc.ic.ac.uk/computing/information-systems/www/tools/translators/rosetta-man

rtftohtml produces HTML from Rich Text Format (RTF) documents containing graphics, tables, text, and equations. RTF is a document-formatting language developed by Microsoft. Many word processing packages (e.g., Word, WordPerfect, and FrameMaker) can read or write RTF format files. rtftohtml runs on DOS or UNIX, and will translate documents produced on DOS or Windows. Each picture in the RTF source will be saved as a separate Windows Metafile Format (.wmf). In addition, links will be created within the output file to the graphic files with the extension .gif. You will have to use graphic conversion software to translate the WMF graphics to GIF format. rtftohtml is available at URL:

ftp://ftp.cray.com/src/WWWstuff/RTF/rtftohtml_overview.html

sorthl is a Perl script written by Earl Hood to sort a Mosaic hotlist. It is available at URL:

http://www.oac.uci.edu/indiv/ehood/

texi2html is a Perl script that converts GNU's Texinfo files to HTML. The program takes Texinfo files and produces HTML files. The quality of the output is close to the printed output. It is available at URL:

http://asis01.cern.ch/infohtml/texi2html.html

Text to HTML is a Perl script that converts plain text files to HTML. It is available at URLs:

http://www.seas.upenn.edu/~mengwong/txt2html.html

http://www.cs.wustl.edu/~seth/txt2html

troff2html converts troff markup to HTML. It is available at URL:

http://cornelius.ucsf.edu/~troyer/troff2html/

WebMaker processes FrameMaker files or books and generates a set of HTML files. It is available at URL:

http://www.cern.ch/WebMaker

WebWorks is a product of Quadralay, which converts documents, including FrameMaker (MIF) and RTF files, to HTML. It runs under Microsoft Windows and UNIX. Information is available at URL:

http://www.quadralay.com/products/products.html

Winh2htm.pl is a Perl script for converting Mosaic hotlists to HTML. It has several options, including the ability to convert and keep intact the submenu hierarchy. Winh2html is available at URL:

http://www.envmed.rochester.edu/wwwrlp/html/winh2htm.htm

w3new is a Perl script that will extract a list of URLs from either your Mosaic hotlist or an HTML document. It will then retrieve the modification dates for each document listed, and it will output an HTML file with the URLs sorted by their last modification time, creating a What's New list of http URLs. It is available at URL:

http://www.stuff.com/~bcutter/home/programs/w3new/w3new.html

Checking HTML documents for errors

An HTML Validation Service is available that will check HTML documents for errors through a forms interface. You are encouraged to set up the program on your own system if you make heavy use of the form. This service (shown in Fig. 10-14A and B) is available at URL:

http://www.halsoft.com/html-val-svc

Figure 10-14

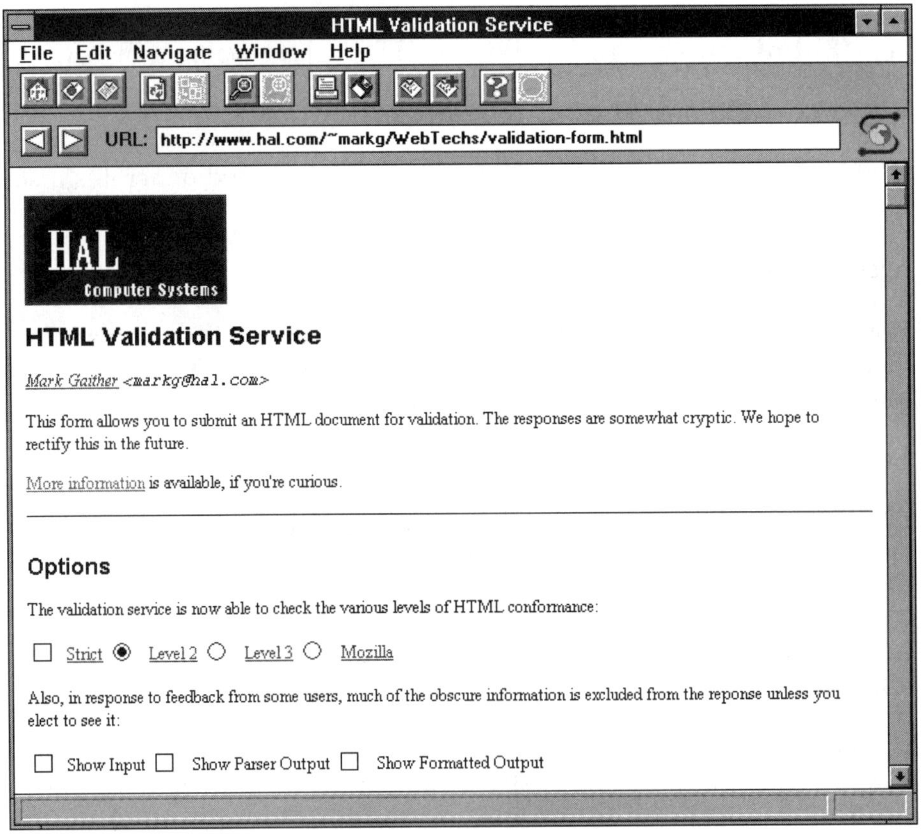

(A) HTML Validation Service

Figure 10-14

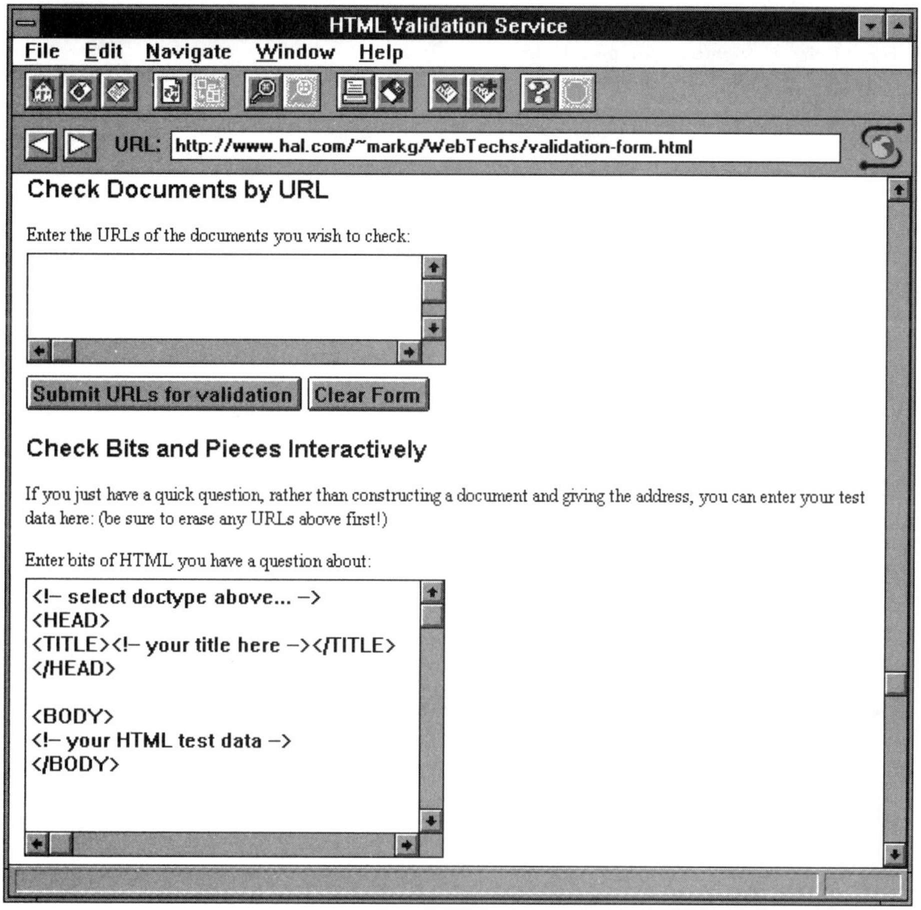

(B) HTML Validation Service (scroll down page)

Weblint is a Perl script that checks HTML documents for errors and is available at URLs:

http://www.khoros.unm.edu/staff/neilb/weblint.html

ftp://ftp.khoros.unm.edu/pub/perl/www/weblint-1.005.tar.gz

You can try out weblint on your documents through a forms interface (shown in Fig. 10-15A and B) at URL:

http://www.unipress.com/weblint

Figure 10-15

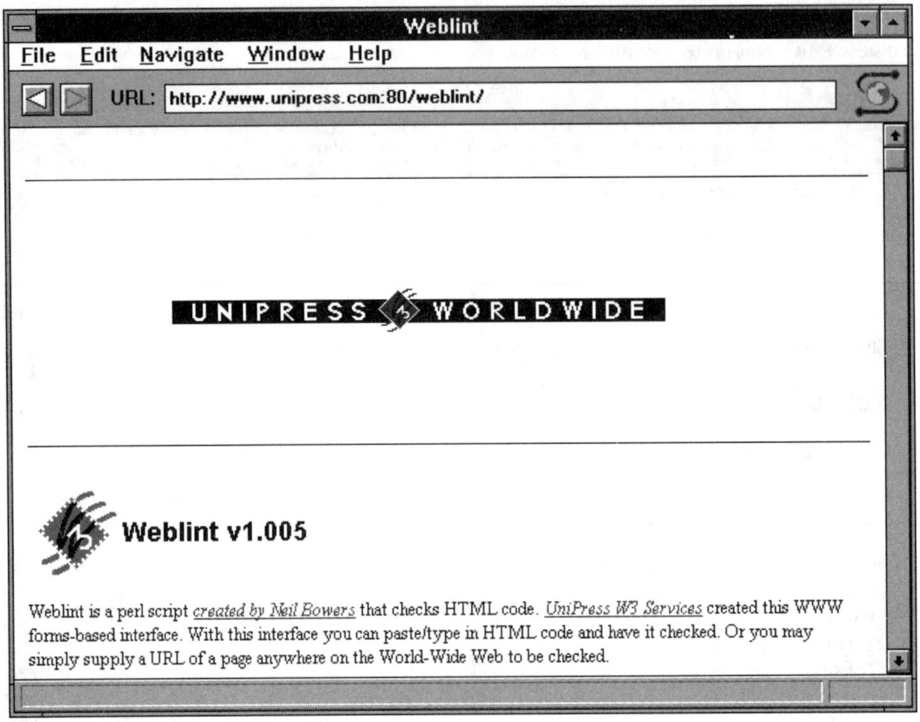

(A) UniPress' Weblint Service

Webtest is a UNIX tool that will check the links in your documents for hyperlinks to nonexistent resources. This is an especially useful tool, given the highly mobile nature of resources on the Web. It is available at URL:

ftp://ftp.eit.com/pub/wsk/doc/README.verify_links

The HTML Check Toolkit for UNIX is available to make maintaining HTML documents easier. The toolkit is available for most UNIX platforms at the URL:

http://www.halsoft.com/html-tk

Figure 10-15

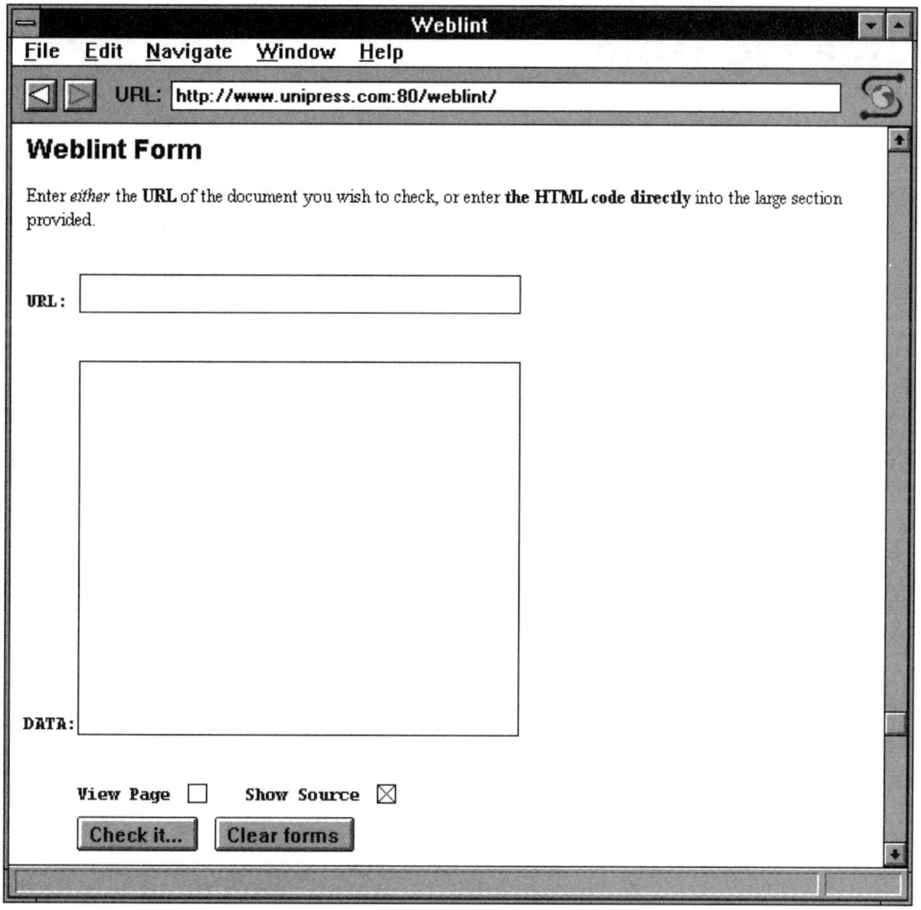

(B) UniPress' Weblint Service (scroll down page)

Advanced HTML tricks

You might not be able to accomplish all you want with the existing version of HTML alone. In this section we introduce you to forms, tables, mail, and graphical image maps as alternatives for presenting information and communicating with the information consumer.

Creating tables

Tables will be a standard feature in HTML Level 3. Unfortunately, at the time this book was written, HTML Level 3 was not widely supported by Mosaic browsers. However, there is a way to use HTML Level 3 markup tags (<tbl> </tbl>) now and convert them automatically to HTML Level 2 preformatted text. This will allow you to design proper tables and install those pages directly when table support arrives in the majority of clients. For a tutorial on creating tables in HTML refer to URL:

http://www.ncsa.uiuc.edu/SDG/Software/Mosaic/Tables/tutorial.html

For a Perl script conversion utility refer to URL:

http://www.stuff.com/~bcutter/home/programs/html_tables.html

Creating fill-out forms

The forms capability extends the Web to a two-way communications vehicle. A form consists of areas of the screen in which the user can input data. Using forms, the user can supply information to the Web sites they access. The data the user enters is sent to an HTTP server that can run a script or program to process the data in an appropriate fashion. Writing an HTML form is easy, but the form doesn't accomplish anything until you configure a Common Gateway Interface (CGI) program on the server side to process the input. Refer to Chapter 12 for more information on gateways.

Common uses of forms include providing feedback on WWW service to administrators, requesting information, even online ordering as shown in Fig. 10-16. Many of the search tools discussed in Chapter 9 allow you to identify search terms and set search parameters through a forms interface. For information on creating HTML forms see URLs:

Figure 10-16

Pizza Hut's order form

http://www.ncsa.uiuc.edu/SDG/Software/Mosaic/Docs/fill-out-forms/overview.html

http://kuhttp.cc.ukans.edu/info/forms/forms-intro.html

http://www.pizzahut.com/comments.html

GetComments is a more general package, also written in Perl, which can handle many different types of comment forms available at URL:

http://everest.cs.ucdavis.edu/~hoagland/getcomments.html

Send mail

You can simply create a link in your HTML document using a mailto: URL that looks like this:

<A HREF="mailto:me@my.address">Send Me Mail</A>

This works great for browsers that support the mailto: URL, but not all browsers support it.

Mailto is a Mail gateway that can be used as a replacement for the mailto: URL scheme by utilizing a form interface. You can get it at URL:

http://seclab/cs.ucdavis.edu/~hoagland/getcomments

There is also a package written in Perl, known as the **WWW Mailto Gateway**, available at URL:

http://www-bprc.mps.ohio-state.edu/mailto/mailto_info.html

Graphical information map

An image map (sometimes referred to as a clickable image) is an inline image in an HTML document. When you click on an area of the image, a link is activated. An excellent image map example (see Fig. 10-17) can be seen at URL:

http://pubweb.parc.xerox.com/map

Click on an area of the map to focus in on successively smaller regions.

Using image maps requires that you create a map file and tell the server about the map file. The way to accomplish this varies, depending on your server and browser. Enhanced Mosaic supports client-side image mapping that allows users to follow graphical maps stored locally. Refer to your server documentation or contact your

Figure 10-17

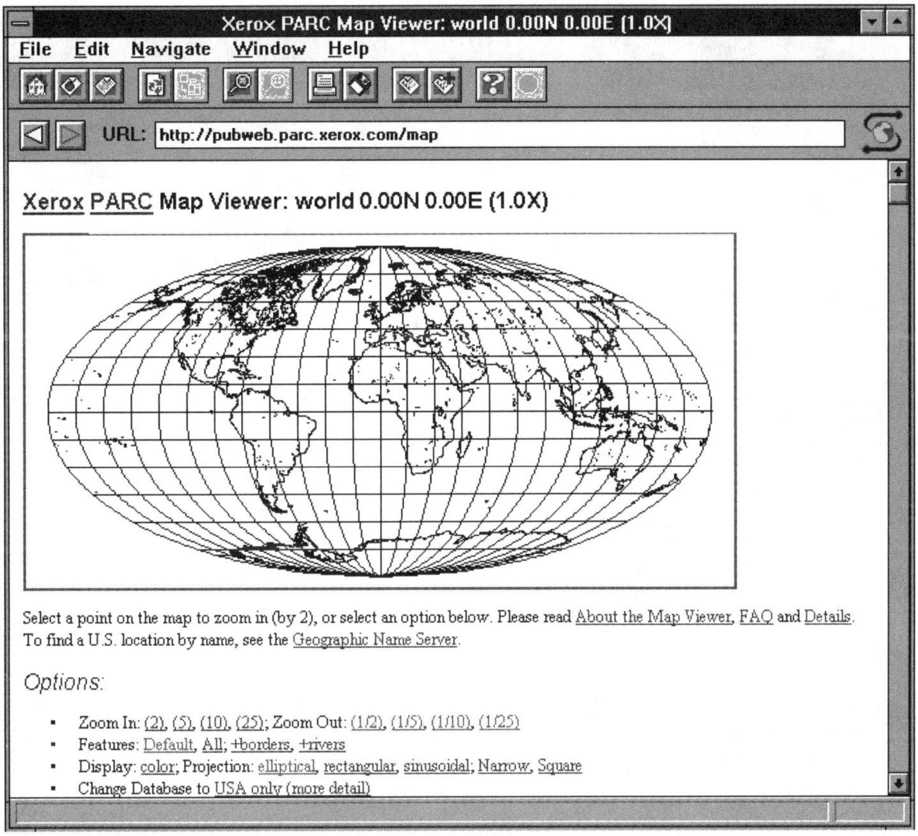

Xerox PARC Map Viewer

Web Server administrator. You can read about image maps and the NCSA server at the URL:

http://hoohoo.ncsa.uiuc.edu/docs/tutorials/imagemapping.html

Mapedit (see Fig. 10-18) is a WYSIWYG image map editing tool for Microsoft Windows and the X Window System available from URL:

http://sunsite.unc.edu/boutell/mapedit/mapedit.html

MapMaker is an X Window System tool that can turn the miniature images created by xv's Visual Schnauzer into an image map. This is

Figure 10-18

Mapedit

useful if you would like to make an entire directory of images available, but note that you should also make textual links to allow those with text-based browsers to download the images for external viewing. It is available from URL:

http://icg.stwing.upenn.edu/~mengwong/mapmaker.html

Glorglox advanced image mapper software for the X Window System lets you make clickable maps with organic and/or discontinuous shapes very easily. It is available at URL:

http://www.uunet.ca/~tomr/glorglox

Summary

It's time to congratulate yourself. You have now graduated to the level of Web publisher with the basic knowledge under your belt to begin to create HTML documents. Are you prepared to take the next step? If so, proceed to Chapter 11 to learn techniques for adding the glitz to your documents. We will introduce you to the intriguing world of multimedia information presentation.

11

Multimedia basics—Adding pizzazz

CHAPTER 11

THE simple definition of multimedia is the integration of more than one medium. Today's powerful computers enable the integration of electronic media combining text, graphics, imaging, animation, video, modeling, and sound. The combination of computers, networks, software, and multimedia provide a powerful vehicle for multidisciplinary collaboration. Learning to interact effectively in media space could open opportunities for creative communications and collaboration.

As you begin to develop multimedia information for consumption by Mosaic users, there are a few things you need to keep in mind.

- The size of the files.
- The dimensions of the display screen.
- The data formats and software needed to decode the information.
- The number of connections and transfers between server and client.

Content providers must be cognizant of the size of the images they provide. The amount of time required to transfer an image, audio, or video file is a critical concern because of the large number of users who might be on slow-speed lines.

The physical size of images should be able to fit within the limits of most displays. One useful way to reduce the size of images on a page is to use thumbnail (postage-stamp size) images hyperlinked to the full-size images. Thumbnail images take considerably less time to download and display. Another option is to provide a clue to the viewer regarding the size of such files, permitting him to decide if he can wait that long for an image to download. Most personal computer displays are 13 to 15 inches wide and can display 640 by 480 pixels. This translates to a window size with a limit of about 500 pixels. To prevent images from spilling off the edges of the window, limit inline graphics to a width of 472 pixels.

Mosaic is open to graphics standards, and thus images might be represented in many different formats. The formats the various browsers support will vary. In practice, the graphics formats you use will be influenced by the availability of support in browsers, the image quality, and whether the format is an open standard or a commercial one subject to copyright or patent fees. For hypertext, HTML is mandated to be supported by all WWW browsers, but for graphics there is no similar standard. An inline image is a graphic (GIF, XBM of JPEG format) that is displayed inline with the text document by Mosaic. An image stored as a separate file (GIF or JPEG) is viewed through an external viewer when the user clicks on a hypertext link. The supported image formats depend upon the capabilities of the installed external viewers.

A new connection is established between client and server for every image to be downloaded. Therefore, including many different images in a single document might be inefficient and slow.

Multimedia types

Following is a comprehensive list of the multimedia file extension types recognized by Mosaic.

Table of Multimedia File Extensions

.au	Sun sound
.avi	MS Video for Windows Audio/Video Interleaved Format
.gif	Graphic Interexchange Format
.html, .htm	HTML document
.jpeg, .jpe, .jpg	Joint Photographic Experts Group
.mid	Music Instrument Digital Interface
.mov, .qt	QuickTime video
.mpeg, .mpe, .mpg	Moving Picture Expert Group
.pdf	Portable Document Format
.ps	PostScript file
.snd	Sun sound
.tiff, .tif	Tag Image File Format
.txt	plain text
.voc	Soundblaster sound
.wav	Microsoft Windows sound
.xbm	X Window System bitmap image

Text file extensions

A great deal of information on the Internet is stored in text format. Such files include full text articles, electronic journals, books, novels, Internet guides, computer software manuals, computer standards, and government documents, plus others. Text files are stored in ASCII format that you can read directly from your computer screen. You can display these files on your screen, download them to your hard or floppy disks, and/or edit them with an editor or any word processor. Mosaic can view text files without the assistance of external viewers.

Compressed text files

Many text files are compressed to save space and transmission time. Compressed files are binary files. You cannot read them on your screen with your text editor or your word processor unless you decompress them. The most popular compression standards used to compress text files are .Z, .zip, .gz, etc. Mosaic will download these files as binary type and use corresponding decompressing software to unpack them.

PostScript

PostScript is a proprietary page-description language developed by Adobe Systems, Inc. PostScript gives you the power and flexibility to create and produce virtually any document with photographic-quality resolution. The PostScript language encompasses all four of the basic elements of the printed page: text, graphics, images, and color. Many applications include printer definitions for PostScript printers. However, often the PostScript produced by applications has a lot of un-optimized header macro definition that tends to create enormous files. You can download a PostScript file in ASCII mode, and send it directly to a PostScript laser printer or any device that contains a PostScript interpreter. Use of the PostScript standard is free. For more information on PostScript refer to URL:

http://www.adobe.com

To read or display a PostScript file on your screen you need a PostScript reader. Free software, such as Ghostview and Ghostscript, is available to display PostScript on your screen. Ghostview is a graphical interface for Microsoft Windows, and is available at URL:

ftp://prep.ai.mit.edu/pub/gnu/ghostview-1.5.tar.gz

Ghostscript (see Fig. 11-1) allows pages to be viewed or printed on an X Window System display and is available at URL:

ftp://prep.ai.mit.edu/pub/gnu/ghostscript-2.6.1.tar.gz

Figure 11-1

Ghostscript

Acrobat Portable Document Format

The Portable Document Format (PDF) is the native format for Adobe Systems' new Adobe Acrobat family of products. PDF is a format for representing text and graphics in a device-independent format. To view PDF files you need Acrobat Reader or Acrobat Exchange installed on your system. Acrobat Reader is free software and is available at URL:

http://www.adobe.com

Figure 11-2

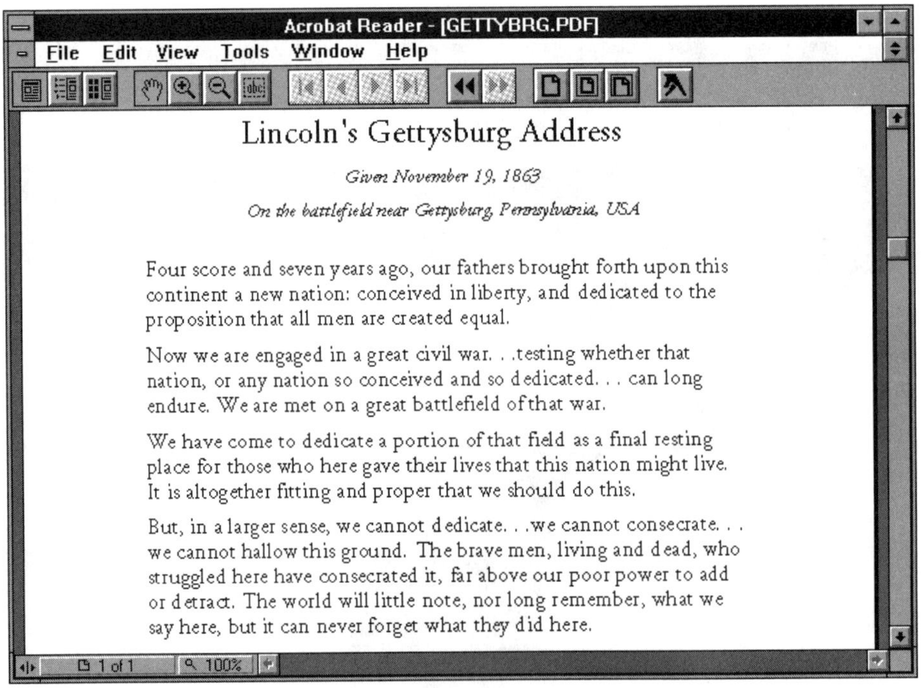

Adobe Acrobat © 1994-95 Adobe Systems, Inc.

Graphics basics

To display graphics, your computer must have a video display system. This typically consists of a monitor and a video card. The capabilities of your video display are important if you want to see quality pictures on your screen.

A digital image is a picture converted to numerical form so that it can be stored, manipulated, and displayed by a computer. Digital images are made up of pixels, short for picture elements. A pixel is a tiny dot, the smallest unit of measure on the screen. The more dots, the greater the detail of the image displayed. The screen resolution is measured in horizontal pixels by vertical pixels. A higher number of pixels produces a higher quality image. For the PC, two standard graphics display resolutions are commonly supported: Standard Video Graphics Adapter (VGA) at 640 by 480 pixels; and Super Video Graphics Adapter (SVGA) at 1024 by 768 pixels.

Color resolution describes the number of colors the screen can display at one time. More colors produce more life-like images. Color resolution is measured in terms of the number of bits used to store the color information for each pixel. Different image formats are capable of holding different quantities of colors. Each format will have a reference to the number of bits per pixel that the format is capable of supporting.

Color Resolution

Bits per pixel	Unique colors represented
1	2
4	16
8	256
16	32,768 or 65,536
24	16,777,216
32	16,777,216

Graphics formats

The file extension of a file containing a graphic image indicates the format of the image or the standard that was used to store the image. The file extension also tells Mosaic what kind of software you need to view the picture. The most commonly used image types in use on the Web are the GIF and JPEG formats.

Common Graphic Image Formats

Format	Bits/pixel
GIF	8
JPEG	24
XBM	1

For more information on graphic formats see URL:

http://www.cis.ohio-state.edu/hypertext/faq/usenet/graphics/top.html

GIF

GIF (Graphic Interchange Format) is a standard format for images that was developed by CompuServe, to be a device-independent method of storing pictures. It allows high-quality, high-resolution graphics to be displayed on a variety of graphics hardware and is intended as a storage and display mechanism for graphic images. GIF has been used extensively on the Web and is supported by all browsers that can handle inline images. Because a GIF image stores 8 bits/pixel (256 colors) it is reasonably well matched to inexpensive computer displays, as well as images with only a few distinct colors, such as line drawings and simple cartoons. GIF remains a popular choice for storing lower-resolution image data.

GIF is the copyright property of CompuServe Incorporated. CompuServe remains committed to keeping the GIF specification open and is organizing an effort to define GIF24. For more information see URL:

http://www.compuserve.com

Interlaced GIFs An interlaced GIF image is saved in four passes instead of one. On each pass, certain lines of the image are saved to the file. As an interlaced image is being downloaded, each line appears at it is received as opposed to being displayed linearly from the top row to the bottom row. This is great to get a quick idea of what the entire image will look like while waiting for the rest. This doesn't do much for you if your Web browser or graphics viewer doesn't support progressive display as the image is downloaded, but nonprogressive viewers will still display the GIF image once it has arrived in its entirety. Versions 87a and 89a of the GIF specification support interlaced images.

Transparent GIFs Transparent GIF images (part of the GIF89a spec) are accomplished using image manipulation software to define one color of the image's colormap to be transparent. These images are useful because they appear to blend in smoothly with the user's display. Some images look better if their background color matches the browser window, making the image appear to float in the window. Not all image-viewing software supports transparent GIFs, in which case the color marked as transparent will be displayed by the viewer. Pages explaining the creation of transparent GIFs are available at URLs:

http://melmac.corp.harris.com/transparent_images.html

http://www.globalx.net/kerry/transg.html

How to create transparent GIF images Here's one way to create a transparent background image:

1. Load the image into one of the graphic software packages listed in the following sections.
2. Isolate the background. If the image does not have a single background color, you will need to touch it up with a paint program. Sometimes you can get a single background color by merging color map entries. The goal is make sure that the background of the image is a single color that isn't used anywhere else in the image. This is important, because any pixel in the picture using that color will disappear (be transparent) when it is finally displayed in a Mosaic window. If possible, make the background color white (e.g., RGB values 255, 255, 255) or light gray (e.g., RGB values 207, 207, 207) so that the image will still

look somewhat transparent when viewed with a browser that doesn't support transparent images.

To determine the color's index, view the image using xv and open the color editing window. Click on a pixel in the background area of your image. Note that a color in the editing window is highlighted. Count colors (starting at 0) from left to right, top to bottom, until you reach the highlighted color. This value is the color's index in the colormap.

3 Make the background transparent. If the image isn't already in GIF89a format, convert it. Giftrans is one package that will convert GIF87a images to GIF89a, and lets you specify which entry in the colormap represents the transparent color. You can also specify the color as an RGB triple or an X Window System color name.

JPEG

JPEG (pronounced jay-peg) is a standardized image compression mechanism. JPEG stands for Joint Photographic Experts Group, the original name of the committee that wrote the standard. JPEG is designed for compressing either full-color or grayscale images of natural, real-world scenes. It works well on photographs, naturalistic artwork, and similar material, but not so well on lettering, simple cartoons, or line drawings.

There are two advantages of JPEG: smaller files and more colorful images. Making image files smaller is a big win for transmitting files across networks, and for archiving libraries of images. The second fundamental advantage of JPEG is that it stores full-color information: 24 bits/pixel (16 million colors). Therefore, with full-color hardware, JPEG images look much better than GIF images. JPEG is far more useful than GIF for exchanging images among people with widely varying display hardware.

For examples of JPEG images, reference any of the following URLs:

ftp://audrey.sait.edu.au/space/AUSROC/JPEG

ftp://audrey.sait.edu.au/twin-peaks/JPGS

ftp://scitsc.wlv.ac.uk/pub/pictures

ftp://src.doc.ic.ac.uk/media/literary/collections/ Online-Book-Initiative/Vatican/exhibit

TIFF

Tag Image File Format (TIFF) was originally developed by Aldus Corporation as a standard method of storing black-and-white images created by scanners and desktop publishing applications. The TIFF standard is commonly found in many paint, imaging, and desktop publishing applications.

XBM

X BitMap is a monochrome bitmap format used in the X Window System graphical user interface.

Which graphics format is best for WWW?

The answer to the above questions depends on what is being stored and how it will be referenced. Generally speaking, JPEG is superior to GIF for storing full-color or grayscale images of realistic scenes, such as scanned photographs. Any continuous variation in color, such as what occurs in highlighted or shaded areas, will be represented more faithfully and in less space by JPEG. GIF does significantly better on images with only a few distinct colors, such as line drawings, buttons, graphs, and simple cartoons. GIF often produces smaller files than JPEG. For example, large areas of pixels that are all the same color are compressed very efficiently by GIF. JPEG cannot squeeze such data as well as GIF does without introducing visible flaws.

Luckman Super Mosaic is capable of displaying inline JPEG images. Others might not be capable and require that you link to them as external images, requiring an external viewer capable of displaying JPEG.

Downloading graphics from the Net

If you see an interesting image in your Internet travels, it is possible to save the image(s) on your local machine. For inline images, use the View Source selection of the Edit Menu to view the HTML source of the document containing the desired image. Find the URL (<IMG SRC="image_URL">). Beware that URL addresses are often relative, in which case you must reconstruct the *full* URL from the URL of the current file (revisit the discussion in Chapter 9 on partial URLs) in order to access the image file. Copy and paste the URL into the Open URL selection under the File Menu. This will download the image to your machine's memory and will launch your external image viewer. Use the Save function of the viewer to save the image to your local disk. For external images, once they are displayed on your screen simply use the Save function of the external viewer.

Icons

Icons are small, thumbnail-sized inline images used to enhance your documents. Many icon repositories are available on the net. Many are referenced at URL:

http://www.yahoo.com/yahoo/Computers/World_Wide_Web/Programming/Icons

Image conversion

Image conversion software allows you to convert one image format to another in order to fit your specific needs. Some software has the capability to serve both functions as an image viewer and an image conversion utility.

Converting GIF files to JPEG is a tricky business, because you are piling one set of limitations atop a different set, and the results can be unsatisfactory. Certainly a JPEG image made from a GIF image will never be as good as a JPEG image made from true, 24-bit color data. Black-and-white images should never be converted to JPEG. You need at least 16 gray levels before JPEG is useful for grayscale images.

With care and a clean source image, it's often possible to make a JPEG image of quality equivalent to the GIF image. But even under the best of conditions, the resulting JPEG image will not look identical to the original GIF image.

Image download shortcut—to save an image file (or any other file) directly to your disk without having Mosaic or a helper application display the image, press Ctrl and click the link that retrieves the image. Then choose the SAVE AS button.

✳ Software for Microsoft Windows

GIF Construction Set GIF Construction Set for Windows is a powerful collection of tools to work with multiple-block GIF files. It will allow you to assemble GIF files containing image blocks, plain text blocks, comment blocks, and control blocks. It includes facilities to manage palettes and merge multiple GIF files together. Among its other functions, GIF Construction Set can create transparent GIF files, add, edit, and delete comment blocks, add nondestructive text to images as plain text blocks, and create multiple-image GIF files and simple animations. To try out the shareware version of GIF Construction Set before you register for it, see URL:

ftp://uunorth.north.net/pub/alchemy/gifcon.exe

GIFTool The do everything GIFTool can be used to create transparent and interlaced GIFs, to manipulate options, to allow batch conversion of large sets of images, and to do many other things. GIFTool is available for Microsoft Windows and the X Window System environments at URL:

http://www.homepages.com/tools

Lview LView Pro (Fig. 11-3) is an image viewer, editor, and converter for Microsoft Windows. It can load/save image files in JPEG, GIF 87a/89a, and other formats. LView Pro requires a 386 or better CPU and offers a wide array of image editing functions. This is a very good, feature-rich program. It allows you to view files, convert different file formats, cut, paste, add text on a picture, print, edit, change colors, adjust the size of the picture, and create a slideshow. Lview Pro is available at URL:

ftp://oak.oakland.edu/SimTel/msdos/windows3/lviewp18.zip

Figure 11-3

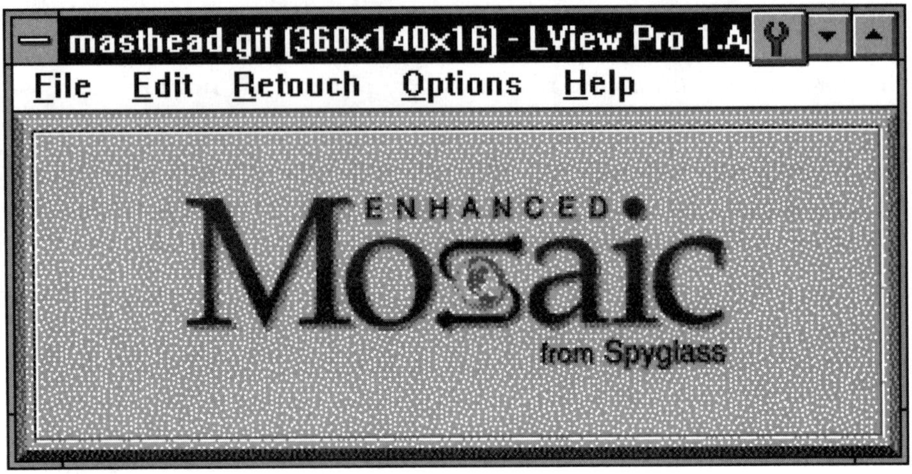

LView Pro © 1993–95 Leonardo Haddard Loureiro.

Paint Shop Pro Paint Shop Pro for Microsoft Windows (Fig. 11-4) has a lot of image-manipulation features, including the ability to save GIF interlaced images. Paint Shop Pro is available at URL:

ftp:// ftp.cica.indiana.edu/pub/pc/win3/desktop/ pspro200.zip

Figure 11-4

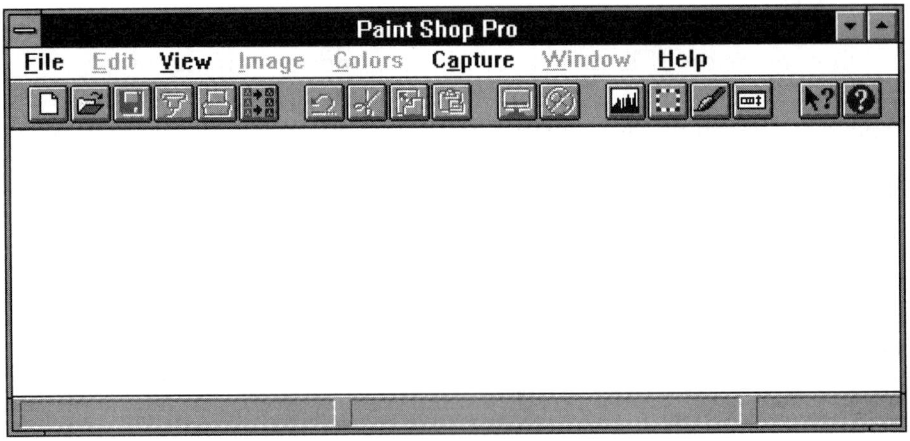

JASC's Paint Shop Pro © 1990–95 JASC Inc.

PhotoLab PhotoLab is an available image processing tool for Microsoft Windows that allows you to view and modify digitized images on your PC. Shown in Fig. 11-5, the program includes features such as print, zoom, rotate, mirror, flip, crop, negative image, resize, and resample. It also offers a variety of effect filters, image combination and type conversion, and adjustments of image color, brightness, contrast, and saturation. The program reads and writes BMP, DIB, GIF, TIFF, and other format images. A video configuration capable of 256 or more colors is recommended. If you have an HP ScanJet IIc color scanner, images can be scanned by PhotoLab. It is available at URL:

ftp://oak.oakland.edu/pub3/win3/graphics/pholab18.zip

Figure 11-5

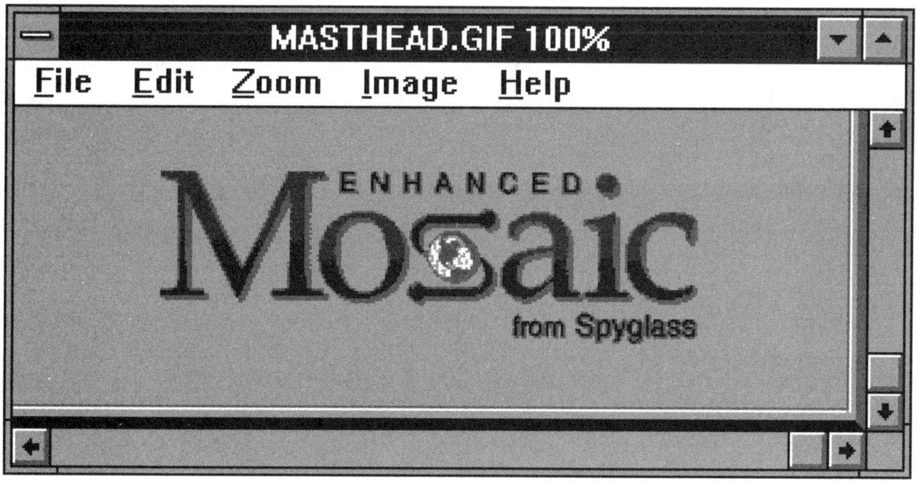

PhotoLab © 1993 David S. Baker.

Graphic Workshop Graphic Workshop for Windows (Fig. 11-6) allows you to convert image files among the most popular file formats, making it possible to use image files from virtually any source in such programs as Ventura Publisher, Windows Paintbrush, PageMaker, Word, WordPerfect, Corel Draw, Deluxe Paint, and others. The current release has a fully resizable window and a menu interface. Its thumbnail mode allows you to preview images as you select them. A powerful keyword-search database of images makes finding graphics in large collections fast and easy. Graphic Workshop

Figure 11-6

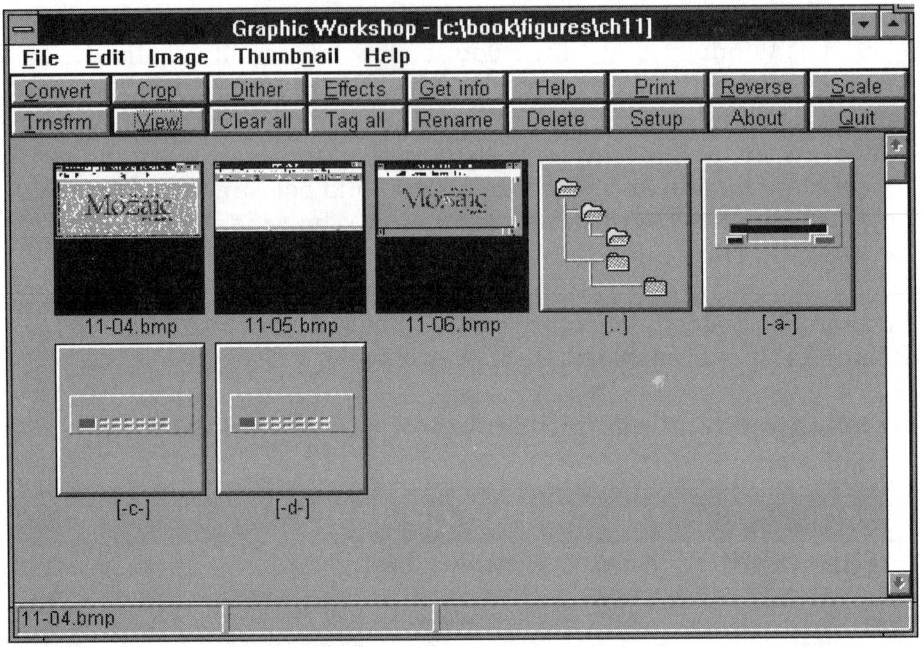

Graphic Workshop © 1991, 1994 Alchemy Mindworks, Inc.

supports more than 30 of the most popular graphics formats. It is available from the URL:

ftp://uunorth.north.net/pub/alchemy/gwswin11.exe

NetPBM NetPBM toolkit, available for DOS and UNIX, offers GIF conversion features. It is available at URLs:

ftp://ftp.cs.ubc.ca/pub/archive/netpbm/ netpbm-1mar1994.tar.gz

ftp://ftp.x.org/R5contrib/netpbm-1mar1994.tar.gz

bCAD bCAD (see Fig. 11-7), a BETA release of bCAD 2.0, is an inexpensive, fully functional, 2-D drafting and 3-D modeling package. The current release is a 32-bit DOS application. However, the Windows 95 version will be available in the next few months. The bCAD demo version limits the size of the file you can save. Note that

Figure 11-7

bCAD

this was not a released product at the time this book was written. This version is still under development, and therefore some features might be not included in the demo release. This demo software can be a useful way to get acquainted with the basics of 2-D and 3-D graphics. It is available at URL:

http://www.lightside.com/~dani/cgi/bcad

Software for the X Window System

GIFTool GIFTool is described fully under Graphics Software for Microsoft Windows.

GIFtrans GIFtrans will transform any GIF image from GIF87 to GIF89. It allows you to also create transparent GIF images. It is available at URL:

ftp://ftp.rz.uni-karlsruhe.de/pub/net/www/tools/giftrans.c

X Viewer xv (see Fig. 11-8) is an excellent interactive image viewer for the X Window System. It supports JPEG, GIF, and many other image formats. It can also do format conversion and image manipulations (e.g., resize, crop, flip, colormap editing). The Visual Schnauzer feature lets you view thumbnail representations of your image files, directories, and other files. Shown in Fig. 11-8, xv is shareware available from URL:

ftp://ftp.cis.upenn.edu/pub/xv/xv-3.00a.tar.Z

Figure 11-8

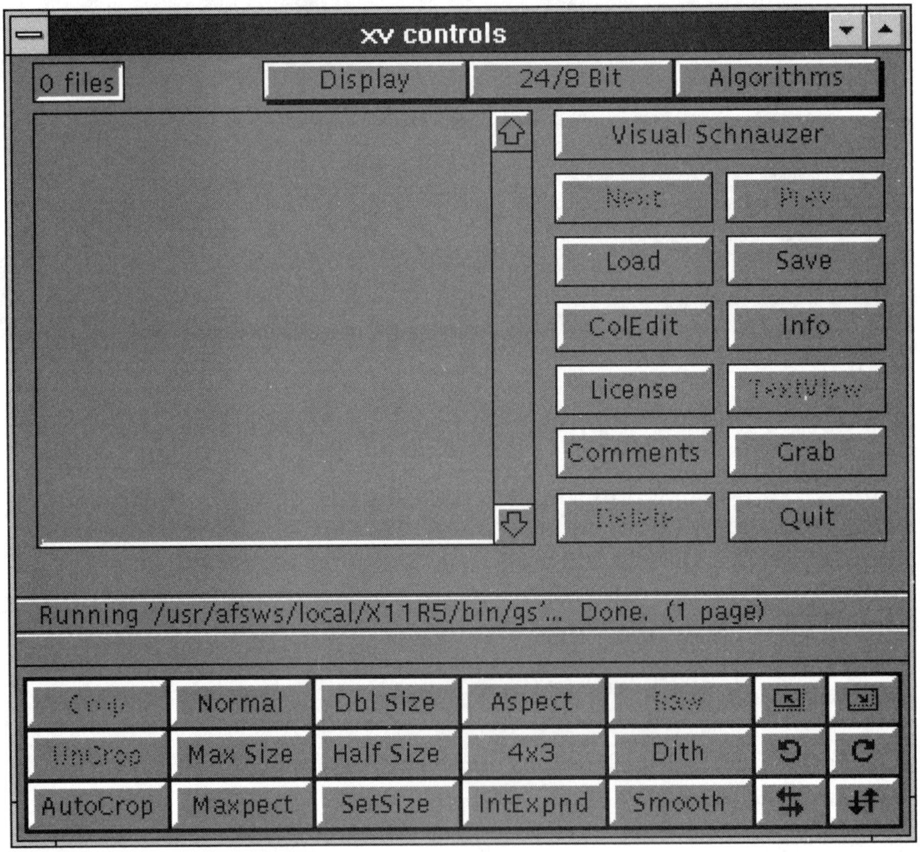

X Viewer by John Brady

ImageMagick ImageMagick (see Fig. 11-9), for the X Window System, is an image processing and conversion package. The ImageMagick viewer (see Fig. 11-9) handles 24-bit displays. It is available at URL:

ftp://ftp.x.org/contrib/applications/ImageMagick/ImageMagick-3.4.tar.gz

Figure 11-9

ImageMagick

PBMPlus PBMPlus Tool Kit is very nearly a de facto standard for conversion between many different formats. It includes tools to scale, quantize, crop, flip, rotate, and do many other graphics operations. It is available at URLs:

ftp://qiclab.scn.rain.com/pub/graphics/pbmplus.tar.Z

ftp://ftp.cc.gatech.edu/pub/software/unix/pbmplus.tar.Z

xloadimage xloadimage (see Fig. 11-10) is a simple image viewer for viewing and converting image files. It is available at URL:

ftp://ftp.x.org/R5contrib/xloadimage.4.1.tar.gz

Figure 11-10

xloadimage

xli xli is a variant version of xloadimage. xli is slightly better as an interactive viewer, but it can't be used as a converter and it supports fewer file formats. xli is available at URL:

ftp://ftp.x.org:/contrib/applications/xli.1.16.tar.gz

XPaint XPaint (see Fig. 11-11) is a reasonably versatile bitmap/pixmap editing tool. The short features list includes the usual paint operations such as Brushes, Spray paint, Pencil, Lines, Arcs, Pattern Fill, Text, Boxes, Circles, Polygons. It also works on multiple images simultaneously; can Cut/Copy/Paste between all active images; can fatbits/Zoom on the image windows. The following file formats are supported: X11 Bitmaps, PPM, GIF, PostScript, XPM, TIFF. XPaint is available at URL:

ftp://ftp.x.org/R5contrib/xpaint-2.1.1.tar.Z

Figure 11-11

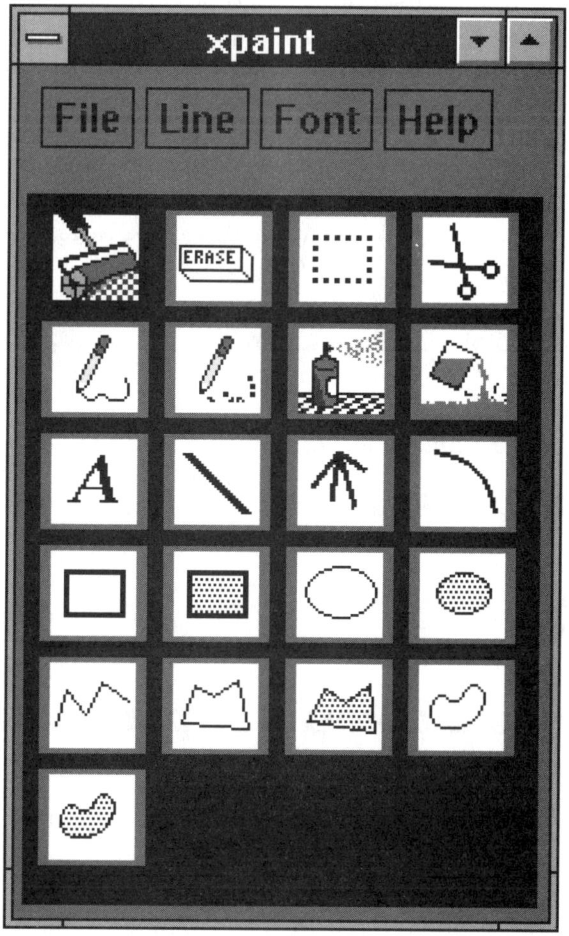

XPaint

Getting images into digital format

The quickest way to start creating images is to make use of a scanner or digital camera to digitize your images. Two options, the HP ScanJet IIcx scanner and the Apple QuickTake 100, are described below. Once in digital format, the image can be manipulated on your personal computer by an appropriate image-processing or conversion tool. The HP ScanJet IIcx is one example of an inexpensive (under $1000) color and grayscale flatbed scanner. The one-pass scanning mechanism delivers high-quality images of everything from black text to color photographs, in seconds. It comes with scanning software. Important features to compare when shopping for scanners include resolution, scanning time, software supported, and interface type.

The Apple QuickTake 100 for Windows is an example of an inexpensive (under $1000) digital camera that allows you to take 24-bit color pictures without using film, and to transfer them quickly from the camera's memory into your Windows-based computer. It comes with Aldus Photostyler software, which allows you to download images into a personal computer directly; display those images in up to 16.7 million colors; and rotate, crop, scale, and zoom-in on images as you edit them for use in your documents.

Key features to consider when looking for a digital camera include: image resolution, color resolution, memory, focus range, flash, and the type interface for transfer to your computer.

Sound

How does a computer play sound?

The sound or music that a computer can play is digitized sound or music. In order to play sound/music in your computer, you need a sound card installed in it. You can attach headphones or amplified speakers to the sound card. Most PCs have an internal speaker that can make simple sounds. Most PCs can play back single channel 8-bit sounds on the internal (1-bit, 1-channel) speaker by utilizing pulse-width modulation, which toggles the speaker faster than it can physically move to simulate positions between fully on and fully off. Software for the PC exists that can play sound on the 1-bit speaker using pulse-width modulation, but it produces disappointing results for anything other than the simple beep.

Sound can be classified into two types: sound data and synthesized sound. Sound data is digital representation of an analog signal, which is typically represented as continuous waveform. When sound is digitally recorded, samples of the waveform are captured at fixed intervals. The more samples taken, the more information stored for each sample, the higher quality the sound. Sample rates, measured in kilohertz (kHz), describe the quality of the sound.

The quality of audio data is determined by three parameters: the sampling rate (the number of times per second the analog wave form was sampled); the sampling resolution (the number of bits per sample); and the number of audio channels sampled.

Suggested Audio Sampling Rates and Styles

Sampling rate/second	Info stored	Style	Channels
8000 kHz	8-bit	U-LAW	mono
22,050 kHz	8-bit	linear unsigned	mono and stereo
44,100 kHz	16-bit	linear signed	mono and stereo

The amount of information stored by sampling just a few seconds of audio is large. Ten seconds of data sampled at the lowest quality (8-bit sample resolution, 8000 samples per second) will produce about 640 kilobits (Kb) of data. At the highest-quality (stereo, 16-bit sample resolution, 44,100 kHz), the same 10 seconds of audio results in 1.7 megabytes (MB) of information.

Synthesized sounds are produced through a synthesizer called MIDI (Music Instrument Digital Interface). When notes are played, a MIDI command is sent to a synthesizer chip, which then produces the sound specified. Because synthesized sounds are stored as simple commands, they require much smaller space than wave form audio.

Sound file formats

The commands needed to play a sound file depend on the file format and the available hardware and software. Most systems can directly play sound only in their native format. You must use a conversion program to play other formats.

MIDI

Music Instrument Digital Interface (MIDI) is a standard for transmitting musical information between electronic instruments and computers. MIDI is able to produce music from sound boards only, which means that you cannot expect to hear human voices or the sound of a dog bark from the MIDI files. However, the quality of music is very good. A MIDI file is small, requiring little disk space. Sample files are available at URLs:

ftp://ftp.cs.ubc.ca/mirror4/freebsd/FreeBSD-current/ports/audio/music/midi

ftp://ftp.crihan.fr/pub/Mirror/Micro/eudora/windows/eudora/dialup

ULAW

ULAW (pronounced as mu-law) is a common sound file found on machines from Sun. Sample ULAW files are available at the following URL:

ftp://ftp.njit.edu/pub/sounds /misc

VOC

VOC Creative Labs's Sound Blaster sample files are available at URLs:

ftp://ftp.cs.yale.edu/WWW/pub/lojban/etymology

ftp://ftp.njit.edu/pub/sounds/misc

ftp://ftp.njit.edu/pub/sounds/movies/aliens

* **WAV**

WAV is an extension for Wave Form Audio File Format. It is a Microsoft Windows 3.1 sound standard. WAV files are digital representations of an analog signal. WAV files are huge data files that take great amounts of disk space. You will need one megabyte of disk space to store a one-minute WAV file. Sample sound files are available at URLs:

ftp://sunsite.unc.edu/pub/micro/pc-stuff/sounds

ftp://julian.uwo.ca/pub/unix/X-windows/X11/ncd-audio/soundsftp.njit.edu/pub/sounds/misc

Sound players/recorders

To play the sound/music on your computer, you need a sound/music player or a viewer. Different formats of music and different types of computers need different kinds of music players. Some software can play one type of format, while some can support several music formats. Some sound/music players have the ability not only to play music, but also to edit, record, and create music. You run your sound/music player on your computer and open the sound/music file within the player. We'll introduce you to some music players. Once you have learned how to find the software, how to download it, and how to use it, you will be on your own way to exploring more on the Internet for music suiting your taste. You will find classical music archives, music companies, record companies, and CDs for sale to mention just a few. Try the URLs:

http://www.magicnet.net/r2/world_of_audio/woa.html

http://stones.com

* **Microsoft Windows software**

MPLAYER Microsoft Sound Recorder comes with Microsoft Windows and can play, record, and edit .wav files.

WHAM Waveform Hold and Modify (WHAM) is a Windows 3.1

application for manipulating digitized sound. It can read and write .wav files, raw 8-bit digitized sound files, and files of several other formats. It can also perform various operations on this sound. WHAM can handle sounds of any size, restricted only by memory. WHAM is one of the recommended sound facilities for Mosaic. It is available at URLs:

ftp://bitsy.mit.edu/pub/dos/web/helper-apps/wham131.zip

ftp://knot.queensu.ca/pub/msdos/winsock/mosaic/wham131.zip

ftp://unidata.ucar.edu/pub/gopherd/gopher-data/anon.ftp/utilities/pc/wham131.zip

ftp://ftp.cic.net/pub/Software/pc/www/viewers/wham131.zip

X Window System software

Soundtool Soundtool is an X Window System program that allows recording, playing, and simple editing of audio files.

Sound file conversion

Like an image format converter, a music format converter is a software used to convert one type of sound format to another to suit your particular player. Unlike image viewers, most sound players cannot convert formats between files. You need specific music conversion software to do that.

SOX

SOund eXchange (SOX) is a universal sound sample translator for the PC and UNIX. It translates sound files from one format to another. SOX works on many different file formats, including .au, .hcom, .raw, .sf, .voc, .auto, .cdr, .dat, .wav, .aif, .snd, and many more. SOX uses file extensions to determine the nature of a sound sample file. If it finds the suffix in its list, it uses the appropriate read or write handler to deal with that file. SOX has an auto-detect feature that attempts to figure out the nature of an unmarked sound sample. It works very well. You can get SOX at URLs:

for DOS:

ftp://ftp.cwi.nl/pub/audio/sox10dos.zip

for UNIX:

ftp://ftp.cwi.nl/pub/audio/sox10.tar.Z

✳ Music Sculptor

Music Sculptor is a product of Aleph Omega Software. It is a MIDI sequencer that is just like a word processor of music. It allows you to play MIDI music; to record MIDI music from an external MIDI input device such as a MIDI keyboard, or from a keyboard window; to edit music by cutting, copying, and pasting measures, adjusting volumes and pitch, naming tracks, and changing channels; to open and save standard MIDI files. Music Sculptor is a Window version MIDI player. It requires a sound card. It works with any synthesizer and sound card compatible with Windows 3.1 or later. It has a very nice user interface and is easy to use. The Track view tells you what kinds of instruments are used to play the music, and other information. The Keyboard Window displays 127 complete piano keys on the screen. You can play the piano by using the mouse or computer keyboard and record your own music. It is fun to use this program. Several MIDI sample files are included in the software package. See URLs:

ftp://freebsd.cdrom.com/.5/cica/sounds/music14.zip

ftp://oak.oakland.edu/pub3/win3/music/music17.zip

✳ GoldWave

GoldWave is software for Microsoft Windows and requires a sound card. GoldWave is a digital audio sound player, recorder, and editor. It can load, play, and edit many different sound file formats, such as .wav, .au, .voc, and .snd files. At the same time, it displays separate graphics for the left and right channels of stereo sound. GoldWave allows you to save and export sounds, and to edit sounds by cutting, pasting, mixing, trimming, and many other options. It is very easy to use and has better sound quality than other players. It is available at URLs:

ftp://freeb sd.cdrom.com/.5/cica/sounds/gldwav21.zip

ftp://ftp.jussieu.fr/pub3/pc/SimTel/msdos/sound/gldwav21.zip

ftp://oak.oakland.edu/pub3/win3/sound/gldwav21.zip

* **Scoptrax**
  Scoptrax is shareware for DOS that plays 8-bit sound files. It can play .voc, .iff, and .snd files, with or without a sound card. It provides about 14 editing functions. Scoptrax has a nice graphic display that allows you to open and save files, choose sample rates, and edit the sound files that are smaller than 550 KB. If you want to play larger files you can use the expanded memory sample player included in this program. You can also convert .au files to .snd format, using ULAW2SND, which is in the software package. The drawback is that, when you want to play large files, you have to remember the basic commands and try different sample and base rates in order to get good quality of sound. However, this is a very nice program. If you don't have a sound card and want to try some music, this is good starting software to use. It is available at URLs:

  ftp://ftp.cdrom.com/.2/simtel/msdos/sound/scoptrax.zip

  ftp://ftp.jussieu.fr/pub3/pc/SimTel/msdos/sound/scoptrax.zip

Digital video

Digital video files are multimedia files that integrate sounds, music, and voices with computer graphics and animation, to present information in an exciting, dynamic way. The videos you can play on your computer are probably different from what you see in the cinema or on TV. Most video files are presented in a small window in your computer screen, and they can only be played several minutes. This is because video files are huge files requiring a lot of disk space.

Some commercial products that can create and play back good quality videos on your computer, including hardware and software, are already available in the market. They are quite expensive. Video recording and playback formats vary with the frame capture size, frame capture rate, and the number of bits of color information stored. Some video compression techniques are available as software-only, or with hardware-assisted playback. Hardware-assisted playback requires a specialized video board not likely to be generally available on the average PC, running Mosaic.

Video formats

MPEG

The Moving Picture Expert Group (MPEG) Study Group was established by the International Telecommunications Union (ITU) in 1991 to develop a group of moving image compression techniques, intended for use in motion video playback applications. MPEG-1 is used to compress motion video sequences stored on CD-ROM and used in PC-playback applications. MPEG-1 image sizes no larger than 720 × 576 pixels, data rates no higher than 1.86 Mbps, and decoder memories are limited to no more than 48 Kbps. MPEG defines these image formats, each recording at frame rates up to 30 frames per second:

- Common Intermedia Format (CIF)—288 lines by 352 pixels
- Quarter Common Intermediate Format (QCIF)—144 lines by 176 pixels
- CIF240—240 lines by 325 pixels

QuickTime

QuickTime is a standard for digital media originally created by Apple Computer, Inc. It brings audio, animation, video, and interactive capabilities to personal computers and consumer devices. Refer to the QuickTime Guide at URL:

http://www.ncsa.uiuc.edu/SDG/Software/MacMosaic/QuickTimeGuide.html

QuickTime 2.0 is significant because it provides larger video at faster frame rates, support for music, and support for interactive television applications. Video on computers is often confined to small windows and played at less than 12 frames per second, making the video appear rough and jerky. QuickTime 2.0 provides greatly increased performance resulting in full-screen videos without the addition of any hardware. This closely resembles what viewers see on television today. At the time this text was written, QuickTime 2.0 for Windows had not been announced.

What do you need on your computer to play a video?

To play video files, you need a relatively powerful PC, a 20-MHz 386SX or better. A true 32-bit microprocessor, such as the 486, is better because it can process and transfer larger amounts of data quickly. Your computer must have at least 4 MB of RAM. Of course, the more memory you have the better. Hard disk space of 80 to 200 MB is recommended. Slow hard disk access time can degrade multimedia performance. A sound card with a pair of external speakers, or a set of headphones, is required to play digitized sound files in high-quality stereo format. A VGA video board capable of at least 16 colors at 640 × 480 resolution is needed, but support for 256 colors is recommended. Software requirements include audio device drivers for different format audio and a video device driver.

Most UNIX workstation configurations are adequate to display video files.

How do you make a video?

The first step is capturing the video source. The source can be an NTSC or PAL signal, such as that from a TV, VCR, or camcorder. Video capture cards convert the signal to RGB (computer video), sample the analog signal a certain number of times a second, and output the results to disk. In choosing a video capture card, the main things to look for are compression capability and image quality. You can capture more frames per second and obtain larger image area (resolution), with more colors, using hardware-based compression. Typical hardware compression (for 16-bit color) achieves a maximum capture rate of 15 fps at 320 × 240 pixels (full screen) or 30 fps at 160 × 120 (quarter screen).

✳ Video software

To play a video on your computer, you need a kind of software called a multimedia player, specifically MPEG player or QuickTime player. These players are also called decoders, because they use software to decode the MPEG or QuickTime compressed codes. Some software allows you both to encode and to decode multimedia files—that is, to make and play the files. Some software only allows you to play back multimedia files.

Software for Microsoft Windows

MPLAYER

Media Player, available with Microsoft Windows, plays video sequences Microsoft Video for Windows Audio/Video Interleaved format (AVI) that can contain audio; supports 11, 22, or 44 kHz audio in 8- or 16-bit-format, audio synchronized with video within 1⁄30 of a second.

Indeo Video Microsoft Video for Windows

This software update is provided to enhance your existing Indeo Video drivers to the latest video technology for compressing, editing, and playing back video on your Intel microprocessor-based desktop computer, using Microsoft's Video for Windows version 1.1d. It compresses NTSC or PAL format files at 320 × 240, 240 × 180, and 160 × 120 pixel resolutions at up to 30 frames per second (fps).

Indio Video is available at URL:

ftp://ftp.intel.com/pub/IAL/Indeo_video/iv32rt.exe

QuickTime for Windows

QuickTime for Windows is bundled with various third party products that support QuickTime for Windows, such as Video clip libraries, software applications, and CD-ROM titles. Look for the QuickTime for Windows logo on the packaging of products. QuickTime for Windows is available for Microsoft Windows systems at URL:

ftp://ftp.support.apple.com/pub/Apple%20SW%20Updates/US/DOS%20%26%20Windows/qt_win/QuickTime%20For%20Windows%201.1.1.zip

Projector

Projector is a Microsoft Windows multimedia file sequencer. Projector can also be used to view animation and images with sound effects or music. It can be used to create custom screen savers, multimedia presentations, or as a file viewer. Projector supports AVI, MOV, FLI, FLC, BMP, JPG, GIF, WMF, WAV, MID, and external file filters. Information on ordering Projector is available ar URL:

http://kspace.com/KM/tool.sys/Nunnally/pages/piece1.html

Software for the X Window System

MPEGTool

MPEGTool, an MPEG player, offers forward, backward, stop, pause, loop commands, and MPEG encoder. It is available at URL:

ftp://atum.ee.upenn.edu in the /dist/pkg/MPEGTool

Xanim

Xanim is an X Window System program capable of displaying various animation formats, including QuickTime, FLI, FLC, IFF, GIF, RLE, AVI, and others. It is available at URL:

http://www.portal.com/~podlipec/home.html

Figure 11-12

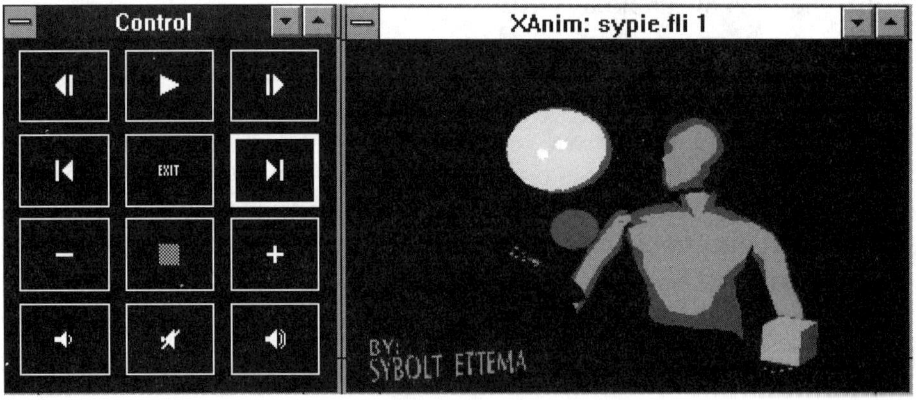

Xanim

How to make an MPEG video on your UNIX workstation

First, you must make a sequence of GIF images in the proper form. Second, you must convert the GIF files to YUV files. Third, you must convert the sequence of YUV files to MPEG, as explained later.

1 Generate a sequence of GIF files. It is important that the GIF have an even number of pixels in each direction. It is often desirable to scale the image data down to a relatively small size (about 400 × 300 or so). This is done so that the resulting video will play back at a reasonable speed and be a manageable size.

2 Before the images can be stored by the MPEG encoder, they must be converted into separate Y, U, and V files. One option is to use a program called ppmtoyuvsplit, which is part of the new netpbm toolkit. A combination of tools from several toolkits might be used in this conversion process. Here is an example:

```
giftoppm $file ¦ ppmtoyuvsplit $file
```

3 Generate the MPEG movie using an MPEG encoder. It accepts a series of separate Y, U, and V files. Here is an example where 100 400 × 300 files from a work directory are encoded into a file called mymovie.mpg.

```
mpeg -a 1 -b 100 -h 400 -v 300 -PF mymovie.mpg
mymovie
```

Finally, enjoy the results. Display the results using an X11-based MPEG display program.

Here's a list of various video/animation archive sites:

QuickTime Walt Disney Studios

http://bvp.wdp.com/BVPM/index.html

Fractal Video Archive

http://www.cnam.fr/fractals/anim.htmlThe Gallery

CERES Videos

http://spocls.larc.nasa.gov/ceres/ceresav.html

Mosaic Network News

http://www.hal.csuhayward.edu/3-d.html

News Reels Archive

http://192.253.114.31/D-Day/News_reels/ News_reels_contents.html

Kaleidospace videos

http://kspace.com/KM/screen.sys/screenlist.html

AVI animations

ftp://phoenix.oulu.fi/pub ftp://ftp-os2.nmsu.edu:/ multimedia/avi

ftp://sun.rz.tu-clausthal.de:/pub/windows/multimedia/avi

Videos of Bari, Italy (AVI)

http://fourier.csata.it/bari.html

MPEG videos

ftp://ftp.iij.ad.jp/pub/mail/mime/mpeg/movies

ftp://etlport.etl.go.jp/pub/ccipr/mime/mpeg//movies

ftp://ftp.cs.wisc.edu/OldFiles/paradise/OldFiles/demo/ video/popeye.gee ftp://uottawa.ca/pub/mpegmipgsun

ftp://mipg.upenn.edu/pub/3DVIEWNIX1.1/MPEG_MOVIES

Fractal Video Archive

http://www.sgi.com/free/gallery.html

Summary

The ability to combine text, graphics, sound, and video into a single presentaton is one reason that the World Wide Web and its associated browser have revolutionized the Internet.

Now that you been introduced to the tools required to produce multimedia information appropriate for the Web, we hope you explore the possibilities and—most important—have some fun!

12

Serving information in the New Internet

CHAPTER 12

WHETHER you are considering serving information in the Internet or on an enterprise-wide basis, the topics presented in this chapter will get you started in the right direction. The tools make it possible for the average PC user to become an information provider. If your interest lies in commercial endeavors, we will give plenty of hints on how to proceed, whatever your pace.

Why consider an Internet presence?

We introduced the potential benefits of establishing an Internet presence in Chapter 3. Establishing an Internet presence means more than simply connecting to the Internet. Establishing a net presence is accomplished through activities such as publishing quality information of interest to others, and establishing appropriate links between your information and other relevant items on the Net.

The Internet continues to experience phenomenal growth in terms of users, hosts, networks, and information. By far the fastest-growing segment of the Internet has been the commercial sector, in which typical applications include customer support, direct marketing, electronic commerce, expanded help-desk applications, low-cost software distribution channels, online marketing, online news services, product information distribution, and product support libraries.

This trend is important to the information consumer, and to entrepreneurs looking for new ways to expand their markets. The information consumer is presented with a new source of timely information. The entrepreneur can explore opportunities in this new marketplace.

There are a few issues to consider before establishing a business presence on the Internet. First, remember that traditional, active-outreach marketing models do not work on the Internet. Also, be aware that a high-performance connection will be costly to install, configure, and administer. Finally, protect your resources. An active hacker community lives on the Internet, so adequate security measures need to be taken.

The culture dictates the approach

As we discussed in Chapter 2, the Internet culture is different from that of the business environment familiar to most professionals. Because no one institution or commercial enterprise owns or maintains the Internet, its user community regards it as a shared resource maintained for the good of all. Their code of conduct is intended to maintain the integrity and efficiency of the Net. Even the uninitiated user is expected to conduct himself or herself in accordance with the standards of the Internet community.

The information exchanged by Internet users must be of demonstrable value and interest. Direct solicitation or promotion of products and services is not tolerated behavior. By the business professional the message should be heard loud and clear—products and information cannot be advertised in a broadcast manner. The community at large will not tolerate unsolicited sales pitches or blatant self-promotion of any form. Violations of this unwritten rule will unquestionably cause the community to retaliate in force, by flaming the guilty party. Flaming refers to sending the offending party unwelcome electronic mail messages condemning the offending action. The word of such abuses spreads quickly among the Internet community, resulting in negative publicity for the offender. Businesses wishing to participate in the Internet must adopt a marketing strategy that involves communications with potential customers in a format that offers content-rich information in a timely manner.

Electronic information distribution is relatively economical. From a technical vantage point, flooding the network with broadcast messages creates massive traffic bottlenecks. From a cultural vantage point, Internet users are interested in specific information and will not tolerate being bombarded with unsolicited information. On the Internet, commercial activity remains much more low key than that found on other networks, such as CompuServe or Prodigy, where you will find advertisements on almost every screen.

The Internet is not a single network; rather, it is a group of thousands of individual networks that have chosen to allow traffic to pass between them. The traffic sent out to the Internet might actually traverse several different networks before it reaches its destination. The use of the network is a privilege, not a right, which might temporarily be revoked at any time for abusive conduct. Some networks may have acceptable-use policies restricting commercial or, more likely, offensive material.

How to establish a presence on the Internet

The number of alternatives for establishing a presence on the Internet continues to expand. An increasing number of third-party Internet service providers are offering to rent electronic storefront space for a monthly fee. Generally, the server is at the service provider's location and is shared by multiple customers. As the customer, you need not be concerned in setting up your own server or establishing the Internet connection. This approach to gaining an Internet presence provides a very attractive alternative in an environment in which many network managers are hesitant to entrust their business transactions to a network that has historically been a hacker's playground.

The services offered by Internet presence providers, Internet publishers, or just plain Internet service providers, range from server setup and connection establishment to home-page creation, document conversion and formatting, and design, plus creative and content-creation assistance. A list of sites offering WWW space for lease is available at URL:

http://union.ncsa.uiuc.edu/HyperNews/get/www/leasing.html

Here are 14 questions to ask when shopping for an Internet storefront. The responses to these questions will affect the performance and quality of your Internet presence.

1. What will it cost?
2. What exactly do I get (number of pages, space, etc.)?
3. Who provides your Internet connection?
4. How reliable is your Internet connection?

5. How big is your Internet connection?
6. Do you have multiple connections for reliability?
7. How big is your server?
8. What backup services are provided for my data?
9. How does my data get updated?
10. Who owns my data?
11. Will you provide me with information on who accesses my data?
12. Will the information on who accesses my data be held in confidence?
13. What other services are offered?
14. Will you help advertise the availability of my storefront?

Questions 1 and 2 are designed to determine what you will be paying for. Is the price based on the number of pages stored or on some other gauge?

Questions 3 through 6 attempt to ascertain the quality of the provider's Internet connection. Is the Internet connection provided by a well-established, reliable provider? Because this is a relatively new business venture for many providers, the long-term viability of any service provider should be considered. What bandwidth will they provide? A low-speed or poor quality Internet connection can hamper the ability of users to view your information.

Questions 7 through 9 help you ensure that your data is safe, timely, and well-served. Question 10 is designed to make sure you retain the rights to all your data placed on the Web. This should be the case whether you or your provider design and implement the data.

You will want an indication of how successful your Web presence is. Question 11 is designed to ensure that your provider helps you determine who is accessing your information, and how often. While such information will be important to you, you probably do not want your competition to have that information.

Question 12 is intended to ensure that the privacy of your customers is maintained. Questions 13 and 14 will help clarify exactly what services the provider is willing to offer. Will they create your pages? Will they design them? Input and update them? What about search capabilities, special forms, etc.?

Serving information

While the focus of this text is HTTP servers, you might need to consider running other information servers to meet all your needs. If that is the case, you might want to consider other Internet books that focus on the more traditional Internet services. It is feasible to run multiple servers simultaneously on a single machine. Thus a single hardware platform can be utilized to serve many information serving needs. For the client side, Mosaic can interact with all four types of Internet servers listed below.

Information servers run programs to handle incoming requests for information. To provide information to the Internet community at large or on an enterprise-wide network basis, you might need an FTP, Gopher, HTTP, and/or a WAIS database server.

FTP servers have the advantage that they might already be set up at your site, they have reasonable logging, and they provide automatic filename indexing (Archie).

Gopher also has automatic title indexing (Veronica) and a fairly simple setup structure. To Gopher, data is either a menu, a document, an index, or a Telnet connection. Hypertext cannot be easily served through Gopher; therefore, set up a Gopher server only if you don't need to serve hypertext.

HTTP servers are designed to deliver multimedia hypertext, and because plain text is a degenerate case of hypertext they do equally well at serving plain text. To deliver hypertext at reasonable speed, use an HTTP server. The main HTTP servers in use are described briefly below. To the WAIS server, everything is an index and everything that is returned from the index is a document.

Setting up your own server

If, after reading the previous sections of this chapter, you believe that a Web presence is for you, and you are not sure whether a service provider can adequately meet your needs, read on. In this section we will try to give you some pointers on the state of the server technology. Keep in mind that this is a rapidly changing area. Many new announcements are coming out daily. Our goal here is to get you going in the proper direction, armed with the right questions to ask. It would be improper for us to try to write the definitive answer on server technology.

At a bare minimum you will need an Internet connection, a hardware platform to run a Web (HTTP) server, HTTP server software, and information to share.

How fast an Internet connection you need will depend on what kinds of things you want to provide on your server. Here are some rules of thumb to use when deciding what kind of connection you need for your server:

Rule #1 It should take less than five seconds to send a page to the client. Five seconds is about how long people are willing wait before getting impatient. External images, audio, and video clips require large amounts of bandwidth. Remember, you cannot predict for certain what sort of access speed the client will have.

Rule #2 Don't worry about simultaneous accesses to your server. Unless you have a site with many servers being accessed from off-site, simultaneous access is not a problem. If you do have such a site, you need as much bandwidth as you can afford.

Rule #3 Remember to factor in your other uses of your Internet connection, because it is likely that your Web server will not be the only use for the connection.

Before you can consider what World Wide Web server is best, you should evaluate the equipment you have available and the type of network connections. A local area network connection is essential with TCP/IP software, configured so that the server workstation is a node on the Internet. If you want only to provide information to local users, placing your information in files on a local or shared disk is also an option. This means, however, that there can be no access to users outside that environment.

Any reliable Intel-based 486 system is a good candidate for a server. If you must use Microsoft Windows as a server environment, give up using the machine for any other purpose. If you are serious about running a server on an Intel 486 platform, there are excellent alternatives to Microsoft Windows. These environments are designed for multiple users and perform true multitasking. This means system resources are well distributed among users and applications. The Windows NT environment, for example, protects applications from one another and from crashing the system by providing each package with its own segment of memory. IBM's OS/2 environment is also stable. Linux is a public domain UNIX for PCs that is popular and widely supported. Finally, several excellent UNIX environments are available. UNIX, Windows NT, and OS/2 all make efficient use of memory and manage system resources well for multi-user access.

Memory is an important consideration. At least 16 Mb of RAM is recommended. A fast hard drive and network adapter card are keys to good performance. Now, if you are planning to put up a server for a large institution, you would be wise to investigate purchasing one or more UNIX workstations to function as your server. Among the supported systems are Digital Equipment, Hewlett Packard, IBM, Silicon Graphics, and Sun Microsystems. When selecting a server in this class, 32MB of RAM is the minimum and 64MB is recommended, but you can probably get by with 32MB until you have some experience to justify the extra expense.

For a server with light traffic, a server with 1 gigabyte of online storage is a reasonable starting point. Be sure to perform backups of your data regularly before you establish a permanent server. Put together a backup and recovery plan, and be prepared to perform frequent backups. The frequencies of your backups will depend on the frequency with which your information changes.

What server software is available?

Commercial quality Web server software alternatives are just beginning to appear. Some vendors are also offering turnkey solutions. This market is very volatile and your options are likely to change dramatically in the coming months. For those brave souls willing to pursue rolling their own Web server, several alternatives are discussed in the following sections.

Servers are available for Microsoft Windows, Windows NT, OS/2, and UNIX systems. For more information on servers and gateways in general refer to URL:

http://www.yahoo.com/yahoo/Computers/World_Wide_Web/HTTP/Servers

Because Microsoft Windows is such a popular end-user environment it is no big surprise that several Windows-based Web servers exist. Windows Web servers are best-suited for a group authoring Web documents, or to share documents among a small group of people. NCSA's HTTPD for Windows is one alternative. NCSA's server supports all the functionality of UNIX servers. It also supports accessing data from other Windows applications, which opens up possibilities perhaps not available with a UNIX server, such as retrieving data from a spreadsheet or word processor. It relies on Visual Basic 3.0 for scripting, so be sure to get a copy of this if you are interested in forms support discussed later in this chapter.

Finally, UNIX has the most Web servers available. The first Web server from CERN was created for UNIX, and new versions are frequently posted at their FTP site. This server, and NCSA's HTTP for UNIX, support basically the same features: the HTTP protocol, authentication, gateways, activity logging, and image maps.

Begin by developing a plan detailing the number of documents you wish to publish, determine the size of your potential audience, and determine how much you can spend on your server project. Use this plan to select a server and software, and a volunteer to run it. Be sure to keep track of usage so it will be easier to justify funding for expansion in the future. World Wide Web is already the most popular client-server information tool on the Internet, and might become as common as electronic mail soon. So think big, or at least in terms of potential expansion.

Microsoft Windows & Windows NT servers

HTTPS

HTTPS is a full fledged web server for Windows NT, which matches all the features in current UNIX servers, including: multiple simultaneous connections, CGIs, clickable image maps, transaction logging, and error logging. It is available via URL:

http://emwac.ed.ac.uk/html/toolchst.html

Windows httpd

The httpd for Windows has most of the features of the UNIX version, including scripts that generate pages on the fly based on user input. It is available via URL:

http://www.city.net/win-httpd

SerWeb

SerWeb is a simple server for Windows written by Gustavo Estrella, and is available at URL:

ftp://winftp.cica.indiana.edu/pub/pc/win3/winsock/serweb03.zip

A Windows NT version of SerWeb is also available, at URL:

http://emwac.ed.ac.uk/pub/serweb/SERWEB.TXT

⁕ WEB4HAM

WEB4HAM is another Windows-based server and is available at URL:

ftp://ftp.informatik.uni-hamburg.de/pub/net/winsock/web4ham.zip

⁕ WebSite

WebSite is an http server for Windows NT or Windows 95 environments and is available at URL:

http://gnn.com/gnn/bus/ora/news/website.html

UNIX servers

⁕ CERN httpd

Information on the CERN's server is available at URL:

http://www.w3.org/hypertext/WWW/Daemon/Status.html

The CERN server has mapping ability to redirect requests, thus acting as a proxy server to allow people behind firewalls to use the Web as if the firewalls were not present.

⁕ EIT httpd

EIT has created the Webmaster's Starter Kit, which installs their Web server on your system via the Web through a painless forms interface. This is recommended for those unfamiliar with server installation. You can learn more about the starter kit and the EIT httpd at the URL:

http://wsk.eit.com/wsk/doc/

⁕ GN Gopher/HTTP server

The GN server is unique in that it can serve both WWW and Gopher clients, in their native modes. This is a good server for those migrating from Gopher to WWW, although it does not have the server-side-script capabilities of the NCSA and CERN servers. See the URL:

http://hopf.math.nwu.edu:70

- **NCSA httpd**
  The NCSA server is available at URL:

  ftp://ftp.ncsa.uiuc.edu/Web/httpd/Unix/ncsa_httpd

- **NCSA Secure httpd**
  The secure httpd server supports transaction privacy and authentication with Secure WWW servers using S-HTTP. It is available at URL:

  http://www.commerce.net/software/Shttpd

- **NetSite**
  NetSite is a commercial offering that is available in two forms—the Communications Server and the Commerce Server. The former has no advanced security features. The latter provides RSA Data Security technology for public-key cryptography. For more information refer to URL:

  http://www.netscape.com/MCOM/products_docs/server.html

- **Perl server**
  Plexus is a server written in the Perl scripting language, for which documentation is available at URL:

  http://bsdi.com/server/doc/plexus.html

- **WN**
  The WN server enables full-text searching of a single html document, which could span many files on a server. It also allows users to search all titles on the server and obtain a menu of matching items. See the URL:

  http://hopf.math.nwu.edu

Okay, but which software is best?

For help in determining which server is best-suited to meet your needs, consult Paul Hoffman's Server Comparison Chart at URL:

http://www.proper.com/www/servers-chart.html

What does a Web server do besides serve documents?

They can log activity. Servers can record the Internet address, time, and request made for each connection. Logging server access is an absolute necessity, both for usage statistics and security. Servers can also protect certain files from nonauthenticated users. Logging, user authentication, and gateway support are important features to look for when selecting a specific Web server.

Advanced features of the Web

In Chapter 10, we introduced some advanced features that require help from the Web server. In this section, we touch on the requirements on the server side to support these functions. For detailed information, refer to the following listed URL and examples. Seeing is believing.

Common Gateway Interface

The Common Gateway Interface (CGI) provides a way to incorporate other information servers into the network of information search systems available through the standard Mosaic interface, integrating information sources such as relational databases with structured query language queries into the hypermedia information environment. Web servers can forward requests for data that neither the client nor the server can access directly, to applications called gateways. Through gateways, the Web can support datatypes and resources not even conceived of when it was invented.

Gateways can allow Web clients and servers to function as WAIS or relational database clients. Data is gathered by the Web client, usually using an HTML form, and is sent to the server along with the name of a gateway program to be run. Then the gateway reformats the data and sends it to an information server, receives a response, and reformats that response as an HTML document that is delivered to the Web client. There are SQL gateways for UNIX to allow you to generate queries to search relational databases, such as SYBASE or ORACLE. (See Fig. 12-1.)

Figure 12-1

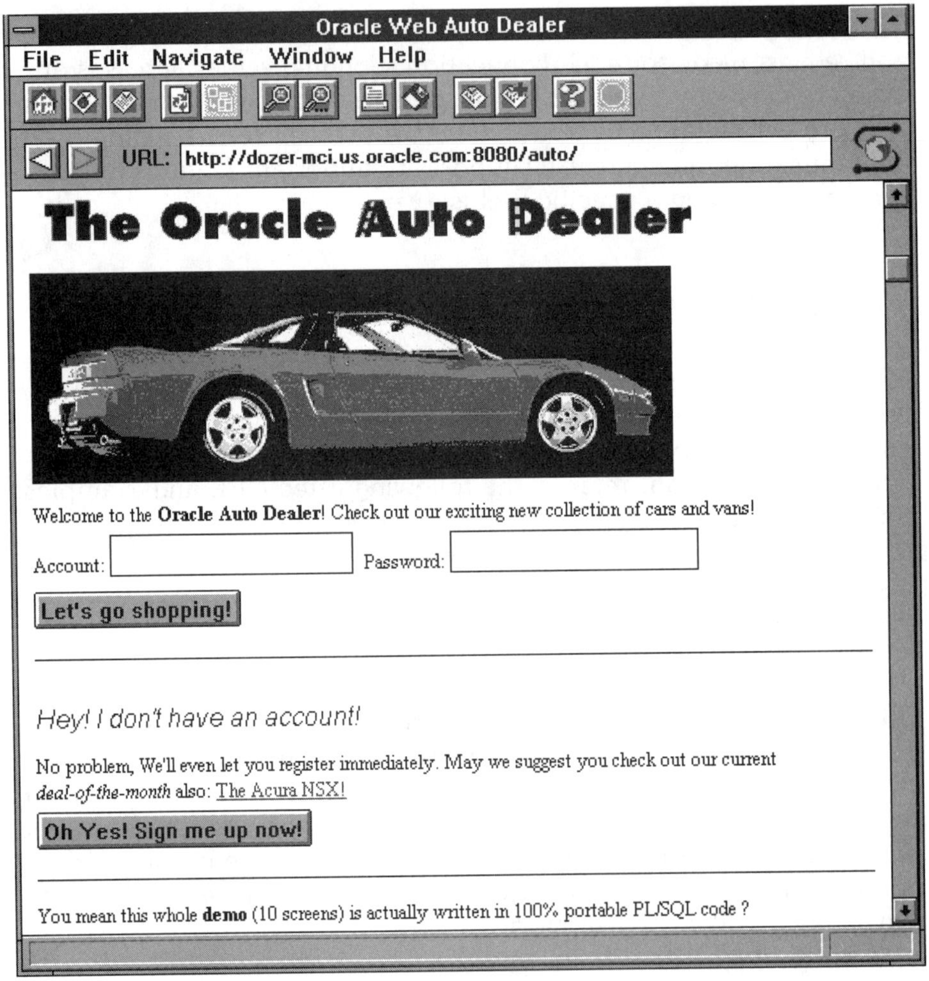

WWW/ORACLE gateway

Searching

A search capability is another consideration with running a Web server. With few exceptions, Web servers do not provide any built-in method of searching collections of HTML documents, nor do they provide direct support for a search of WAIS or relational databases. There are a few options, depending on the platform you are using. For UNIX, GN has limited built-in searching that might be sufficient for your needs. Then there is freeWAIS, which provides relevance feedback and Boolean full text searching. WAIS is a widely used full-text indexing, search and retrieval engine available on the Internet. There is also a commercial version of WAIS that does all freeWAIS can do and more, and comes with technical support. See Fig 12-2. The public domain WAIS software is also available for Windows NT. See URLs:

ftp://ftp.cnidr.org/pub/NIDR.tools/freewais/freeWAIS-0.202.tar.Z http://www.wais.com

Figure 12-2

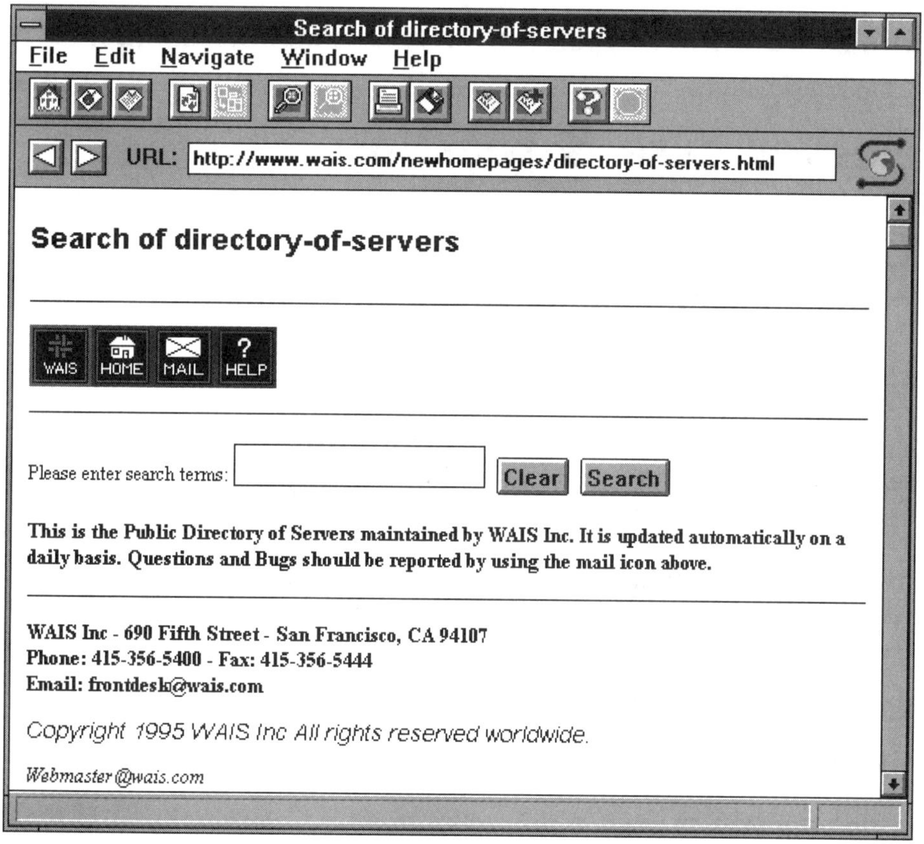

WAIS directory search © 1995 WAIS, Inc.

Proxy server

Many corporate networks are protected from the Internet by firewalls. Only limited access (e.g., electronic mail) has traditionally been allowed through the firewall. The proxy server approach allows the best of both worlds by allowing users on machines protected by a firewall to access the Web, while at the same time retaining the firewall protection of the corporate network from Internet hacker attack. A proxy server is a specialized HTTP server that provides access to the outside world for people inside the firewall. The CERN httpd can be configured to run as a proxy server. Furthermore, it is able to perform caching of documents, resulting in faster response times. For information see URL:

http://www.w3.org/hypertext/WWW/Daemon/Status.html

Server care & feeding

Can you restrict & control access to your server?

All major servers have features that allow you to limit access to particular sites, and many clients have authentication features that allow you to identify specific users. For more information, see your server documentation or reference the tutorial on security and user authentication with the NCSA server at URL:

http://wintermute.ncsa.uiuc.edu:8080/auth-tutorial/ tutorial.html

Can you protect your server from robots?

As illustrated in Chapter 9, programs that automatically traverse the Web can be quite useful. However, if not engineered carefully, robots can place undue loads on the servers they visit. Every so often someone will write a *depth-first* searching robot that brings servers to their knees. Fortunately, well-behaved robots on the Web follow a simple protocol by which you can keep them off your server if you wish. To learn about the emerging standards for exclusion of robots from areas in which they are not wanted read the document *World-Wide Web Robots, Wanderers and Spiders* at URL:

http://web.nexor.co.uk/mak/doc/robots/robots.html

Keep statistics on access to your Web server

HTTP servers are able to record the Internet address, time, and object requested for each server access. Keeping track of server access will be important to help you justify additional bandwidth, effort, hardware, etc. HTTP servers also log unsuccessful attempts in an error log.

When the information HTTP servers are in the position to save is of a personal nature it should clearly be treated in a confidential manner. Its handling might even be constrained by law in certain countries. Server providers should ensure that such material is not distributed without the permission of individuals and networks identified by the published results.

HTTP servers logs are plain text files that you can process to generate statistical reports, using your favorite processing tools. Or, you can try one of several readily available tools.

Getstats (see Fig. 12-3) is a versatile HTTP access log analyzer that provides reports for various time periods with a high degree of flexibility. Add-on packages have been written to generate reports in HTML, and also to generate graphs. For more information see URLs:

http://www.eit.com/software/getstats/getstats.html

ftp://ftp.eit.com/pub/web.software/getstats

Figure 12-3

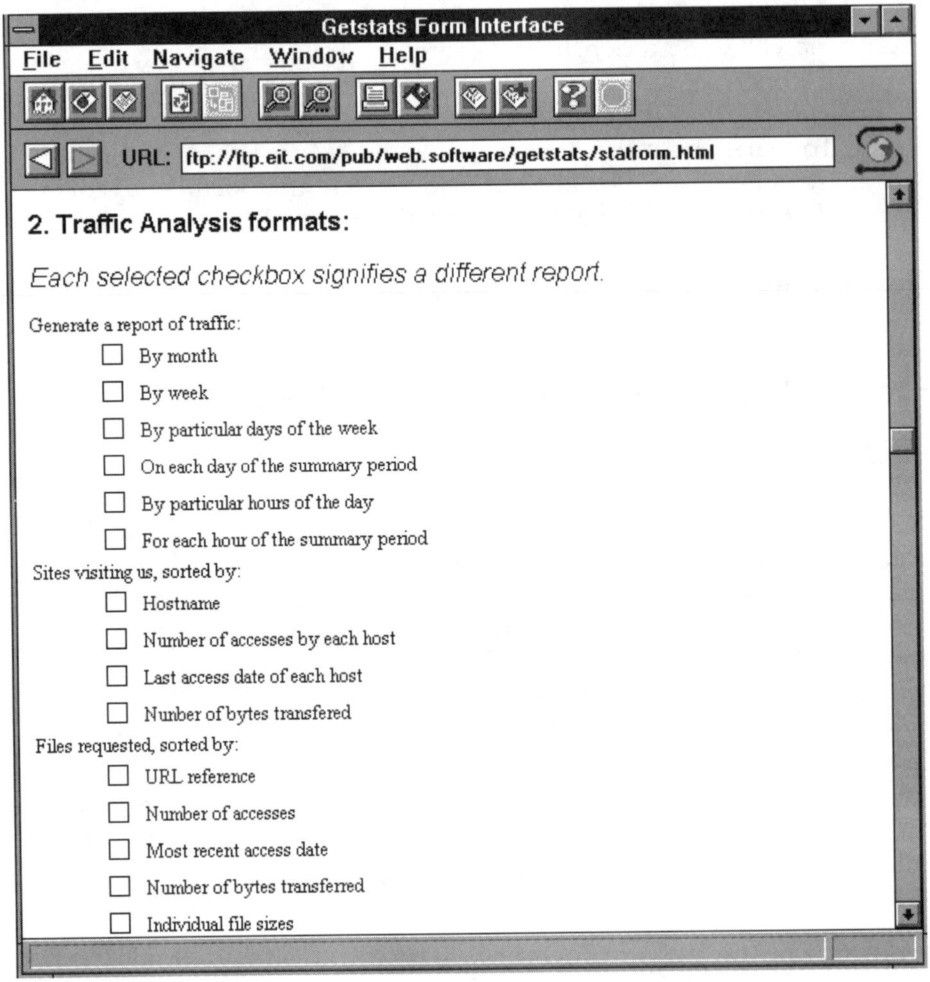

Getstats

WebStat is a package that supplies Web access statistics on usage by domain, country, etc., with daily, weekly, monthly, and annual reports available. For details, see the WebStat Home Page at URL (Fig. 12-4):

http://www.pegasus.esprit.ec.org/people/sijben/statistics/advertisment.html

Figure 12-4

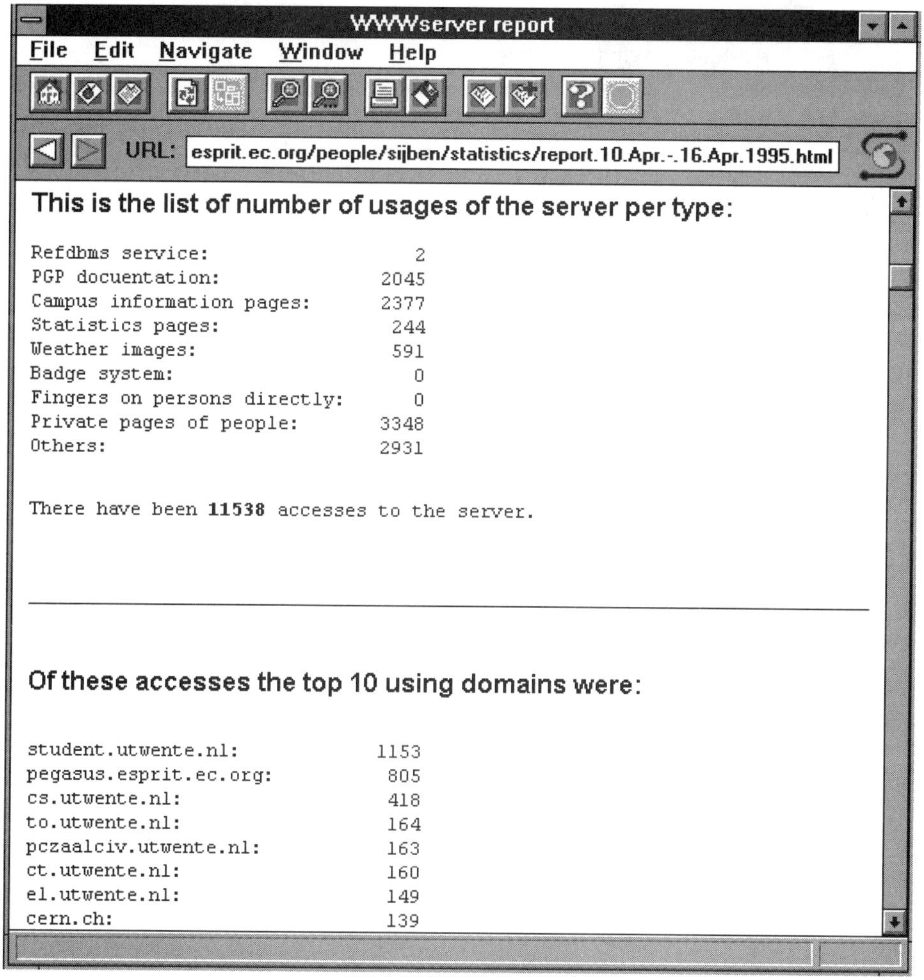

Webstat

Wusage (see Fig. 12-5A and B) generates simple weekly reports in HTML, with inline image graphs displaying server growth and the distribution of accesses by continent. You can also exclude irrelevant accesses (e.g., inline images and local machines) from the results. For more information read the Wusage Home Page at URLs:

http://siva.cshl.org/wusage.html

ftp://isis.cshl.org/pub/wusage

Figure 12-5

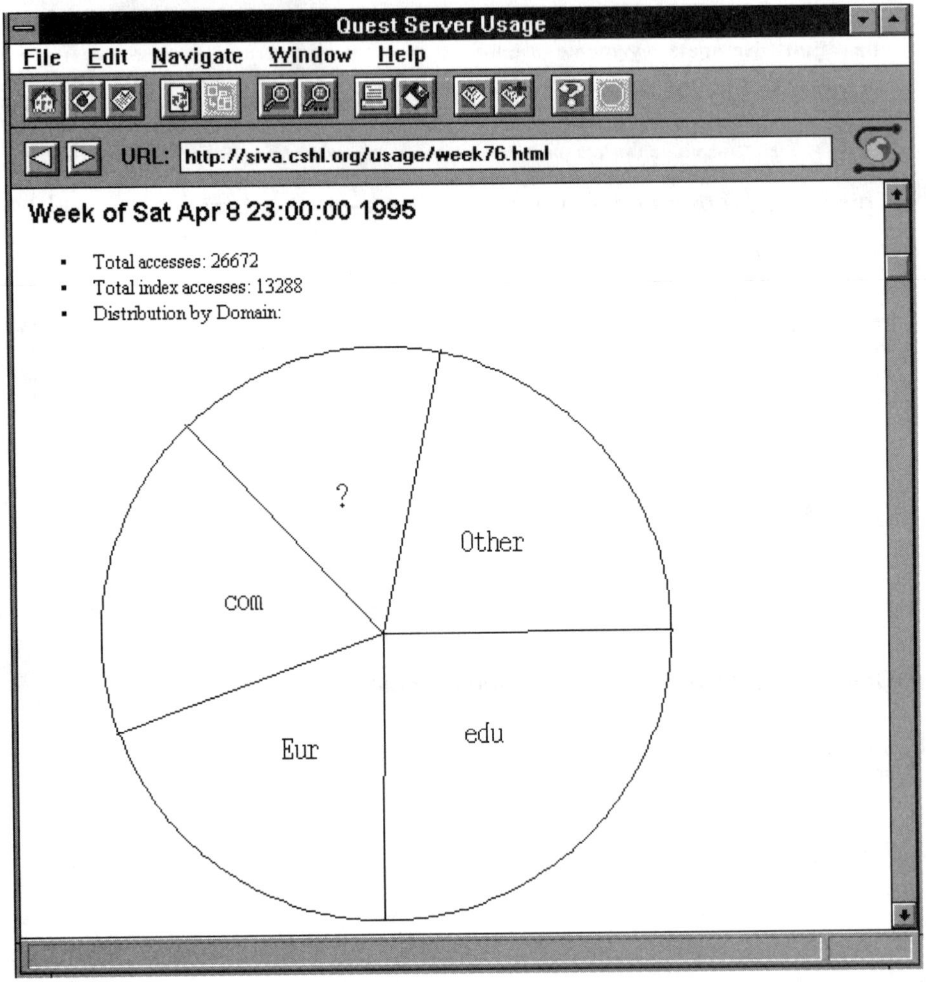

(A) Wusage

Figure 12-5

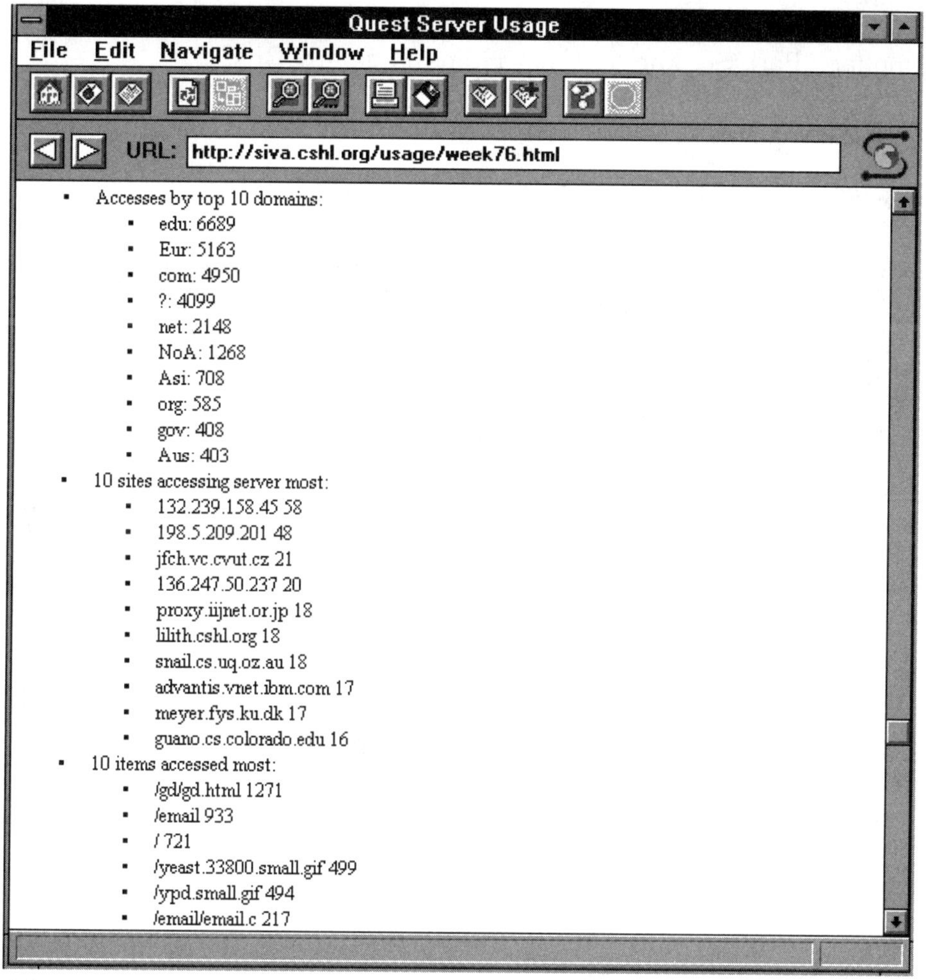

(B) Wusage (scroll down page)

wwwstat (see Fig. 12-6) is a full-featured log analyzer written in the language Perl. See the wwwstat Home Page at URLs:

http://www.ics.uci.edu/WebSoft/wwwstat

ftp://liege.ics.uci.edu/pub/arcadia/wwwstat

Figure 12-6

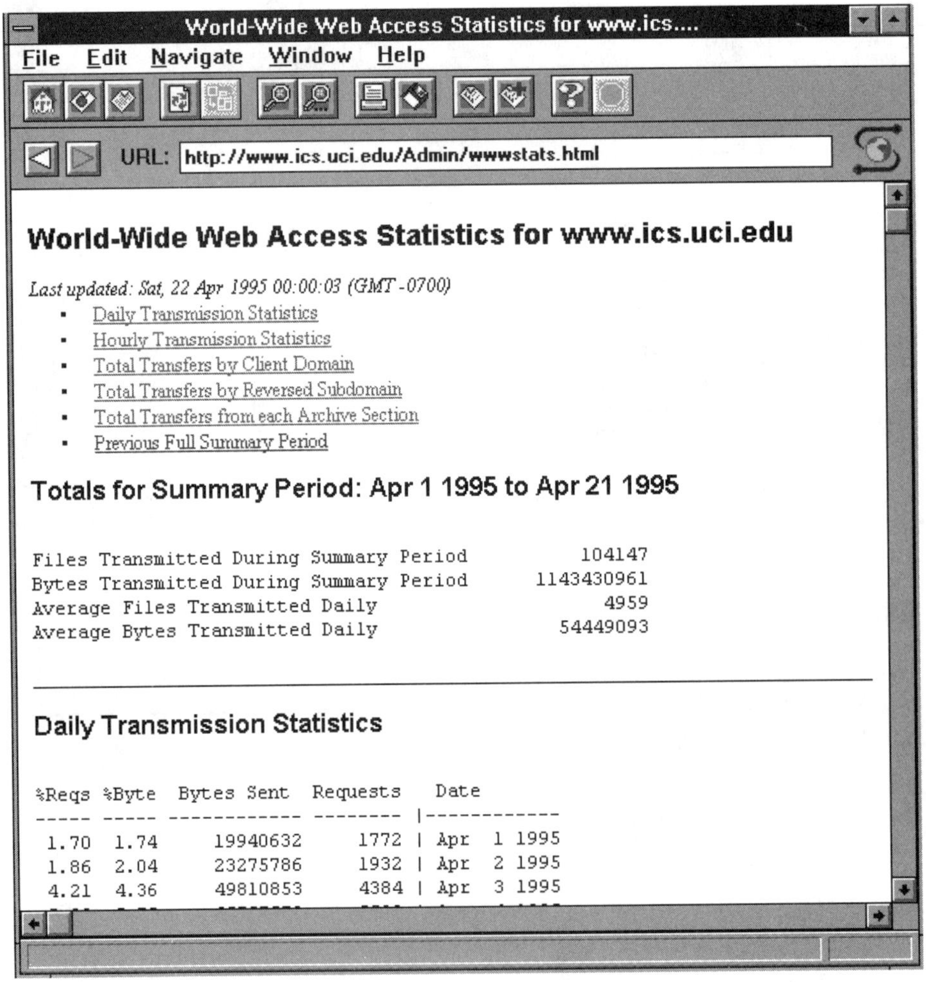

wwwstat

gwstat is a package (shown in Fig. 12-7) that produces GIF graphs from the output of wwwstat at URL:

http://dis.cs.umass.edu/stats/gwstat.html

Figure 12-7

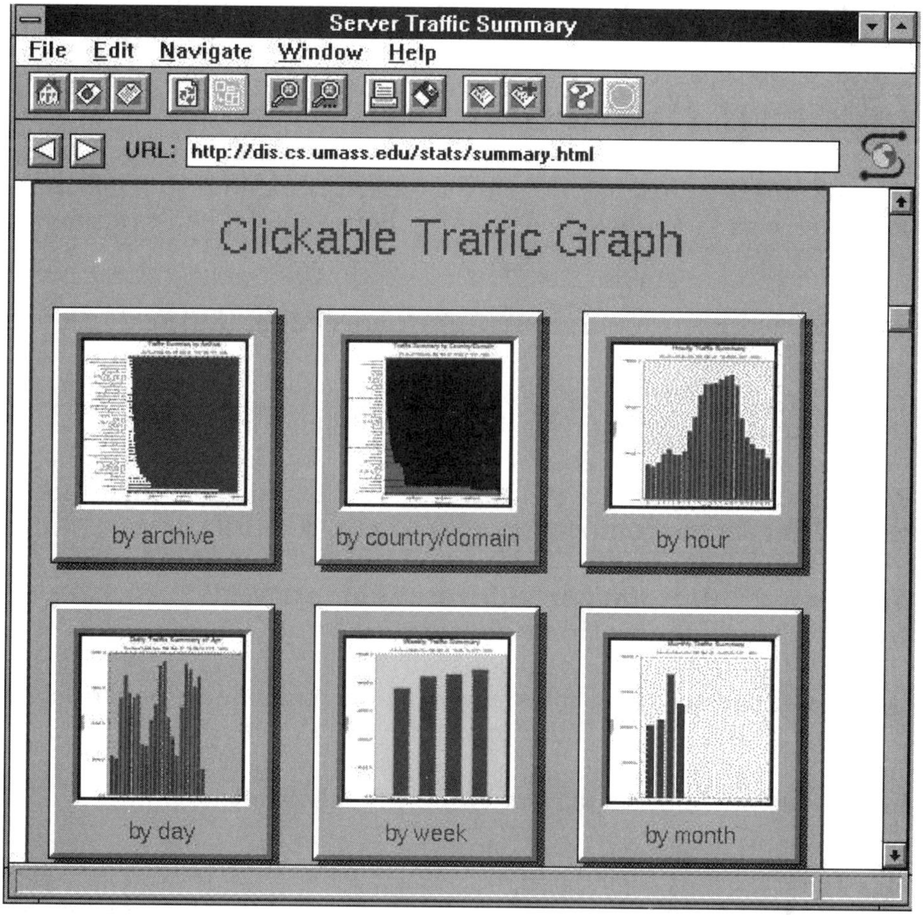

gwstat

There are also ways to include access counts in your individual documents. Then, as people access your HTML documents, they get an idea of how popular a document has become. For more information see URL:

http://melmac.corp.harris.com/access_counts.html

Getting the word out

As you can see in Chapter 9, you can do several things to publicize your new Web server or other offering. For example, you can submit it to the NCSA What's New Page at URL:

http://www.ncsa.uiuc.edu/SDG/Software/Mosaic/Docs/whats-new.html

Details on how to submit your listing are included in the NCSA What's New Page. You can also register with W3 Consortium. The W3 Consortium maintains the WWW Virtual Library and other lists. For information on contributing information, see URL:

http://www.w3.org/hypertext/DataSources/WWW/Geographical_generation/new-servers.html

You can also submit your information to the maintainers of various catalogs, such as the ALIWEB index at URL:

http://web.nexor.co.uk/aliweb/doc/aliweb.html

Making the Net safe for commerce

Many network managers are simply unwilling to entrust their networks, much less their business transactions, to a network that has historically been a hacker's breeding ground. Improved reliability and security are major requirements. Various security schemes have been proposed to handle the new breed of Internet transactions. Among the proposed solutions are digital cash, RSA, SHTTP servers, and digital signatures.

Browsers such as Luckman Interactive's Super Mosaic, based on Enhanced Mosaic version 2, include security modules (third-party programs) that allow Mosaic to communicate with secure servers using various security protocols. When Mosaic accesses a secure server it activates the security module required by that server. If the required module is not installed on your system you will need to obtain and install the correct module. Security modules and instructions for installing and configuring modules should be available from servers that require that module.

The following modules are pre-installed:

- **First Virtual**. Supports an Internet payment system from First Virtual Holdings, Inc.
- **Digest Authentication**. Uses MD5-encrypted passwords for authorization to receive an HTTP reply.
- **Basic Authentication**. A basic, nonsecure protocol supported by nearly all WWW servers. A user name and password are sent to the server in UUENCODED form. This method can be used to limit access to a server.

Security in the client is not the complete solution. Servers and clients both need to implement compatible security schemes. Future Web servers will include some form of encryption and authentication capabilities, allowing sensitive data to be handled as servers become more selective about which clients receive information. Such improvements in security will facilitate more commercial interest in the Internet and the Web.

Secure HyperText Transfer Protocol (SHTTP) addresses the issues of authentication and transaction verification. With applications that support Secure HTTP, sensitive information, such as credit card numbers, can be encrypted and securely exchanged. In addition, users can affix digital signatures that cannot be duplicated, permitting auditable digital contracts.

The Secure HyperText Transfer Protocol (SHTTP) could become the preferred method for implementing RSA-based public key systems in clients and servers. On the client browser side, Secure-HTTP represents another scheme based on a set of extensions to HTTP. It also covers some nonpublic, key-based systems, but its strength remains in the handling of public key encryption. SHTTP should be implemented wherever digital signatures and other public key-based schemes are needed.

There is a lot of work in progress (both research and commercial) attempting to define specific changes in the communication protocol and the WWW to implement various forms of security. A wide variety of security needs and concerns exist, ranging from no security to military-grade security to the security of monetary transactions.

It might seem that it takes a lot to get started, but actually, the difficult part is simply getting started itself. Once you begin the process you will find you get swept away by the excitement surrounding the evolving nature of this technology. Take the time upfront to address the issues of content, effort, and security, and make your presence known.

13

Positioning for the future

IN Chapter 2 we introduced the notion of the NII, more commonly referred to as the Information Superhighway. In Chapters 3 through 9 we uncovered a lot of new tools to speed your journey through the New Internet. Chapters 10 through 12 prepared you to begin serving information on the Internet. At this point you might be asking yourself, "So what's left? Is this the end of the road?"

Our answer is . . . this is just the beginning! New doors are opening at an unprecedented rate. The new technology is no longer limited to a few researchers and educators. The tools and technology are becoming available and affordable for the masses.

Our goal in this chapter is to explain many of the forces influencing the evolution of the Internet. These trends, and many more like them, are likely to encourage new ways to collaborate, to enhance your economic potential, to work with information effectively, and to make changes that might help you lead a more satisfying, challenging life. This chapter will give you a taste of what we think the future has in store.

Could this be the information superhighway?

Speculating about the "Information Superhighway" has become a national obsession. It holds the promise of dramatically changing the ways business is conducted, through telecommuting, multimedia, and distance learning to name just a few applications. Additional new applications will open up vast new markets in information services, and in support applications in strategic areas such as health care, education, manufacturing, commerce, finance, and government. The information superhighway, originally coined by the Clinton Administration, proposes to bring two-way audio, video, and data services to the masses, nationwide.

The Information Superhighway concept of a ubiquitous information access network evolved from the current global Internet. And yet, although widely publicized by the media as being *here already*, a few of the key components have yet to fall into place. Equitable entry and access costs, and the need for widespread deployment of services to sparsely populated geographic areas, are basic requirements.

Today's Internet is the world's largest collection of decentralized computer networks. It is estimated that more than 45,000 computer networks now connect more than 2.2 million computers to one another. At least 20 million people in 137 countries send and receive information through the Internet.

Much of the Internet's success has come about because the suppliers of content and conduits have remained separate. Those in control of the distribution channels have not been able to dictate the selection and pricing of the information. "Well," you might ask—"what's missing?" The successful deployment of the Information Superhighway vision will depend on the success of each of the following components:

- A network infrastructure must be constructed, capable of carrying two-way digital information.
- Devices required to access, deliver, and process the information and services must be powerful, affordable, and user-friendly.
- The kinds of information, entertainment, public data, and commercial product sales and services to be offered will be determined in the marketplace by private industry and public institutions, based on consumer demand.

The network will require a large capacity (bandwidth) fiber-optic infrastructure to deliver multimedia.

- End-user facilities will require megabits (millions) per second bandwidth, scalability, and affordability. They must also support voice, video, and data at varying quality-of-service levels.
- Access network must provide gigabits (billions) per second bandwidth, and interactive broadband access to the home capable of two-way multimedia, at affordable prices.
- Backbone network facilities must provide terabits (trillions) per second capacity at dramatically lower costs.

The likely candidates to build the necessary infrastructure are the cable television companies and telecommunications carriers. The telephone companies must upgrade or acquire infrastructure. One possible way would be through partnerships with cable TV companies who already have fiber-optic networks. Cable TV companies have the fiber-optic network and access to programming technologies. Local phone companies have the reach (access to homes and businesses) and switching technology. Cross ownership of cable TV firms and telephone companies would allow phone companies to provide video services and cable companies to offer competing local telephone services. Long-distance and local phone companies are entering an era of competition in the local and long-distance arenas.

In the near future, the cable TV and local telephone networks will look increasingly similar, as the regulatory environment changes. Similarly, the lines between the local telephone companies and the interexchange carriers will blur. Deregulation will play a huge role in redefining relationships between cable companies and local and long-distance telecommunications providers. The potential for new business opportunities in the telecommunications industry has raised the level of activity as the cable television and telephone companies vie for a piece of the action. Neither sector is particularly well-suited to meet the challenges currently before them.

Here are just a few of the problems facing the cable and telephone industries:

- Enormous amounts of distributed storage will be required to deliver the proposed services.
- Control and billing software will be critical in the deployment.
- No standards exist for two-way interactive high-bandwidth communications.
- No proven market exists for these services—who is likely to buy them?

Some argue that regulation can be too much of a good thing, contending that too much regulation harms innovation, freedom, and openness. But not enough regulation results in chaos. Deregulation will play a key role in making the necessary infrastructure and services available; ideally, it will encourage private investment, promote and protect competition, provide universal access to the network, and encourage flexibility.

The information networks of today will likely become on-ramps. They will be connected to, and will feed information to, the Information Superhighway, and will include corporate networks, telephone networks, interactive TV, bulletin boards, online services, and the Internet.

Consumer devices (*access appliances*) will likely result from the convergence of computer, telecommunications, and television industries. Set-top boxes are likely to give way to personal computer monitor-bottom boxes. PCs provide a personal experience and a level of control and flexibility to personalize the user's access to information. PCs are becoming the consumer device of choice, but are still too hard to use and too costly. Consumers will demand that the devices used to access the services provide customizable navigators, transparent connectivity, extreme simplicity, reliability comparable to that of today's television sets, and total security from unwanted transmissions and monitoring.

Announcements of new business alliances between telecommunications carriers, service providers, and commercial enterprises have become commonplace. A number of similar, well-funded commercial endeavors are underway in an attempt to be first to market or to establish dominant positioning within the potential marketplace for interactive television, information access, and consumer services. Companies are proceeding with ambitious technological experiments such as the Time Warner trial, demonstrating an interactive multimedia network to residences in Orlando, Florida. As the industry rises to the challenge of solving these technical problems, the players jockey for position in an as-yet undefined competitive landscape.

While issues and opportunities surrounding the market remain to be fully understood, many are making large investments in pilot programs to test various technologies and their market acceptance. However, there are still no widely deployed or in-production systems sophisticated enough to support the popular vision of the Information

Superhighway as a medium capable of meeting virtually all the entertainment, communications, and information needs of an entire community.

Is this the end or just the beginning?

1994 was a critical year in the evolution of the Internet, beginning with the National Science Foundation's phasing-out of its financial support of the NSFnet, the largest portion of the Internet. Major changes were implemented in how the infrastructure is funded and managed. Commercial service providers began playing an increasingly important role.

NSF awarded $50 million in contracts to telecommunications companies to develop the next-generation Internet services. NSF awarded contracts for Internet interconnect services to Ameritech, Pacific Bell, and Sprint. Three Network Access Points (NAPs) were put into operation in Chicago (Ameritech), New York (Sprint) and San Francisco (Pacific Bell), as neutral meeting places where Internet providers agree, based on bilateral agreements, to exchange traffic. MFS Datanet, Inc. manages a fourth NAP in Washington, DC. In the context of the new architecture, service providers called Network Service Providers (NSPs) connect end users to the Internet. NSPs connect to the NAPs in order to exchange traffic with other NSPs. This new network architecture, driven by unproved technology, was implemented with some degree of uncertainty, frustration, and confusion. It will drastically alter the way the Internet operates, and the result will be decentralized oversight of Internet operations.

The concept that the Internet is not a single network, but instead is a collection of networks, means little to the end user. You want to do something useful, to run a program or access some unique data. You shouldn't have to worry about how it's all stuck together. Consider the telephone system—it's an Internet, too. Pacific Bell, Bell Atlantic, AT&T, MCI, British Telephony, and others, are all separate corporations that run pieces of the telephone system. They worry about how to make it all work together; all you have to do is pick up the phone and dial.

Ignoring cost and commercials, with regard to your own phone system you probably don't care if you are dealing with MCI or AT&T. Dial the number and it works. You only care who carries your calls when a problem occurs. If something goes wrong, you have to know who to talk to because only one of those companies can fix it. They talk to each other about problems, but each phone carrier is responsible for fixing problems on its own part of the system. The same is true of the Internet, and the same will continue to be true of the Superhighways of tomorrow. Coordination of providers will be essential to the overall operation and usefulness of the Net.

What'll they think of next?

The global nature of the Superhighway has already spurred new ways of interacting. Many of these new areas are in the early stages of development. The possibilities are endless. We have talked about many of these applications throughout this book. How might the following list of considerations change the way you live and work?

- Customer support
- Product information distribution
- Online marketing
- Software distribution
- Electronic commerce
- 24-hour access to services
- Online news services
- Interactive educational experiences
- Distance learning
- Customized entertainment
- Information sharing for social, political, and life-enabling purposes

- Improved access to medical records and specialists from remote locations
- Automating current health care procedures and tasks
- Infotainment or information on demand
- Telecommuting

Here are a few of what we consider the most interesting emerging applications.

* **Digital libraries**
  Today, libraries are moving toward electronic distribution of text to become libraries without walls, transforming libraries from guardians of tradition to catalysts of vast change. Digital library projects are underway at many institutions. Topics being explored include the archiving of enormous volumes of data, efficient search and retrieval mechanisms, and the economies of electronic publishing. From the Internet today you can search the catalogs of thousand of libraries across the world. The Library of Congress catalog is just one example. See URL:

  http://lcweb.loc.gov/homepage/lchp.html

* **HotJava**
  HotJava is one of many new Web browsers. What makes it different, however, is that it builds on the Internet browsing techniques established by Mosaic and then expands them by implementing the capability to add arbitrary behavior. The information viewed in other browsers is limited to text, illustrations, low-quality sounds and videos. The transparent acquisition feature of HotJava frees developers from the limitations of fixed media types like images and text and lets them do whatever they can dream of. HotJava provides a way for users to access applications in a new way. Software transparently migrates across the network.

  World Wide Web content developers no longer have to worry about whether or not some special piece of software is installed in a user's system. HotJava's dynamic capabilities are made possible because it is written in a new language called Java™. Briefly, think of Java as a simplified, portable version of C++. The central difference between HotJava and other browsers is that while other browsers have a lot of detailed, built-in knowledge of the different data types and protocols necessary to navigate the Web, HotJava understands essentially none of them. This essential difference results in great flexibility and the ability to add new capabilities easily. For more information see URL:

http://java.sun.com/1.0alpha3/doc/overview/hotjava

✳ Intelligent agents

Intelligent agents will be employed to lend some degree of artificial intelligence to automate tasks on behalf of individuals. One early prototype example of this application is the Relevant Personal Edition Personal Digital Newspaper (PDN), which allows users to receive customized daily news via Internet e-mail. Each PDN will arrive at the customer's desktop, personally indexed and in an easy-to-read graphical format. PDN locates the news that matters to the individual, so that he or she will spend less time looking for critical business news and more time acting on it. Relevant Personal Edition, which relies on the DowVision News Service, includes the full text of *The Wall Street Journal*, the Dow Jones News Service, *Barron's*, the Dow Jones International News Services, Press Release Wires, and *Professional Investor Report*. For more information see URL:

http://www.ensemble.com/relevant.html

✳ MBONE

MBONE stands for Multicast Backbone, which is a virtual infrastructure on top of the Internet for Multicast IP services. It was adopted in 1992 as an outgrowth of the first two IETF *audiocast* experiments (IETF is the acronym for *The Internet Engineering Task Force,* which is responsible for short-term technical deliverables across the Internet—see Chapter 3), in which live audio and video were multicast from the IETF meeting site to destinations around the world. A semi-permanent IP multicast testbed was established to carry the IETF transmissions and to support continued experimentation between meetings through a cooperative, volunteer effort. The IP Multicast Backbone facilitates distributed applications to achieve time-critical near-real-time communications over wide area IP networks. Various software packages have been developed (both research and commercial) that make use of the multicast capability to demonstrate video and audio streams over the Internet.

Typical uses of this technology include transmission of meetings, lectures, and presentations of general interest to a portion of the Internet community. Examples include IETF meetings, working group meetings, NASA Shuttle Coverage, delayed rebroadcast of WWW conferences, etc. The MBONE has been a useful proof of concept experiment. The bandwidth requirements for the transmission of audio and video streams depends on the number of simultaneous conversations. Typically, audio is carried at 32 or 64 Kbps, video at up to 128 Kbps per stream. Therefore, if 10 people started video conferences from your site over a T1 (1.54 Mbps) circuit, the circuit would be overloaded. Other more robust protocols will follow to handle the demands of real-time audio and video streams. The promise of easily transmitting real-time audio and video communications is likely to have an effect on where we live and work.

Virtual reality

Virtual reality can be defined as the presentation of computer-generated, multisensory information that tracks a user in real time. The applications for this technology are far-reaching. Imagine a medical professional being able to navigate through the human body (remember the film *Fantastic Voyage*?). Operations could be performed on a 3D model without the need for cadavers. Other areas this technology is being applied to include education, architecture, science, medicine, military, flight simulation, art, and entertainment.

The Virtual Reality Modeling Language (VRML) is a language for describing multiparticipant interactive simulations—virtual worlds networked via the global Internet and hyperlinked via the Web. All aspects of virtual world display, interaction, and inter-networking can be specified using VRML. It was conceived in the spring of 1994 at the first annual WWW Conference in Geneva, Switzerland. Tim Berners-Lee and Dave Raggett organized a session to discuss Virtual Reality interfaces to the Web. Several attendees described projects already underway to build 3-D graphical visualization tools that interoperate with the Web. Attendees agreed on the need for these tools to have a common language for specifying 3-D scene description and WWW hyperlinks—an analog of HTML for virtual reality.

It is the intention of its designers that VRML become the standard language for interactive simulation within the Web. The first version of VRML allows for the creation of virtual worlds with limited interactive behavior. These worlds can contain objects that have hyperlinks to other worlds, HTML documents, or other valid MIME types. When the user selects an object with a hyperlink, the appropriate MIME viewer is launched. When the user selects a link to a VRML document from within a correctly configured WWW browser, a VRML viewer is launched. Thus VRML viewers are the perfect companion applications to standard WWW browsers for navigating and visualizing the Web. Future versions of VRML will allow for richer behaviors, including animations, motion physics, and real-time multi-user interaction. For more information refer to URL:

http://vrml.wired.com

What challenges lie before us?

Current challenges include the need to design networks and computer systems with sufficient intelligence and capacity to manage the billions of transactions the Superhighway will foster; to make the technology open and easy to use; to guarantee the privacy and security of transactions; and to arrange for financial settlements.

Privacy in the brave new world

We will need comprehensive privacy-protection policies to enable companies and individuals to conduct business on the information highway, and as a fundamental right to be extended to all travelers. As telecommunications and networking rapidly move more information to more users, concerns are being raised about how the information might be stored or used. The preservation of confidentiality and personal privacy must not be compromised. Privacy policies are needed in this brave new world of electronic commerce, to protect personal information relating to health, finance, spending, and other areas.

Among other things we must be able to authorize transactions in real time, prevent fraud, protect confidentiality and privacy, make exchanges nonrefutable, and create alternative methods to create binding agreements. Potential solutions may involve cryptographic solutions, hardware solutions, and digital signatures.

Have you seen the future yet?

If not, you will! Many organizations are discovering ways to bring these ideas, and many other visions, to reality in the near future. In this brave new world of electronic information, the journey is half the fun.

A

Contents of the CD-ROM

The CD-ROM accompanying this book contains Mosaic software for both personal computers running Microsoft Windows 3.1 and UNIX workstations running the X Window System. The software originated at Spyglass, Incorporated, but is distributed and supported by Luckman Interactive.

All support questions should be directed to Luckman Interactive Technical Support, 213-468-1021.

Microsoft Windows Files

Luckman Super Mosaic is a customized product based on Spyglass Enhanced Mosaic version 2. The software is packaged on the CD-ROM as if it was written in compressed format onto two floppy disks. The setup program (SETUP.EXE) resides in the DISK1 directory.

Installation under Microsoft Windows is explained in Chapter 6.

Spyglass Enhanced Mosaic version 2 is supplied on the CD-ROM in executable form for seven UNIX platforms as shown:

AIX.tar	IBM RS/6000 running AIX
ATT486.tar	AT&T 486 architecture
AlphaOSF.tar	DEC Alpha running OSF
HP.tar	Hewlett-Packard running HP-UX
IRIX5.tar	Silicon Graphics running IRIX version 5
Solaris.tar	Sun running Solaris version 2
SunOS.tar	Sun running SunOS version 4.1.X

Installation under UNIX is explained in Chapter 5.

B

Finding Mosaic software on the Internet

If you find that you need either a different binary or a different version of Mosaic than are available on the CD, you will need to go to the Internet to get the software. There are a growing number of locations on the Internet to watch for Mosaic and related software.

You might want to install other software, including viewers for multimedia-like capabilities. A variety of external viewers provide Mosaic with enhanced capabilities. We discuss the most popular viewers available at the time this book was written in the following sections. Refer to the indexes listed for more up-to-date listings of available software.

One thing that you must be aware of is that many Microsoft Windows binaries are compressed on the Internet with a package known as PKZIP. PKZIP is a shareware package from PKWare Shareware that is not included on the CD due to a licensing restriction. You need to get PKZIP from the Internet, using the URL:

ftp://ftp.ncsa.uiuc.edu/PC/Windows/Contrib/pkz204g.exe

Once you have downloaded PKZIP and PKUNZIP you can use it to uncompress all compressed files. You will know if a file is compressed with PKZIP if they have a file extension of .ZIP. If you see this, you will know that you need to uncompress it before you can use it on your machine. Note that you should read the licensing information for PKZIP, and send the required amount of money to the authors of PKZIP to ensure that you don't violate the license agreement. Once you have retrieved and installed PKZIP you can begin to download the appropriate viewers and use PKUNZIP to uncompress and extract the files. A simple example is:

```
PKUNZIP LVIEWP1A.ZIP C:\LVIEWP1A
```

where LVIEWP1A.ZIP is the name of the particular ZIP file that you have downloaded and C:\LVIEWP1A is a directory that you have chosen to unwind the ZIP file into.

For a comprehensive list of WWW browser software refer to the URL:

http://www.yahoo.com/Computers/World_Wide_Web/Browsers

You can get the NCSA Mosaic and related software for Microsoft Windows from the URL:

http://www.ncsa.uiuc.edu/SDG/Software/WinMosaic/HomePage.html

For NCSA Mosaic for Unix and the X Window System references use the URL:

http://www.ncsa.uiuc.edu/SDG/Software/XMosaic/faq-software.html

You can get the latest Chameleon package from the URL:

http://www.netmanage.com

You can get the latest Netscape package from the URL:

http://www.netscape.com

As discussed in Chapter 7, each viewer is responsible for a particular type of support, including video, audio, and graphics.

Microsoft Windows viewers

Adobe Acrobat Reader
ftp://ftp.ncsa.uiuc.edu/Mosaic/Windows/viewers/acroread.exe

Ghostscript
ftp://ftp.cs.wisc.edu/pub/ghost/aladdin/gs333w32.zip

Lview Pro
ftp://ftp.ncsa.uiuc.edu/Mosaic/Windows/viewers/lviewp1b.zip

Mpegplay
ftp://ftp.ncsa.uiuc.edu/Mosaic/Windows/viewers/mpegw32h.zip

QuickTime
ftp://ftp.ncsa.uiuc.edu/Mosaic/Windows/viewers/qtw11.zip

WPlany
ftp://ftp.ncsa.uiuc.edu/Mosaic/Windows/viewers/wplny09b.zip

Configuring viewers with Enhanced Mosaic

It is a good idea to create separate subdirectories on your local hard disk to ensure that you keep different viewers in different directories. Once you have downloaded and uncompressed the appropriate viewers for your machine you need to configure each of them. You must either copy the appropriate files into the designated locations or run the SETUP.EXE that comes with the particular viewer.

UNIX and X Window System viewers

Adobe Acrobat Reader
http://www.adobe.com/Acrobat/Acrobat0.html

Ghostview
ftp://ftp.cs.wisc.edu/pub/ghost

Mpeg_play
ftp://tr-ftp.cs.berkeley.edu/pub/multimedia/mpeg

Xv
ftp://ftp.cis.upenn.edu/pub/xv

Enhanced Mosaic support for external viewers is configured by selecting Helpers from the Edit pulldown menu as described in Chapter 7.

C

Table of international country codes

Most Internet domain names worldwide end with the two-letter international code of the host country. These codes are provided here for your convenience, to help you recognize the locations of the Internet resources you visit.

AD	Andorra
AE	United Arab Emirates
AF	Afghanistan
AG	Antigua and Barbuda
AI	Anguilla
AL	Albania
AM	Armenia
AN	Netherland Antilles
AO	Angola (Republic of)
AQ	Antarctica
AR	Argentina
AS	American Samoa
AT	Austria
AU	Australia
AW	Aruba
AZ	Azerbaijan
BA	Bosnia-Herzegovina
BB	Barbados
BD	Bangladesh
BE	Belgium
BF	Burkina Faso
BG	Bulgaria
BH	Bahrain
BI	Burundi

BJ	Benin
BM	Bermuda
BN	Brunei Darussalam
BO	Bolivia
BR	Brazil
BS	Bahamas
BT	Bhutan
BV	Bouvet Island
BW	Botswana
BY	Belarus
BZ	Belize
CA	Canada
CC	Cocos (Keeling) Isl.
CF	Central African Republic
CG	Congo
CH	Switzerland
CI	Ivory Coast
CK	Cook Islands
CL	Chile
CM	Cameroon
CN	China
CO	Colombia
CR	Costa Rica
CS	Czechoslovakia
CU	Cuba
CV	Cape Verde
CX	Christmas Island
CY	Cyprus
CZ	Czech Republic
DE	Germany
DJ	Djibouti
DK	Denmark
DM	Dominica
DO	Dominican Republic
DZ	Algeria
EC	Ecuador
EE	Estonia
EG	Egypt
EH	Western Sahara
ER	Eritrea
ES	Spain
ET	Ethiopia
FI	Finland
FJ	Fiji
FK	Falkland Islands (Malvinas)
FM	Micronesia
FO	Faroe Islands
FR	France
FX	France (European Ter.)
GA	Gabon
GB	Great Britain (UK)
GD	Grenada
GE	Georgia
GF	Guyana (Fr.)
GH	Ghana
GI	Gibraltar
GL	Greenland
GM	Gambia
GN	Guinea
GP	Guadeloupe (Fr.)
GQ	Equatorial Guinea
GR	Greece
GS	South Georgia and South Sandwich Islands

GT	Guatemala
GU	Guam (US)
GW	Guinea Bissau
GY	Guyana
HK	Hong Kong
HM	Heard & McDonald Isl.
HN	Honduras
HR	Croatia
HT	Haiti
HU	Hungary
ID	Indonesia
IE	Ireland
IL	Israel
IN	India
IO	British Indian O. Ter.
IQ	Iraq
IR	Iran
IS	Iceland
IT	Italy
JM	Jamaica
JO	Jordan
JP	Japan
KE	Kenya
KG	Kyrgyz Republic
KH	Cambodia
KI	Kiribati
KM	Comoros
KN	St. Kitts Nevis Aguilla
KP	Korea (North)
KR	Korea (South)
KW	Kuwait
KY	Cayman Islands
KZ	Kazakhstan
LA	Laos
LB	Lebanon
LC	Saint Lucia
LI	Liechtenstein
LK	Sri Lanka
LR	Liberia
LS	Lesotho
LT	Lithuania
LU	Luxembourg
LV	Latvia
LY	Libya
MA	Morocco
MC	Monaco
MD	Moldavia
MG	Madagascar (Republic of)
MH	Marshall Islands
MK	Macedonia (former Yugo.)
ML	Malli
MM	Myanmar
MN	Mongolia
MO	Macau
MP	Northern Mariana Isl.
MQ	Martinique (Fr.)
MR	Mauritania
MS	Montserrat
MT	Malta
MU	Mauritius
MV	Maldives
MW	Malawi
MX	Mexico
MY	Malaysia

MZ	Mozambique
NA	Namibia
NC	New Caledonia (Fr.)
NE	Niger
NF	Norfolk Island
NG	Nigeria
NI	Nicaragua
NL	Netherlands
NO	Norway
NP	Nepal
NR	Nauru
NU	Niue
NZ	New Zealand
OM	Oman
PA	Panama
PE	Peru
PF	Polynesia (Fr.)
PG	Papua New Guinea
PH	Philippines
PK	Pakistan
PL	Poland
PM	St. Pierre & Miquelon
PN	Pitcairn
PR	Puerto Rico (US)
PT	Portugal
PW	Palau
PY	Paraguay
QA	Qatar
RE	Reunion (Fr.)
RO	Romania
RU	Russian Federation
RW	Rwanda
SA	Saudi Arabia
SB	Solomon Islands
SC	Seychelles
SD	Sudan
SE	Sweden
SG	Singapore
SH	St. Helena
SI	Slovenia
SJ	Svalbard & Jan Mayen Is.
SK	Slovak Republic
SL	Sierra Leone
SM	San Marino
SN	Senegal
SO	Somalia
SR	Suriname
ST	St. Tome and Principe
SU	Soviet Union
SV	El Salvador
SY	Syria
SZ	Swaziland
TC	Turks & Caicos Islands
TD	Chad
TF	French Southern Terr.
TG	Togo
TH	Thailand
TJ	Tadjikistan
TK	Tokelau
TM	Turkmenistan
TN	Tunisia
TO	Tonga
TP	East Timor
TR	Turkey

TT	Trinidad & Tobago
TV	Tuvalu
TW	Taiwan
TZ	Tanzania
UA	Ukraine
UG	Uganda
UK	United Kingdom
UM	US Minor Outlying Isl.
US	United States
UY	Uruguay
UZ	Uzbekistan
VA	Vatican City State
VC	St. Vincent & Grenadines
VE	Venezuela
VG	Virgin Islands (US)
VN	Vietnam
VU	Vanuatu
WF	Wallis & Futuna Islands
WS	Samoa
YE	Yemen
YT	Mayotte
YU	Yugoslavia
ZA	South Africa
ZM	Zambia
ZR	Zaire
ZW	Zimbabwe

D

HTML reference guide

Tag	End tag/attribute	Description
<HTML>	</HTML>	Starts/ends document
<HEAD>	</HEAD>	Starts/ends header
<TITLE>	</TITLE>	Starts/ends title
<BODY>	</BODY>	Starts/ends body
<H#>	</H#>	Starts/ends heading text
<P>		Starts new paragraph
 		Inserts line break
<HR>		Inserts horizontal rule
<EM>	</EM>	Starts/ends emphasized text
<STRONG>	</STRONG>	Starts/ends strong text
<B>	</B>	Starts/ends bold text
<I>	</I>	Starts/ends italic text
<U>	</U>	Starts/ends underlined text
<ADDRESS>	</ADDRESS>	Starts/ends address format
<BLOCKQUOTE>	</BLOCKQUOTE>	Starts/ends text in blockquote format
<PRE>	</PRE>	Starts/ends preformatted text
<DL>	</DL>	Starts/ends glossary

Tag	End tag/attribute	Description
<DT>		entry in glossary
<DD>		term definition in glossary
<UL>	</UL>	Starts/ends unordered list
<OL>	</OL>	Starts/ends ordered list
<LI>		entry in a list
<IMG>		inserts inline graphic
	SOURCE	defines image source file
	ALIGN	defines text alignment
	ALT	defines alternate text
<A>	</A>	HREF defines link destination
	NAME	gives symbolic name to anchor

Glossary

access provider A company that provides a connection to the Internet.

analog Waveform fluctuations represented electrically as an infinite number of values.

Archie A network service that searches FTP sites for files.

ASCII American Standard Code for Information Exchange.

bandwidth A measure of network capacity, usually stated in terms of bits per second.

browser Software that provides an interface to the World Wide Web. Also, a program that allows a person to read hypertext. The browser gives some means of viewing the contents of computers, and of navigating from one computer to another.

client A program that requests services of another program. Normally the browser is a client of a data server.

compression Reducing the size of a transmission or file through computer programming, thus allowing more information to be transmitted in less time.

cyberspace The online world of computer communications networks, where people interact without face-to-face contact.

digital Information represented as digits.

electronic mail Text-based messages sent and received over a computer network.

FAQ Frequently Asked Questions. Inquiring minds have to know.

fiber-optic networks Communications networks that use glass fibers and laser technology to transmit information at the speed of light.

File Transfer Protocol (FTP) A common method for transferring files across networks.

Finger A service that responds to queries and retrieves user information remotely.

firewall One of several ways of protecting a network from unwanted traffic.

GIF Graphic Interexchange Format. An 8-bit, 256-color, indexed color-file format, introduced by CompuServe in 1987 as a medium for exchanging compressed pictures.

Gopher A text-based, menu-driven information service.

graphic Data that can be rendered on the screen by virtue of an encoding algorithm.

image Data representing a picture or drawing. An image is represented by an array of pixels.

ISDN Integrated Services Digital Network; it represents the next major push by the telephone companies to provide higher-speed, lower-cost dial-up lines in the home and work environment.

JPEG Joint Photographic Experts Group format; this is an industry standard for compressing 24-bit and 8-bit color, and gray image files; also 16.7 million colors compression standard for 24-bit color.

home page The first page of information in a hypermedia document. WWW's default document.

HTML HyperText Markup Language is an Internet protocol that is required on clients for transmission of text, menus, and simple online help information.

HTML+ Lightweight delivery format for browsing and querying information in a web globally distributed over the Internet; a superset of HTML.

HTTP Hypertext Transport Protocol is a network protocol for retrieving hypertext information, such as compound documents, using an extensible set of formats. The protocol used by WWW servers to move information across the Internet.

hyperlink A reference point in a document for linking information.

hypermedia A multimedia document that contains and links text, audio, and video embedded in formatted documents.

hypertext Text that is not constrained to be linear; text that, when selected, has the ability to present connected documents; text that contains links to other text, graphics, videos, or sound. You select a link by clicking on it.

MIME Multipurpose Internet Mail Extensions standard defined for transmitting mixed-media files over networks.

MPEG Motion Pictures Expert Group standard for the digital representation and compression of video images.

multimedia The integrated use of two or more communications media—text, graphics, video, and/or audio.

navigation The process of moving from one node to another through hypertext web.

netiquette The appropriate behavior and styles for users of computer networks, especially the Internet.

newbie Internet term for new users.

NNTP Network News Transfer Protocol, a common method by which articles over Usenet are transferred.

pixel Short for "picture elements," the elements of color created on a display surface.

PPP Point-to-Point Protocol is a direct connection protocol standard that lets two computers communicate via a physical link.

protection The prevention of unauthorized users from reading or writing a particular piece of data. Also known as authentication, or access control.

QuickTime Apple format for computer movies.

RFC Requests for Comment are Internet standards documents.

SLIP Serial Line Interface Protocol; it allows data to be exchanged between computers.

SVGA A higher resolution version of the VGA standard; 800 × 600 or 1024 × 768 pixels, and up to 24 bits can be used to define the color of each pixel.

Telnet A program that allows users to remotely access computers across networks.

URL Uniform Resource Locator is the Web addressing system, with syntax that lets objects be addressed using HTTP and other common network protocols, such as FTP, Gopher, and WAIS.

Veronica A network service that allows users to search Gopher systems for documents.

VGA Video Graphics Array developed by IBM. It has become the dominant standard for PC graphics. Two different modes: 640 × 480 pixels (4 bits) and 320 × 200 pixels (8 bits).

viewer Application external to Mosaic for handling non-HTML file types.

Video for Windows Microsoft video format for Microsoft Windows.

WAIS Wide Area Information Servers is a service that allows users to search for information among Internet databases.

Web A set of information sources (nodes) interconnected by links.

WHAM Waveform Hold and Modify; recommended audio player for Microsoft Windows.

Whois A name lookup service.

Winsock Windows Sockets specification defines a network programming interface for Microsoft Windows, based on the socket paradigm made popular in the Berkeley Software Distribution from the University of California at Berkeley.

WWW The World Wide Web initiative to create a universal, hypermedia-based method of access to information.

Index

Illustrations are in **boldface**.

I

N

O

P

W

X

Y

About the authors

Steve Karlovsky has served Argonne National Laboratory since 1990 as computing consultant, instructor, and Webmaster and Internet specialist. He has more recently founded Netnautics Incorporated (**http://www.netnautics.com/**), an Internet consulting and training firm based in Naperville, Illinois. Steve delivers Internet seminars and workshops throughout Chicagoland. He holds a Master of Science degree from the University of Illinois at Urbana-Champaign. Over the last twelve years he has worked with users of virtually all classes of systems, from PCs to large supercomputers.

Kevin Leininger is the Director Reengineering at DevTech Associates, a systems integration consulting firm based in Naperville, Illinois. Kevin consults on UNIX and open systems technologies, and assists corporations with utilizing information technology in the reengineering process. He has earned an MBA from the University of Chicago. He speaks frequently at major UNIX conferences, has authored several books for McGraw-Hill, and currently serves on the Readers Advisory Board for UNIXWORLD's Open Computing.

Linda Winkler joined Argonne National Laboratory (**http://www.anl.gov/**) in 1982, where she has been active in planning, designing, installing, and troubleshooting local and wide area networks. Linda earned a BS in Computer Science and an MS in Management from Purdue University. She is active with the Internet Engineering Task Force (IETF), which is responsible for setting the techical direction of the Internet.

CD-ROM WARRANTY

This software is protected by both United States copyright law and international copyright treaty provision. You must treat this software just like a book. By saying "just like a book," McGraw-Hill means, for example, that this software may be used by any number of people and may be freely moved from one computer location to another, so long as there is no possibility of its being used at one location or on one computer while it also is being used at another. Just as a book cannot be read by two different people in two different places at the same time, neither can the software be used by two different people in two different places at the same time (unless, of course, McGraw-Hill's copyright is being violated).

LIMITED WARRANTY

McGraw-Hill takes great care to provide you with top-quality software, thoroughly checked to prevent virus infections. McGraw-Hill warrants the physical diskette(s) contained herein to be free of defects in materials and workmanship for a period of sixty days from the purchase date. If McGraw-Hill receives written notification within the warranty period of defects in materials or workmanship, and such notification is determined by McGraw-Hill to be correct, McGraw-Hill will replace the defective diskette(s). Send requests to:

McGraw-Hill, Inc.
Customer Services
P.O. Box 545
Blacklick, OH 43004-0545

The entire and exclusive liability and remedy for breach of this Limited Warranty shall be limited to replacement of defective diskette(s) and shall not include or extend to any claim for or right to cover any other damages, including but not limited to, loss of profit, data, or use of the software, or special, incidental, or consequential damages or other similar claims, even if McGraw-Hill has been specifically advised of the possibility of such damages. In no event will McGraw-Hill's liability for any damages to you or any other person ever exceed the lower of suggested list price or actual price paid for the license to use the software, regardless of any form of the claim.

MCGRAW-HILL, INC. SPECIFICALLY DISCLAIMS ALL OTHER WARRANTIES, EXPRESS OR IMPLIED, INCLUDING, BUT NOT LIMITED TO, ANY IMPLIED WARRANTY OF MERCHANTABILITY OR FITNESS FOR A PARTICULAR PURPOSE.

Specifically, McGraw-Hill makes no representation or warranty that the software is fit for any particular purpose and any implied warranty of merchantability is limited to the sixty-day duration of the Limited Warranty covering the physical CD-ROM only (and not the software) and is otherwise expressly and specifically disclaimed.

This limited warranty gives you specific legal rights; you may have others which may vary from state to state. Some states do not allow the exclusion of incidental or consequential damages, or the limitation on how long an implied warranty lasts, so some of the above may not apply to you.